Birthing Fathers

Birthing Fathers

The Transformation of Men in American Rites of Birth

RICHARD K. REED

RUTGERS UNIVERSITY PRESS

NEW BRUNSWICK, NEW JERSEY, AND LONDON

LIBRARY OF CONGRESS CATALOGING-IN-PUBLICATION DATA

Reed, Richard K., 1954–
    Birthing fathers : the transformation of men in American rites of birth /
Richard K. Reed.
       p.   cm.
    Includes bibliographical references and index.
    ISBN 0-8135-3516-6 (hardcover : alk. paper) — ISBN 0-8135-3517-4 (pbk. : alk. paper)
    1. Childbirth—Social aspects—United States.   2. Birth customs—United States.
3. Labor (Obstetrics)—United States.   4. Natural childbirth—United States.
5. Fatherhood—United States.   6. Fathers—United States—Psychology.   7. Fathers—
United States—Attitudes.   8. Men—United States—Attitudes.   9. Father and infant.
I. Title.
    RG652.R44 2005
    618.4—dc22   2004011740

A British Cataloging-in-Publication record for this book is
available from the British Library.

Copyright © 2005 by Richard K. Reed

Manufactured in the United States of America

Dedicated to Anna and Austin

CONTENTS

ACKNOWLEDGMENTS

First and foremost I thank my life partner, Lisa Chatillon. She introduced me to feminist ideas long ago, literally labored through my introduction to fatherhood, and shared her books on both topics as I developed my own perspective on birthing. I remain indebted to her scholarly critique of the first draft and for her generous support throughout the long months of writing.

Special appreciation goes to Robbie Davis-Floyd. She first suggested I write this book and offered unstinting advice and support along the way. Her work not only guided me through my own birthing, but became central to this analysis. Her comments contributed enormously to the development of this manuscript.

Of the many birth-class teachers who opened their classes to me, I want to especially thank Mary Stanchak and Julie Walker. They are spectacular trainers and warm human beings and their classes showed me how wonder-filled birth training can be.

I want to express my gratitude to Jim Spickard and an anonymous reader at Rutgers University Press. Their careful reading and constructive criticisms are sterling examples of intellectual generosity. Jen Moran's keen editorial work saved me from a variety of both grammatical and conceptual errors. Kristi Long accepted this project with enthusiasm and moved it quickly, the greatest favor an editor can give. I'd also like to express my gratitude to my colleagues at Trinity University, whose supportive community fosters both scholarship and sanity. Franke Johnson and Irma Deleon deserve special mention for keeping the trains running on time.

Perhaps most important, I wish to thank the fathers who told me their stories, especially those new fathers who gave up scarce time and energy to share memories. I can only hope that what I heard will foster wonder-filled birthing experiences for future fathers.

Birthing Fathers

1

American Fathers and Hospital Childbirth

It was as if a part of me hadn't woken up until then. Something innate, I really started to feel a small voice talking to me and I was listening to it. I never heard it before then; and it was so very, very deep—very, very special—and very, very strong.

—Mark

Kevin hunched forward in the booth of the coffee shop, rolling the mug slowly in his calloused hands. "We didn't really know what we were getting into; hell we didn't even know we were going to get pregnant." His shock of blonde hair and his slight, muscular frame suggested an inner tension that energized his slow movements. He looked up at me, catching my eye for just a moment. "But once Sara was born, I was blown away, I was totally into it."

Kevin's baby entered the world one hot July night. "I had watched a lot of those birthing-class videos and every time I'd be like, 'Oh man, this looks terrible.' But it wasn't like that when Sara was born. It was magical." Kevin's eyes started to fill with tears as he talked about wrapping himself around the little being, or how she grasped the air with tiny hands, arched her back, and opened her perfect, pink mouth. Even six months later it was clear that for that moment, and from that moment, Kevin's world was engulfed by this new little person.

Kevin is destined to become a new kind of father. Gone are the days when Dad's job was simply to keep his daughters well dressed and his sons straight. Today's fathers change diapers and brush hair, pack lunches, and bandage scraped knees. The ideal father is no longer the stern patriarch or distant provider, but a warm and accessible caregiver. Dr. Spock and Penelope Leach, child-rearing specialists, put dads next to moms on the covers of their books and Bill Cosby was raised to God-father status as he bantered with his TV teenagers.

1

For generations, most dads have carried out their loving duties, quietly painting cribs and coaching Little League. The image of the new father emphasizes qualities that have been considered secondary in men's role in the family. Rather than authorities, fathers can be nurturers. Although they may still drive the car, dads are now responsible for doing laundry, sweating over homework, and comforting sick kids. In addition to being strong, they are expected to be empathic and understanding fathers. Despite the stresses of being overworked and underpaid, these new fathers are finding time and energy to be full parents. While media focus on absent and uncaring fathers, almost half of American men have reduced work time to be with their kids, and three-quarters would like to do so more (Griswold 1993, 245).

What do we know about these new fathers? Although academia has devoted decades to studying motherhood, we have only recently become aware of fathers. In the past, research focused on the economic man, the political man, and the physical man—but rarely the family man. When fathers were noticed, it was for their faults. Public interest and national research about dads focused on their failures: absent fathers, uncaring fathers, teenage fathers, abusive fathers, and unmarried fathers.

Only in the last decade have social scientists discovered fathers and uncovered a multifaceted phenomenon. Anthropologists study the evolutionary importance of fathers; historians have traced the changing place of fathers in families and society; psychologists point out that babies form powerful ties to their dads, which are important for the child's psychological and social development; and sociologists trace the roles of men as parents and how those ties change over the life span. In all these various fields, it is clear that a man's relations with his children are not only important for the children, but for dad's identity and place in society as well.

Men and Birth

Academic treatises did not turn my attention to fathers—I stumbled across fatherhood when my daughter was born. After years of working to be a man, a husband, a friend, and a son, I somehow became a father without thinking about what it meant. I attended to my little daughter in those first months, hardly aware of the change that was taking place in me. When my son was born several years later, I realized that I had become one of these people called "fathers." But I was not a father in my own father's image; I had become a new kind of father. My interest was piqued. Who had I become? How had it happened? So I set out to understand the transformation of men into social beings who have all the complex rights, responsibilities, hopes, dreams, fears, and frustrations of being fathers.

Trained as an anthropologist, I had developed some of the tools to explore this phenomenon. I had spent years with South American Indians and witnessed the rituals of fatherhood in other societies. I knew that culture underlies phenomena that often seem immutable, such as the practice of medicine. Plus, I am a good listener. So I searched my field notes, mined the library, and began to collect stories from the experts—other fathers. More than fifty men shared their memories, plans, thrills, and concerns as fathers. I found men in doctors' offices and birthing classes, at family reunions and business meetings, on the street and in coffee shops. Following my own inclinations, these conversations focused on the process by which men took up the mantle and assumed the role of fatherhood. We discussed the deliberations, the preparations, and the reality of joining children in a lifetime of becoming. These men talked about sharing pregnancy, birth, childhood, and adolescence with partners and children. They recounted the difficulty of letting go as grown children leave home to enter the world. Most of all, we talked about birth: that of fathers and that of their babies.

I discovered that inside every father is a birth story he wants to tell. Despite the fact that we rarely hear men talk about childbirth, these men relished the opportunity. They have powerful and personal stories of what they did and how it felt. Each father had his own unique and intense memories. One talked about the feel of his partner's belly during contractions, another about the mixture of boredom and fear; some could describe the smallest detail in the first sight of their babies, and many waxed poetic about the feeling at first holding the new being. I became their willing audience.

Anthropologists do not survey large numbers of random and anonymous individuals: we record the more complex perspectives of a smaller number of people who share a common experience. The men with whom I talked came from what we might call the mainstream of American birthing. Most were middle-class men in long-term relationships with their partners. They went to birthing classes, gave birth in hospitals, and returned to work soon after. Although I talked with home birth, gay, adoptive, teenage, and single fathers, I did not try to include all their fascinating stories in this book. Instead, I focus on a more standard birthing story as it has played out for fathers in the conventional medical establishment.

Being an anthropologist, I compared these men's experiences with those of fathers in different societies. I returned to Paraguay and talked with Guaraní fathers and to the library and combed the ethnographies of other anthropologists. I found that pregnancy and birth were powerfully important to dads in those cultures. They rarely caught babies and cut cords, but each group had its own way of including fathers. Library research showed that throughout European history men took part in birth. In the stories of Strabo and Elizabethan sonnets, men take their place next to pregnant and birthing women. I eventually came to see that even the American men we considered so removed from birthing, those twentieth-century fathers in maternity waiting rooms, were intimately and directly involved in their children's birth. Each society and each historical period had its own means of recognizing the importance of fathers to birth, and the importance of birth to fathers.

I came to realize that today's fathers had taken part in a grand experiment in new fatherhood. In a self-conscious effort to foster this nurturing role, our society has invited men into the chamber to share the birth of their own babies. Couples who experienced the sexual revolution and chose alternative lifestyles (or at least heard about them) wanted to share birth. Men whose own fathers never set foot on a maternity ward sought to share these most intimate and powerful moments with their partners and babies. And they were transformed. Although every man has a unique experience and each enters fatherhood in his own way, men returned from the birthing room with a new and profound commitment to their children, their partners, and themselves. Birthing had become the rite of passage for every man who wants to become this new kind of father.

Kevin's Birth Story

Kevin was twenty-seven when his wife Laura discovered she was pregnant with their first child. The news came as a bit of a shock. They had not been intending to have children quite yet, as they had been hoping that Kevin's new contracting business would be strong enough to provide a stable income and allow Laura to stay home with the new baby. But Kevin greeted the idea with good-natured anticipation, and enjoyed sharing the news with his friends and family.

"It was something we were talking about, but nothing we had wanted to happen right then. But, then again, it happened and we were real excited."

From early on Laura made it clear that she wanted him to be part of the process; not that either one of them had any clear idea of what that meant. Kevin dutifully went to Laura's first prenatal checkups, sitting self-consciously in the room with the painted giraffe and thumbing magazines with covers showing pictures of gurgling babies as the physician asked questions and poked at Laura. It all remained an abstract concept until one day when Kevin saw the blurry image of their fetus in the sonogram. He could make out the pulsing heart on the green, glowing screen and felt a new sense of wonder and pride. He took the printout to work the next day and had a good time showing it around. The younger guys on the crew could not have cared less, but those who already had kids took the time to trace out the little being in the shadowy image. He tucked the picture in his wallet and kept it.

As Laura began to show, Kevin was transfixed by the magic of her bulging belly and began to feel the reality of their pregnancy. More than an image, it was there between them as they hugged. It spurred him to finish the baby's room and put the last touches on the deck, a project that had been delayed by their previously busy lives. He worked even longer hours, paid down some debt, and put their finances in better order.

Kevin first attended birthing classes with the same sense of duty as he had in the first prenatal checkups. It was in these classes that I first met him, looking vaguely embarrassed, holding the pillow and quilt that they sat on in class. He stared at the medical drawings on the wall to avoid eye contact with the seven other pregnant couples. Sitting in the coffee shop some months later, Kevin recalled, "I think I'd only read a little bit and I wasn't real convinced yet." After the first class, however, he went with enthusiasm. Kevin continued, "By the second week I had finished reading 'Husband, Coach, Childbirther'—I forget what it's called. And it clicked with me. I was, like, 'Wow, Laura, this is great! We really get to do this.' There were things for her to do all the time. She had to do her Kegels, all her little exercises and stuff. And I was getting excited because I knew what I was supposed to do. Every night I would massage her and made sure she did her exercises."

The first contractions came one Sunday afternoon two months later. Looking back, Kevin would recount the joy he felt in this early stage and the appreciation he developed for Laura's power of concentration and strength. "I timed the contractions, because our biggest fear was getting to the hospital too early. She called a friend and we ordered a pizza and just waited. At about three in the morning she started having some real good contractions, so we said, 'Okay, let's go.'" He brought the car around, got the suitcase, and drove carefully along the prescribed route to the hospital. As Laura pulled inward into her body, Kevin took care of admission and made sure they were given the kind of birthing room they had chosen. Everything was going according to plan.

In the hospital, the nurse got them settled, hooked up an IV for liquids, and put a fetal monitor around Laura. Kevin enjoyed watching the sweeping blue arcs that traced contractions and the shorter jagged lines of their baby's heart. They gave him a way of defining contractions without asking Laura, and it was reassuring to know that the baby was in good shape. The machine changed the atmosphere, however. The beep of the machine filled the quiet and, as time went on, the paper spilled forth onto the floor beside the bed.

They labored for hours, but sometime in midmorning the nurse came in, checked Laura's cervix, and let them know they were making little progress. Laura seemed to have gotten stuck, her cervix not expanding beyond four centimeters. It was holding in the baby. As time wore on the strain and tediousness began to take its toll, making both of them tired and irritable. The feeling of being a smoothly functioning team began to disappear. Kevin reported, "We were left alone in this room and she kept thinking that she had to go to the bathroom, but the baby was just pressing on her bladder. She was hooked up to all these things—IV and the monitors and all that stuff—and she'd want to just get out of bed. Then she'd get mad at me for not trying to help her. It was just a lot of . . . we weren't connecting."

Soon after, the nurse came back in and suggested that an epidural might relax Laura and speed progress. They had not planned on anesthesia, they had not wanted it, but given her condition, they were ready for a little medication. "Really," Kevin admitted, "I couldn't wait for them to give her the epidural." With the medication, Laura fell quickly to sleep. The fetal monitor continued to beep out its paper trail, with a clear record of Laura's silent contractions, and reassurance of the baby's strong heartbeat. Kevin had the time and energy to dig out the video recorder and tape Laura looking serene on the pillow.

"It was about that time that the doctor stopped by, took one look, and said, 'Well, let's break her water and see if that will speed things up a little bit.' I think they were starting to worry. It was taking a long time and she was getting tired. So they broke the water and I think that worked because she was ready to go in about an hour and a half." Kevin remembers that in those final minutes before delivery, he and the nurse made a good team. "I was on one side of Laura and the nurse was on the other side and we both had the back of her knees over our arms and we would hold her legs up so that she could bear down some weight on our arms so that she could push. And we were counting and helping her breathe."

The physician finally arrived and, in what seemed like a few short minutes of pushing, the top of the baby's head came into view. Then, in single powerful push, the head popped through into the world. The sight of the little blue-white scrunched face was shocking. Kevin held his breath. He looked at his wife's face. Laura was trying to sit up and see, but a nurse held her shoulder and the doctor said, "Wait, just two more pushes. Now give me a big one." Then, with the obstetrician's help, a little shoulder and arm appeared next to the head. Finally, even before she could push again, the entire body of a little being slid quietly into the physician's waiting gloves.

Kevin went numb; his mind was drained of all thought. He was overcome by exhilaration as he watched the flesh turn pink and was electrified as he saw the little face work its delicate lips. Almost as an afterthought, he craned his neck to see whether it was a boy or a girl. "It's a girl!" he called out to Laura, and the word reverberated through their world. "Yeah, she did it," he remembered. "She just pushed her out. Just to see that was wonderful. Such a relief."

The physician held the little girl for a minute, then handed her to a nurse, and turned to Kevin. "Well, here's your part," he said with a smile, and offered the new father a pair of surgical scissors. Kevin took the scissors with a sense of detachment and found himself being ushered into place beside the kneeling obstetrician. "I was thinking, 'Oh man, I don't know,'" remembered Kevin. The doctor held the cord for a few more seconds, then as the pulsing faded, he held out the section to be severed. "I did cut it. And it was a lot tougher, thicker than I thought it would be. I had to snip it twice. I kind of forgot that blood would squirt out and stuff. But I was real excited, and I was real happy."

Finished, Kevin turned to the warming table to watch his new daughter being wiped down and swaddled in clean cotton cloth. Then, with warmth and gentleness, the nurse handed the little being to him. "Here," she said, "do you want to take her over to Mom?" He gathered up the little bundle and placed her in Laura's waiting arms.

Birth Changes Men

Twenty years ago we discovered that men are important in birthing; now we must realize that birthing is important to men. Gathering men's birthing stories proved to be a most valuable means of exploring the topic. After talking to dozens of men, I chose eighteen for more extensive interviews. I interviewed most of these men several times in the months before and after birth.[1] Fathers talked about c-sections, vaginal births, miscarriages, and adoptions; they told about waiting, watching, and holding their baby against their chests. They expressed their anxiety, bravado, empathy, and incompetence. Every story was different; every father had his own intense experience. Some loved it; others were riven by fear; most were moved to tears, and some to laughter. A father named Mark put it this way: "Right when [my son] was born, I was kind of almost numb. I was in a daze. Not a daze; I was kind of out of it—overwhelmed." No two fathers had the same experience: all fathers are affected differently by the birth of their babies. Despite their uniqueness, however, the stories contain several common threads that relate to the more general cultural construction of fathers' role in birth.

Men's stories confirmed my own experience that fathers are created in birthing children. Women seem to quietly grow into motherhood as they feel their bodies grow rounder with the baby. Fathers are aware of no such biological experience. As fathers wait for birth, they take care of mothers, babies' rooms, and gassing up the car—but do not attend to themselves. They enter the hospital thinking about the moms' pain and the babies' health. They wait, wonder, and worry—and then are blindsided by one of life's most intense experiences. In a moment that is unexpected, unrecorded, and all to often unrecognized, the intensity and emotion of birth fires the crucible for a man's great transformation into a nurturing father.

Identity is only one part of the change to fatherdom: the event also reshapes a man's social world. I remember the wonder, joy, and relief I felt as I cradled my newborn daughter. I had this new, profound human connection. In a moment that is experienced by fathers with great power but little self-awareness, birth brings men into the middle of a child's world and moves infants to center stage for newly born dads. As I held her, engrossed in her little fingers, she was forging other changes in my social world. Only later would I discover the new script I had in relation to my wife, and the ways we would adjust to our changing roles.

Talking to other men, I have become acutely aware of how parents come to a new understanding of each other and their relationship as they struggle with the presence and demands of a new baby. At a greater level, for which the anthropologist has a special appreciation, birth reshapes the tie between a father and the larger society. Once a man has passed through the portals of his child's birth, we look at him differently, no matter how involved he was or was not. Whether new fathers like it or not, they are changed in the eyes of friends, relatives, acquaintances, religion, and the state.

The Medium: Fathers' Rituals

We know little about the birthing practices of contemporary American fathers. At first glance this is surprising, as social scientists have been studying birthing for almost a hundred years. As early as 1908, a German folklorist named Arnold van Gennep documented pregnancy and childbirth practices around the globe, considering them as important as ceremonies of initiation and marriage. The last decade has produced an extensive anthropological literature analyzing birthing in contemporary hospitals. This literature has analyzed the place of mothers, babies, doctors, staff in hospital birthing—but not fathers (see, for examples, Leavitt 1986; Davis-Floyd 1992).

We have been very aware of the importance of fathers in birth in other cultures. As early as 1557, the French missionary Jean de Léry first visited the ancestors of the Guaraní, the Tupinamba, near the bay of Rio de Janeiro and watched fathers take a central role in birth.

> I saw for myself the father receive the child in his arms, tie off the umbilical cord, and cut it with his teeth. Continuing to serve as a midwife, but unlike ours over here [France], who pull on the noses to make them more beautiful, he, on the contrary, pushed in his son's nose and crushed it with his thumb; this is done over there with all children, who are thought to be prettier when they are snub nosed. As soon as the baby has come out of the mother's womb, he is washed clean and immediately painted all over with red and black by the father, who then lays him down, without swaddling him, in a cotton bed hung in the air. If the child is a boy, the father makes him a wooden sword, a little bow and arrows feathered with parrot plumes; then, placing it all beside the infant, and kissing him, he will say to him, his face beaming, 'My son, when you come of age, be

skilled in arms, strong valiant, warlike, so that you can take vengeance on
your enemies.' (Léry [1578] 1990, 154)

In fact, anthropologists have been eager to analyze fathers' birthing ritual
in other societies. When reports such as Léry's found their way into anthropological accounts, the self-satisfied "civilized" world was regaled with tales of
"primitive" South American Indian men lying in hammocks, writhing in pain,
and calling out—as their wives gave birth quietly nearby. In his 1861 book *Das
Mutterrecht*, a single example of a genre that became quite popular, and one of
the first great monographs in anthropology, the Swiss jurist Johann Jakob
Bachofen found this imitative behavior both strange and counterintuitive. He
tried to explain it as a failed attempt for fathers to declare their paternity in
societies where mothers held dominant power, a temporary problem that would
ultimately be solved by social evolution toward patriarchy.

If anthropology has analyzed birthing in contemporary society, and fathers-
in-birthing in other cultures, why are we so ignorant of the importance of birth
to American fathers? The answer lies in the fact that American fathers were considered extraneous to the process. Social scientists like Bachofen assumed that
modern society had evolved beyond the point of believing that fathers had a
place in birth. Throughout most of the nineteenth and twentieth centuries,
fathers were excluded from birth. Men were recognized as making a small
(albeit significant) contribution to conception, but not throughout pregnancy,
labor, and delivery. The lore, rituals, and especially the biology of birth were a
feminine domain. Women's discussion fell to hushed tones when a man entered
the room; physicians asked fathers to leave during prenatal checkups, and hospitals barred fathers from watching the delivery of their own children. In fact,
fathers were often blamed for this traumatic event, rather than considered part
of its resolution. I remember stories of my own grandmother helping deliver a
child in the 1940s. As the husband waited anxiously outside the room, she
observed, "He'd better worry; he's the one who got her into this mess." After
hospital birth, the newborn was delivered from the mother and then exhibited
to the newly minted father from behind the sterile safety of the nursery's plate
glass window.

Fathers' role in birthing babies has changed dramatically in the last two
decades. American families broke down the barricades that isolated men from
pregnancy and birth. Couples fought to bring fathers into birth with legal peti-

tions, statistical arguments, and financial leverage: and they won. Some of the fathers I interviewed had experienced firsthand radical changes in the practice of birth. They were restricted from the birth of their first child (for the good of the mother and baby), only to be expected at the birth of the later ones (for the good of the mother and baby).

In a remarkably brief period, men have gone from being excluded from birth, to being admitted, then invited, and finally, expected in the delivery room. Fathers are not just observers of birth, but active in the entire birthing process. They attend baby showers, go to birthing classes, and share the intimate, everyday details of their partners' pregnancies. At the hospital, they join the fray with enthusiasm, apprehension, excitement, and fear—not to mention stopwatches, birthing manuals, and video cameras. They bring juice, hold hands, and struggle to find words of support. In the final moments, fathers catch babies, cut cords, and hold their new infants to their chests. After decades of being the offstage antagonist in the drama of birth, dads have become important players in the limelight.

The various roles for men in birthing emphasize the importance of culture in determining our practice of birth. If we can change the birthing team in a few short years, the cast of characters is obviously not determined by biology. Our attitudes, ideas, norms, and values decide how and with whom we birth our babies. This is not to deny that biology provides a basic structure for reproduction. Birth has been patterned by millions of years of physical evolution to assure the continued survival of the species, and much of the process happens without individual decisions or cultural norms. According to a biological clock, hormones activate muscles and prepare tissue for parturition, the amniotic sac breaks, contractions start, and the child begins its slow path down the birth canal toward physical independence. But to ignore the ways culture organizes biological birthing is like suggesting that our culture's cuisine is dictated by the biological drive that accompanies hunger. Few gastronomists (or anthropologists) would care to suggest that Americans' preference for limp fried potatoes (or English choice of crisp ones) is a function of basic human biological needs. Likewise, when Americans prepare to give birth, we approach it through the lens of our own culture.

The fathers I talked with, more than most anthropologists, are aware that whatever the biological substrate, childbirth is carried out according to a plan that is designed by the medical community and taught to birthing parents. Birth is an intensely personal event, especially because individual experience of exhilaration, anxiety, pain, and pleasure are closely intertwined. But a closer analysis of birth shows that few activities are defined by fathers themselves. Mothers, nurses, obstetricians, as well as families and the general public, offer very specific sets of guidelines for fathers' actions in the hospital birthing room.

Ritual

Rather than think of father's part in birth as pragmatic action, it is helpful to see his performance as ritual. Anthropologist Catherine Bell (1992) points out that secular ritual can be distinguished from pragmatic behavior by two primary characteristics. First, ritual behavior is carried out according to cultural dictates, rather than for practical effect. The chants uttered in Zuni birthing rooms and the "lying-in" practiced by Japanese men have little direct affect on the biology of parturition. They are not demanded by the immediacy of the birth, but by a cultural template that defines what actions various participants take during the process of birth. Even pragmatic aspects, however, can sometimes take on ritual formality. The physician's lab coat was originally designed to protect his clothes, but today it is far more important as a means to define his social position and role in the medical setting. Doctors who rarely enter the laboratory or examining room don the costume before seeing patients.

Second, birth ritual communicates to an audience. The physician's coat is designed to be "read" by staff and patients. It symbolizes a social position with rights and responsibilities of rank. It suggests the relative position of others and demands a specific treatment in return. As such, ritual often communicates to those engaged in the ritual themselves. For example, the doctor may feel especially like a doctor when wearing a lab coat. In Jewish tradition, baby boys are circumcised with family and friends in attendance. This bris milah ceremony communicates the child's transformation to membership in the larger community, and as the parents and attendants take part they come to a new realization about their place in their child's life and in the larger community.

Ritual is more than action; it also defines and is defined by the space in which it occurs. Ritual space is carved out of the ordinary world to provide an arena for the performance of formalized symbolic performances. The action of ritual infuses the three physical dimensions, as well as the fourth—time, through which it moves—defining and transforming them. Ritual space, in turn, heightens the symbolic meaning of social action. The stations of the cross in a Catholic Church and the central altar at a Masonic lodge give meaning to ritual, even as they are defined by the symbolic activity.

Two contemporary scholars of ritual, David Chidester and Edward Linenthal (1995), point out that a wide variety of common areas in everyday American life are defined by secular rituals. Historical sites, gyms, and gambling casinos are organized to express and reinforce the symbolic meanings of the activities they contain. In a study of contemporary birthing, anthropologist Robbie Davis-Floyd (1992) shows that the same is true in hospitals. As nurses usher visitors out of the room, the space takes on new meaning as sterile and the birthing mother (in being allowed to remain) is transformed into someone special. The hospital, home, and birthing centers become defined as "special" by the way that they reinforce the messages of the ritual actions. As fathers are asked to leave the delivery room or allowed to stay, they are identified as outsiders or insiders, respectively.

An analysis of fathers' birthing as ritual calls attention to the fact that their actions are less for practical effect than for their power to communicate messages. As a Guaraní father cuts the umbilical cord with a bamboo knife, the act is more than efficient birthing procedure. The knife becomes a symbol of power and masculinity, and the act communicates change in the father, his partner, and their new child. Likewise, as the American father helps pregnant mom up the stairs or mops her laboring brow, the act has more to do with messages than with the physical exigencies of pregnancy and birthing.

Ritual meanings of birth do not derive from ritual itself, but from more general understandings of birth and babies, fathers and mothers, and health and illness in the larger society. The father's presence or absence makes sense—and only makes sense—in the larger cultural context. Being accepted or rejected defines and redefines the father's new role and his relations with his baby, his partner, and his community.

Rites of Passage

Gennep realized that childbirth was a special kind of ritual, which he called a "rite de passage." Like puberty and death ceremonies, he recognized that birthing rituals mark one of life's major changes. "The life of an individual in any society is a series of passages from one age to another and from one occupation to another. Wherever there are fine distinctions among age or occupation groups, progression from one group to the next is accompanied by special acts" ([1908] 1960, 3).

Passage rites are characterized by periods of isolation from general society, called "liminality." Removed from the previous identity and shorn of the rights and responsibilities that it entailed, the initiate makes the transition to a new social role. Then, with fanfare and ceremony, the individual is reintroduced to society, with a new persona and place in the group. In boot camp, for example, civilians abandon their previous identity as they enter the military. They are literally and figuratively shorn of their previous identity, giving up hair, clothes, and personal pasts. Even the distinction conferred by a college degree is temporarily left behind. The hazing and homogenizing process of military life and drills reduces any remaining differences between the recruits—even to the most basic distinctions that our society makes between races and class. Being a recruit negates all previous and future identities. Only graduation from basic training provides relief from this liminal state, integrating graduates into the social milieu of the military with a new identity as soldier, sailor, or airman.

Why do *men* perform childbirth ritual? How do these socially constructed rituals affect men's ideas of themselves, their relations with their partners and children, and their positions in the larger society? This book argues that an American father's assistance in birth is a rite of passage to fatherhood. Like boot camp and fraternity initiation, birth ritual separates men from society, imposes its symbolic processes on them, and finally reintegrates them into conventional society as changed beings. On one hand, men are transformed as individuals, acquiring the new identity of fatherhood; on the other, the birthing rite of passage provides public recognition of his new social position. As a man's attention is focused on the infant newcomer, he enacts rituals that change his own roles and relationships: he is transformed and transforms himself into one of these men we call a father.

What of the fathers who do not attend birth? The older men I talked with were often relegated to hospital waiting rooms. They recounted long waits on hard benches in the halls of officious maternity wards. But they were no less engulfed by birth. They waited and worried and sat and smoked, and then made the classic trip to the nursery room window to set eyes on their new bundle of baby. I came to see their isolation as an anxious vigil. Although they were removed in space from mothers' labor and delivery, these fathers enacted a scripted performance that focused directly on the momentous social event at hand. Would anyone suggest that sitting shiva is unconnected with the burial of a loved one, or that the Irish wake was not a ritual?

Aware of the rituals we enact during parturition, I became curious about our other rituals of childbirth. I knew from my previous research among indigenous peoples of South America, that from the first days of conception, Guaraní fathers perform ritual proscriptions that anthropologists call "couvade." They cannot eat venison, shoot monkeys, or have sex when their wives and lovers are pregnant. As birth draws near they cannot enter the forest to hunt. When contractions start, some men even take to their hammocks to writhe and moan like a birthing woman.

The rituals of childbirth do not end with delivery. As a father comes to know the new being, he depends on a ritual template for the all-consuming first minutes of his new relationship. In past generations, a father made the trip to the nursery room window for the ritual viewing of his infant in the arms of a uniformed nurse. Today, he is more likely to hold the little being to his chest and lovingly count fingers and toes. He stares into the bluish eyes and gurgles a happy welcome. Whether in his arms or through a window, the introduction is every bit as scripted as the ritual handshake of new acquaintances, or the first kiss of an adolescent.

Thus, in studying birth as a rite of passage to fatherhood, I do not restrict myself to the brief period in the hospital. Birthing begins with conception, perhaps before, and does not end immediately after parturition. Our own practice of isolating or integrating fathers in pregnancy, at birth, and beyond is clearly just as much a ritual as the behavior of the Tupi-Guaraní father in the sixteenth century.

How does birthing ritual change men into fathers? Although intensely personal, birth is a social event. The mother, father, and child, as well as attendants and relatives, engage in actions that carry powerful messages to all concerned. A man sees himself defined and redefined in the eyes of his partner, the nurses, and the rest of the birthing team. Their shared perception becomes the crucible in which he forges his new identity, relations, and role.

In past generations, fathers were restricted to the maternity waiting room, mirroring the emotional isolation considered appropriate for the family patriarchs. The opening of delivery room doors to men demanded revisions in our rituals of reproduction. As their family roles changed to emphasize nurturing over authority, fathers' needed a new birthing script. Who wrote this script? In the United States, obstetricians themselves reintroduced men into birthing. Doctors Lamaze, Bradley, and Dick-Read argued for childbirth with less intervention from medical systems and more direct support by fathers. With the stroke of these obstetricians' pens, birthing rituals were created whole cloth almost overnight. Fathers were told to train and support their wives in pregnancy, to comfort and coach them in labor, and to catch the baby and cut the umbilicus. Men assumed their new ritual responsibilities with care and enthusiasm.

The Message: Fathers, Babies, Partners, and Society

What is the message that these intense rituals carry? If timing contractions is symbolic, what is the message? If sitting in a waiting room is a passage rite, passage into what? My interviews uncovered a variety of messages embedded in birth performance, and in each case fathers are changed in their self-concept and social relations. For example, as a husband pants with his laboring wife, he shares her experience and comes to a new understanding of her place in his world. As a father cuddles the newborn, he is overwhelmed by the understanding that this new being is henceforth a part of himself and his life. Finally, with a handful of cigars, a father communicates to fellow workers his new role as father, even if the cigars are made of chewing gum. In the following sections, the rituals of pregnancy and childbirth are analyzed for their messages concerning a father's identity; his connection to his baby; his relations with his partner; and his place in the world.

Fathers' Role and Identity

Birth messages change men into fathers. As a newborn makes its way into our world, a man takes up the mantle of fatherhood and is forever altered. Often unconsciously and usually with little preparation, men assume one of the most engrossing identities of life. Fatherhood reaches deep into the soul, more profound than religion, more demanding than a job, and more permanent than marriage. Fatherhood is a fundamentally new identity: a new way of feeling, thinking, and being in the world.

Sociologists have defined "role identities," self-concepts that correspond to particular positions that individuals occupy in society. A husband comes to think of himself in self-images that develop out of his relationship with his wife, drawing on his ideas of what a husband is in his society. Unlike personality, individuals develop a variety of these role-identities throughout life, based on the various roles occupied in the family, at work, and in the larger society. Men, for example, develop ideas of themselves as breadwinners, lovers, sons, and friends based on the social roles they occupy in different groups.

In fatherhood, procreation creates a new identity that conforms to men's new and renewed relationships in society. One father recalled to me, "They took her [the baby] to the nursery and I remember walking through the halls in that getup, you know, the suit, and going to see my family and friends and feeling like, you know, really, like, wow, I'm a father. This is really weird." This identity joins previous self-concepts, often jockeying with other identities in shifting hierarchies. A man's identity as a fraternity brother, for example, recedes as he assumes responsibility for his new son.

As we shall see below, the rituals of pregnancy, labor, and delivery communicate a new series of ideas and identities to participants. In pregnancy and childbirth, during birthing classes and while assembling the crib, men consciously work on skills that they consider fatherly, while they unconsciously form an image of themselves as fathers. What determines a man's commitment to fatherhood? Recent research suggests that the level of investment a man makes in his identity as a father is determined by his relations with others, especially his partner. In a survey of 184 married fathers, wives' opinions ranked among the most salient factors in determining a man's commitment to his role as father (Pasley, Futris, and Skinner 2002, 136): if a man thinks that his wife values his parenting skills and activities, he is far more likely to consider fatherhood as central to his identity.

Childbirth, therefore, becomes a structured means to develop the identity of this new father in activities and relations with babies and partners. The process of pregnancy becomes ritualized in birthing classes and routine chores, like assembling the crib. In labor and delivery, hospitals and physicians provide these scripts. Davis-Floyd (1992) has pointed out that most of the activities of hospital birthing carry powerful symbolic meaning for all concerned. As ritual, medical practice transforms a man's idea of himself as a man and a father. As he cuts the umbilical cord, he has a greater effect on his own sense of self than on the two individuals he is symbolically disconnecting.

Bonding with Babies

Despite the popular perception that fathers sit on the sidelines while newborn babies and mothers form strong relationships, recent research has shown that neonates form similar attachments with fathers. The process has been given a variety of labels: bonding or attachment, if one is focused on the child; engrossment, if one is thinking about the father. In landmark studies in the 1970s, psychologists detailed both sides of the relation. Michael Lamb (1977) studied babies' attachment to fathers, showing that babies experience the same level of stress when fathers leave their field of vision as when mothers do. Looking at fathers' relations with their infants, Martin Greenberg and Norman Morris found that fathers have a strong and visceral attraction to their newborns, and begin to form powerful and enduring relations to the new beings. One father, Nicolas, remembers the experience this way: "They gave me the baby just a couple of minutes after he was born. He was crying a whole lot and I started talking to him. And this always struck me, is that my voice kind of soothed him and he stopped crying after a while and I don't know whether he could hear me or not because I have a very deep voice or if he recognized my voice from talking to his stomach. And so I did realize and my wife noticed that, too. She goes, 'He stopped crying. He heard his dad and stopped crying.'"

The argument below extends psychological awareness of father-infant bonds to look at the ritual process in which the new relation is forged. Few sociologists would expect the time at the altar to be the fundamental force in creating the bond between the new couple. Similarly, it is unlikely that the time that a man spends in the birthing room is the primary influence on his connection with his child. The rituals of childbirth, however, begin long before the baby's arrival. From the first word of the pregnancy, to birthing classes, the telling of family and friends, labor, delivery, and afterward, a father experiences a complex series of rituals that focus his time and attention on the new being with whom he will be closely tied. These rituals create the context in which fathers and babies experience each other and their new relationships.

Companions in Parenthood

Childbirth ritual allows men to create and recreate their relationships with their partners: a child forces every man into a new relation with his partner-in-parenthood. The period of adjustment to parenthood is a time for new and exciting ideas and cooperative activities for couples, but also a time of greater potential conflict and confrontation. The increased stress and distress that a couple suffers in the first months of their baby's life has been well documented by a variety of studies. During the process of pregnancy and birth, couples learn new aspects and identities of each other, some of which they had never known (or previously found easier to ignore). The pressures of a new baby cause parents to feel less satisfaction with their relationship and the quality of their communication. The arrival of a child also brings a host of new responsibilities. Individuals find that a new level of cooperation is demanded by the child's presence. Decisions need to be made about the child, and with an infant that needs constant care, a couple is forced increasingly to coordinate time and activities. (For additional discussion of this topic, see Miller and Sollie 1980; Cowan and Cowan 1992; and Tomlinson 1987.)

The ritual of childbirth emphasizes the joint aspect of the endeavor of reproduction. For fathers, communicating their commitment and cooperation is especially important. Kevin, for example, looked back on the other benefits of laboring together. "It brought Laura and I real close and that helped. I think that that really helped strengthen our marriage, just going through that experience together and knowing what each other's roles were and supporting each other and helping each other." Like Kevin and Laura, couples that practice labor during pregnancy enact the joint process of physically producing the baby. As they perform the rituals of birth, they act out the dependence they have on one another. As they join together around their new baby, they realize the importance of each other as parents and partners.

Fathers, Birth, and Society

Childbirth does not create a relationship simply between a man and child or woman; it creates and recreates roles and relationships between men and the larger society. It establishes new ties with kin, as well as the political, social, and religious institutions of society. Birth challenges the place of men in their social world: men alter their old social identities by establishing their new roles and relations as fathers.

When babies arrive, there are a host of forms to file and things to do. They need social security numbers and birth certificates; they might need a christening or a bris; their names need to be added to insurance policies, birth registries, and W-2 forms. Each of these tasks gives a child an identity with the state, the church, and the myriad people who will touch or be touched by the new life.

Each bureaucratic act also demands that a father declare his new social position. Babies need parents or guardians to act as their official representatives, and fathers (and mothers) find themselves declaring their new status as they stand up at church or sit down with the human resources officer at work.

Ritual not only transforms the participants, but the larger society. Therefore, birthing becomes a venue to change fatherhood itself. After decades of being considered stern authority figures, dads are increasingly idealized as nurturers of their children. This social change occurs as different and often conflicting perspectives and voices compete for control over the meaning of symbols. As new, younger parents raised voices against the idea that mother's place was in the home and father's place was at work, the 1950s image symbol of the father in business suit or work shirt is replaced by Robin Williams fighting for his children as Mrs. Doubtfire.

Victor Turner, an anthropologist working with the Ndembu of West Africa, pointed out (1977) that ritual not only mirrors reality, but also creates reality. Ritual symbols are both *of* the real world and symbols *for* the real world; they become templates through which we take action to create new social relations. Turner took Gennep's concept of the rite of passage into the social realm, asserting that ritual not only reflects or communicates existing social realities, but can create and recreate social norms. In hospital birthing, for example, bringing men into the delivery room reflected the more intimate bonds of couples, and also helped create a new, more nurturing father.

On another level, birth provides an arena for negotiation of conflict with the larger society. Issues of conflict between class, gender, age, or ethnic groups compete with one another to define the meanings of social forms. Various perspectives compete to define the meaning of ritual and roles in the larger society. As men discover and create their identity and relations of fatherhood, they are brought into negotiation with various powerful actors, who are themselves negotiating diverse and often conflicting relations.

Fathers had to fight their way into the birthing room. Throughout most of the last century, hospital policy prohibited fathers from watching the birth of their babies. In newspapers, legal briefs, and medical journals, physicians argued that fathers were unnecessary to birthing and a danger to mother and child. Couples responded with a popular movement that created new birthing rituals that forced hospitals to include fathers. Physicians and hospitals acquiesced in an attempt to assure busy maternity wards.

What were the ideological conflicts that underscored the fathers-in-birthing debate? The following suggests that hospital birthing is characterized by a biological perspective that ignores the social, spiritual, and psychological aspects of birth. Since fathers are primarily participants in these unrecognized facets of birthing, they were excluded from birthing rituals. This, in turn, reinforced the definition of birth as a biological enterprise. The new birthing rituals, which include fathers, recognize and legitimize the social, spiritual, and psychological aspects of birth. Fathers' fight was part of the effort to redefine birth as a multifaceted event, and birthing became the ritual arena to negotiate the conflicting ideas about birth and the family.

Reinventing Birth: Inventing Tradition

In the past, anthropologists understood culture as a static entity that societies accumulated over a long time in response to a given environment. Traditions, they suggested, were inherited with a continuity and organization analogous to a natural object. Unchanging and internally coherent, cultures stood as templates through which societies acted in the world. Thus, anthropologists could characterize most of the world's nonindustrial societies as mired in the distant past. Without the capacity to change, these "traditional" societies relived the lives of their ancestors, locked in the inefficiency of the preindustrial era and the irrationality of the prescientific society.

A second and more useful conception of culture that gained prominence in the 1970s suggested that culture was constantly changing, reformulating in response to the environment and human knowledge. As knowledge is invoked in the world, it adapts to new physical and intellectual environments. Like the river that can never be stepped into twice, culture is the flowing body of symbolic relations that is never repeated in precisely the same manner. As the swirling eddies of water cut away the sand on the bank, they change the course of the river and send future water along an ever-changing course.

Like a shifting river, each couple that has gone forth to birth has changed American birthing ritual. In response to the demands and experiences of fathers and mothers, doctors and staff, American society has developed new roles for men to act out in the birthing room. In the nineteenth century, fathers acted as assistants in birthing, boiling cloths and providing another pair of strong arms when they were necessary. In the first two-thirds of the twentieth century, the tradition of ritual seclusion in the hospital waiting room was created. The last three decades have seen yet another tradition created for men and birth. As husbands become increasingly companions to wives and nurturers to babies, they are invited back into the delivery room. Childbirth classes teach husbands to time contractions and coach laboring women. They are trained to minister to mothers and catch newborns. They swaddle babies and record the event for posterity on video cameras; they do those things befitting a loving husband and caring father.

But couples do not write or enact birthing ritual in a social vacuum. Babies are birthed in a cultural milieu that dictates what will happen and what it means. This is especially true in hospital births, where codified policy dictates process, and where meanings and methods are defined by a long tradition of medical practice. The couple who write their own wedding vows must contend with prevailing religious doctrine if they choose to be wed in a church, synagogue, or mosque. Likewise, as America's families began to request new birthing practices that included fathers, they confronted hospitals, physicians, and staff with entrenched ideas and practices.

What happened when couples chose to have fathers as spiritual, social, and psychological participants in birth? The new concept of fathers-in-birthing encountered established medical norms that defined dads as extraneous and incidental. The enactment of the rituals created conflict, as new symbolic practice entered into dialogue with the meanings and messages of medical tradition. The confrontation of these two cultures is the context for fathers' experience of birth. Its effect is clear in Kevin's discussion of the birth experience.

The Problem

Kevin loved the birth experience and would not have missed it for the world, but there was another side to Kevin's birth story. As time went on, he began to be bothered by nagging doubts and questions. Could he have done more to help Laura? Why, if they were going to have an epidural, had he spent the time studying massage? Who decided that he was to cut the cord? Why could he remember his baby's face so well in those eighteen seconds after birth, when he could hardly remember what Laura looked like over her eighteen hours in labor? When I interviewed him some months after the birth, Kevin was able to put words to some of the incidents that left him feeling as if something were wrong. In some ways, the process seemed to create emotional distance, not empathy.

He talked about not being able to defend Laura from the intrusions of the nurses; in retrospect it seemed she was being poked and prodded by nurses who spoke a language all their own. The object of their attention was the woman whom he loved and wanted to help. She was hurting and scared and there was nothing he could do to help but hold her hand. He couldn't even muster the confidence to assure her that everything was all right. "She was really hurting and I was real stressed out because I just didn't know how to help her, I guess. I kind of felt like there really wasn't very much for me to do because it seemed like it was just all medical. Then once they got her on the drugs, I was really kind of out of the picture. There was a recliner in there and I just rested, I just read. I'd look at her and look at the monitors."

Despite his overall positive feelings about birth, part of Kevin felt that he had failed to help his wife with either her pain or her battle with the medical system. "I feel like I should have done something, but I didn't know what to do. I was real naïve, I guess. We were real naïve about what was going on."

Fathers' birthing stories, like Kevin's, show that many men experience ambivalence about their childbirth experience. On the one hand, they feel the elation of joining with their partner to bring a son or daughter into the world. On the other, they walk away feeling that something was missing, or that they did something wrong. Rather than full members of the birthing teams, they feel peripheral to the birth of their babies. Although they feel joined in birthing, they walk away with a new sense of distance from their partners.

This book explores fathers' childbirth experience through the lens of the anthropologist, as social ritual that has been programmed according to American cultural norms. Rather than focus on the unique character of Kevin's relations with Laura, the staff, the obstetrician, and his baby, it is useful to see the process as scripted performance. His elation, disappointment, involvement, and displacement are defined by the larger cultural framework of American medicine and society.

The Biomedical Model

The ideas and traditions that underlie the practice of American birthing conform to what has been called the "biomedical model" (Rothman 1982). Just as the prayers and hymns of the Lutheran Church are organized around religious beliefs about the power of God, the rituals of labor and delivery in a hospital setting are organized by a set of medical assumptions and definitions. In the same way that religious knowledge provides a consistent and universal concept of the world and its workings, medical knowledge offers a coherent and comprehensive way of thinking about the body and its functioning.

Scientific knowledge, as it developed in the Enlightenment, was dependent on analyzing and classifying the human body according to form or function. Drawing on the mind-body dualism posited by Descartes, medical knowledge came to understand the body as an entity that could be described through a universal category and analyzed as an objective fact. The machine metaphor allowed medical specialists to analyze the body as a series of interrelated parts that could be disassembled and analyzed in isolation.

In birthing, the medical model suggested that the body of the pregnant woman could be understood as the object of description and analysis. Labor and delivery could be defined as the functioning of that machine through a process. The baby was the end product of the functioning of the body as machine. The medical model distinguished the mother and baby's experiences from the objective fact of birthing, and rendered the former unnecessary for understanding the true nature of birth. Four basic assumptions underlie the medical model of birthing: dualism, universalism, essentialism, and individualism. Beginning with these perspectives, medicine has created an understanding of birth that governs the actions and attentions of all participants.

Mind-Body Dualism: You Are Not What You Think!

In adopting the Enlightenment model of science, medical knowledge separated the mind and body, distinguished between the experience and the process, and rendered the body an object to be acted upon, not a subject of action. Descartes allowed modern philosophy to distinguish the mind from the body, but in doing so permitted natural philosophers to identify the body as an independent entity. The human body was freed from the thinking apparatus that gave it consciousness, freed from the spiritual aspect that gave it soul, and freed from the experience of being human.

The distinction between body and mind builds directly into a model of health that distinguishes the natural from the cultural. The physical body as a natural entity is separated and distanced from its socialized aspects. The biological body is defined by its mechanical functioning, and the cultural knowledge of the mind is considered unnecessary to understanding or acting upon the body.

Recent medical anthropology argues that by adopting this Cartesian understanding of the body, medical discourse rejected more holistic perspectives that integrate emotions and spirituality into our understanding of human beings. The biomedical model identified the essence of humanity not in the thinking mind, but in the acting body. By separating the mind and the body, the Cartesian dualism allowed the medical model to place primacy in the sphere of the body. Curing the body would heal the soul; the human spirit went the way of the flesh (Jacobus, Keller, and Shuttleworth 1990).

The medical profession assumes that the scientific understanding of birth is a fact that exists in the real world, not a cultural construction or subjective perspective. By attempting to derive a purely objective understanding of the material world, the medical model excludes what it considers biases and perceptions that are patterned by subjective understandings based on particular cultural frameworks. Thus, the objective reality described in the scientific literature purports to transcend all cultural categories and understandings.

Universalism: Bodies as Men

The second assumption of the biomedical model proposes a universalist model for the body and health that describes the body as an ideal type, reducing it to a stereotype that may not conform to any actual object. The enormous diversity of human waist sizes is reduced to a continuum, which provides the data to define a norm, which serves as the basis for the definition of the human waist. More than simply describing the world, this universal waist size then becomes the measure for the evaluation of waist sizes in the world. Individuals are compared against the medical definition and defined as either normal or aberrant. To put it in a more contemporary metaphor from the popular book *Men Are from Mars, Women Are from Venus* (Gray 1993), the biomedical model would mandate that, "*All* men are from Mars, *all* women are from Venus!"

This universalizing tendency in the biomedical model has implications for our understanding of birth. From the first medical understandings of the body, the male form was considered not simply superior, but was used as the standard for evaluation of all bodies. The definition of the human body *was* the male body. Simply by being different, the female body was considered both abnormal and inferior. This androcentric bias has a profound impact on our understanding of pregnancy and birth. The state of pregnancy is not only suggested to be abnormal in that it is singularly female, but it is especially abnormal; the more pregnant a woman becomes, the more her body diverges from the conventional and by definition the more unhealthy she becomes. Thus, in popular parlance, the medical model proposes that "men are from Mars and women are not!"

Essentialism: Getting Down to the Nitty-Gritty

The medical model not only assumes that bodies are all that counts and that only men's bodies count, but defines men by the bodies that they occupy. The concepts of "man" and "woman" are created around the manifestation of their physical forms. This focusing solely on the biology of the body reduces the purpose and the performance of the body to its physical nature. This third assumption of medical understandings, essentialism, reduces every individual to either a male or female being—then explains the perceived differences between men and women on the basis of the physical differences. So men and women are not only different, but all distinctions between the two genders are understood on the basis of physical factors.

The essentialist perspective leads medical practice to localize illness in specific physical processes. This is called the doctrine of specific etiology. Each disease has a specific biological cause and the removal of that problem will result in the restoration of the healthy functioning of the body as machine. (For more discussion of this, see Freund and McGuire 1991.) Just as the body could be isolated from social, psychological, and spiritual aspects of the person, so health can be reduced to a smoothly running machine and illness defined in a malfunctioning of the body.

Individualism: Alone with Your Body

Identifying the body as a biological object implies that illness is a characteristic of specific individuals, the fourth assumption. The biomedical model recognizes the individual as an entity that can be removed from his or her social milieu. The body as a physical entity is perceived as bounded and distinct from its physical context. The individual, in the same way, is understood to be distinct from the social context in which she or he exists. Not only is the body defined as an individual attribute, but health and disease are also understood to rest in the characteristics of the individual. Pathogens are seen as invaders of individuals and disease is understood as the breakdown of individual bodies. The fundamental unit of analysis of health is the individual, not the group. This theory does not deny that many physical ailments have a social component, but asserts that health and the disease are aspects of the individual, not society. Thus, in the biomedical model, alcoholism, hypertension, and depression are defined by physical symptoms of the individual and treated as diseases that rest in the attributes of that individual.

Biomedicine and Birth

The biomedical model, therefore, defines birth as an objective and universal process. The subjective experience of a woman in birth is subsumed into a universal model of a biological process of birth. In fact, her subjective experience is no longer even relevant. As Ernest Hemingway so succinctly wrote in the words of his father, responding to a woman in labor, "Her screams are unimportant. I don't hear them because they are unimportant" (Hemingway 1972). But the biomedical model does not simply define birth as biological process; pregnancy is defined as an abnormality in the normal physical state of the human body. If the normal body is not pregnant, the pregnant body is abnormal and by definition pathological. Given that the conventional biological state is defined to be the masculine body, pregnancy exaggerates the female qualities of a woman's body, making it even more aberrant than at other times.

The biomedical model also isolates pregnancy from the mother and the larger social milieu. Medical knowledge places the locus of pregnancy in a single organ of the female body. A woman's state of pregnancy emanates from the uterus that is transformed by the presence of the fetus. Like a machine with a misshapen part, a woman's body suffers the discomfort of disequilibrium. This disease has a specific cause that needs to be remedied before she will regain health. Just as the uterus is treated as a pregnant organ that can be isolated from a woman's body, so the pregnant woman is treated as a diseased individual who can be separated from her social context. The friends and family who share a woman's life are treated as unnecessary to the understanding of her condition, and the cure can be affected without their involvement. In short, pregnancy and birth in biomedical terms are an abnormal biological condition, rather than a normal social process.

These definitions lead to practices that are designed to maintain not the woman's own process, but that of the medically defined "normal" process. The goal of the medical system is to take a woman in a diseased state and return her to her conventional (almost) healthy condition. The physician is a technician with the interventions necessary to return the mother to normalcy. The obstetrician and medical interventions become appropriate and normal to the process of a successful delivery of the baby.

Birthing, Identity, and Power

In recent studies of childbirth, anthropologists have become aware of the importance of social control in determining the practice of birth. The biological act of birth is a social arena that creates and renews power relations. These point out that throughout history, birth has been considered a natural event; experienced women helped mothers birth their children at home. As physicians took over delivery in the nineteenth century and moved it into hospitals in the twentieth century, however, childbirth became redefined as a biological process to be managed by technicians. Mothers lost control of birthing to medical specialists who considered pregnancy an illness, and medical technology the cure. Where previously women birthed babies, now doctors delivered them. (This literature deserves a careful reading that cannot be offered in this brief space. As examples, I would recommend: Eakins 1986 and Oakley 1984 concerning the social control of birthing; Goldsmith 1990 on its history; Corea 1985 or Leavitt 1986 about technology and birth; and Scully 1994 on birthing as disease.)

Davis-Floyd argues convincingly that from the moment a woman enters the hospital, she is subjected to a ritual that redefines the birth as a biological event. She is stripped of her clothes, isolated from her family, and subjected to the poking and prodding of strangers. This highly structured rite of passage drives home the idea that she does not control herself or her birth, and transforms her into a biological object. She only need submit to technical control of the medical institution and the physician who will deliver her baby. When that baby is born, he or she undergoes a similar passage rite. Whisked away to the dehumanizing environment of the hospital nursery, the infant is institutionalized first, and only later ceremonially granted to the mother. She and her new baby are released from the hospital with new identities heavily influenced by our technical and patriarchal society.

Fathers and Birth: A New Perspective

Great care has been taken in developing fathers' place in birth activities. Whether in waiting or delivery rooms, men have a highly structured role to play in the process of birth. But my discussions with Kevin, Mark, and other men point out several aspects of birth that have been ignored. First, rather than being a distant observer or a technical support, fathers' experience at birth can be one of profound involvement. Although we think of men as peripheral observers of birth, they have an intensely subjective experience. More than involved, men are deeply transformed in the process, and exit as new (or renewed) fathers. Second, many men experience conflict at birth and leave feeling that something was missing. Even when it produced healthy mothers and babies, fathers suggest that they had misgivings about their experiences of birth and the relations that it fostered with their partners. Understanding that birth is accomplished according to a ritual that has ideological underpinnings allows us to better understand these fathers and their powerful and ambivalent experiences at birth.

The rituals designed for men's birthing are enacted by couples who seek to share the intimacy and power of birth as they draw together as a couple and family. However, they enact the rituals within the restrictive context of the biomedical model of birthing. This assumes that pregnancy is a biological condition of the mother and charges the birthing team with removing a healthy baby from the mother's body. Fathers are called upon to support and collaborate with medical institutions in returning mothers to their pre-pregnancy states and are expected to minister to mothers' and babies' biological needs.

Focusing on pregnancy and birth as a physical condition of mothers ignores the subjective experience and social connection that fathers have with birthing. By identifying birth as a physical process, the medical model denies the spiritual and emotional aspects of the event. By treating the physical condition as an individual attribute of mothers, fathers are defined as insignificant. In adopting the biomedical model of birth, we deny fathers' independent relationship with and experience of pregnancy and birth.

These are especially clear in fathers' pregnancy rituals, where men share the experience of fetal gestation. Couvade rituals are recognized in cultures around the world and historically in our own society. They remain common, though unacknowledged, in American culture. For example, most men reduce sex during pregnancy; they think that it is dangerous or wrong or both. But this sexual proscription is more taboo than medical practice. There is no biological reason to reduce sex—especially at a time when many women want more. (Women often enjoy sex and achieve orgasm more easily during pregnancy.) The biomedical model of birth ignores the existence of this contemporary couvade or, when that is impossible, defines men's pregnancy experience as pathological. By shifting out of the biomedical model of birth, couvade activities of American men stop being psychological pathologies and become rituals of transformation that have important social ramifications.

Being aware of the cultural content of birthing ritual points to the messages that were carried by traditional hospital birthing ritual, where men were isolated in maternity waiting rooms. The worried father smoking in isolation can be seen as performing a ritual role. Waiting rooms become symbolic chambers to hold men in a liminal state of ritual seclusion. Rather than dictated by birth itself, fathers were removed to enact the medical definitions and practices of birthing. Hospital birth was organized around the belief that the body was a biological object. The abnormality of pregnancy could be "cured" by the intervention of a physician and medical technology. Not only did birthing fathers reinforce the subjective and social nature of the birthing woman, but also the father's presence threatened the masculinity and the superiority with which the physician approached the mother. Fathers could be effectively neutralized in the sterile confines of the waiting room.

If men were antithetical to medical practice, why were they integrated into contemporary birthing rooms? Obstetricians themselves defined the new and alternative birth methods. They conflicted with standard medical practice, but not biomedical definitions of the body and birth. The major architects of new birthing, Dick-Read, Lamaze, and Bradley, consider birth a biological process. Mothers are taught to retreat from their social and spiritual selves into their animal nature. Fathers are trainers in practice and coaches in labor; they help the staff administer bedpans and ice chips, but fathers' principle task is to assure that mothers (or, more specifically, mothers' bodies) perform as efficient birthing machines. Fathers are included, but only if they collaborate with medical staff and corroborate the definitions that biomedicine imposes on birth and mothers.

If we consider birth a series of rituals that define pregnancy, labor, and delivery, how are fathers taught the methods and messages of medical ritual? Most men know little of birthing culture prior to pregnancy. Excluded from the feminine lore, they depend on birthing classes to learn about birth. For many men, this is the first ritual arena for their introduction to fatherhood. In the dark and quiet of the class, couples simulate birth. Like the Guaraní couvade, fathers learn to share pregnancy with their partners. They breathe together as if they were both in labor. But birthing classes carry other messages about birth as well: parents are taught the biomedical perspective of birth. Rather than an arm of the women's health movement, most birthing classes are managed by hospital administrations. With a curriculum that is tailored to the hospital where they will birth, couples are taught methods that conform to the conventional practice of birth.

Understanding the biomedical basis of American birth ritual sheds new light on what fathers' experience of birth. My conversations with men show that they are transfixed and transformed; they feel deeply and intimately connected with their partners and babies; and the intense worry of labor gives way to the profound excitement of seeing and holding their new babies. But understanding birth as ritual draws attention to the relation of this personal and subjective experience with the structured and formal process that is defined by society. As the biomedical model defines birth as a physical process undertaken by a female body, the subjective experiences of birthing fathers become insignificant. While many fathers feel an intense connection with their partners in birth, our medical ideology of birth only recognizes the importance of these social relations in facilitating biological delivery. While a father may feel profoundly important in his baby's life, our model of birth suggests that, being men, fathers have little to offer these new beings.

It is not surprising that many fathers experience a deep ambivalence in the roles that they are offered in the rituals of labor and delivery. Trained to help mothers in labor, fathers are asked to ignore their own experience. Despite the verbal messages that they are important to birth, fathers usually find their role quickly superseded by nurses and physicians as they are relegated to the observers and the (video) recorders of the process. Although taught that birth is an intimate event to be shared with mothers and babies, fathers are expected to collaborate with staff in biomedical procedure. In the end, men often find themselves co-opted by physicians, reinforcing the power of the medical process to enact its own rituals of transformation over the mother, and accomplishing this same purpose with the father in the process.

Finally, biomedical practice ignores the importance of birth as a rite of passage to fatherhood, denying the role of birth ritual in initiating and developing a relationship of the father with his new child. This book argues that men's participation in birth provides an important window for men to develop relationships with their children. Following the trial of labor and exhilaration of delivery, the satisfaction of holding his baby provides the father with an arena to create and strengthen his relation with this new very important person in his life.

2

Couvade in Society and History

We observe each loving husband, when the wife
Is labouring by a strange and reciprocal strife
Doth sympathising sicken.

—Robert Heath, "Clarastella" (1650)

In June 2002, international news services reported that doctors had implanted an embryo into the abdomen of a thirty-five-year-old man. The fetus was said to be developing normally and the world could follow its progress at the Web site of the father, Mingwei Lee, and his partner Virgil Wong (Lee and Wong 2002). After frantic scrambling (What did this mean for my research!), I discovered that Lee, when not online, was a performance artist whose work defies traditional concepts of humanity and masculinity. Although *virtually* pregnant, he was not *actually* pregnant.

Lee's artistic imagination challenges our scientific understanding of men and birth. For the last century, medical research has defined childbearing as an activity of mothers. Nevertheless, there is nothing new about virtual pregnancy for fathers. Across cultures and through time, men have nurtured their children in pregnancy, labored through birth, and presented their newborn progeny into this brave, new world.

We think of American fathers' involvement in birth as a recent innovation in social life, as if contemporary fathers in maternity wards are exploring brand-new terrain. It is true that fathers have only recently become the birth assistants, massaging mothers' backs and catching babies. But there is another form of participation in which fathers, themselves, have experienced pregnancy and birth. Rather than physically carrying the baby or coaching the mother, fathers have performed pregnancy and birth in ritual. Called "couvade" in the anthropological literature, these rituals range from minor changes in food and behavior to more explicit identification with the mother, in which dads actually act out the pregnancy, labor, and birth.

"Male birthing" was recorded in the first written works of European culture, two centuries before Christ. The Greek poet Apollonius Rhodius (262 BC–190 BC) reported that when Argonauts sailed in the Black Sea, among the Tibareni of Pontus, they discovered that, "When wives bring forth children to their husbands, the men lie in bed and groan with their heads close bound; but the women tend them with food, and prepare childbirth baths for them" (1912, 377). Later explorers brought similar reports from South America, India, Siberia, and Japan. In one famous example from the thirteenth century, Marco Polo returned from Chinese Turkestan with reports of men performing labor in the place of their partners. "When a woman has given birth, and the baby is washed and swaddled, the husband takes the wife's place in the bed and stays there for forty days with the baby beside him. All his friends and relations come to see him and to congratulate him. . . . So the wife gets up immediately, after giving birth, does the housework and waits on her husband in bed" ([1298] 1984, 107). Polo's observations entered into the popular imagination centuries later through artwork, and Samuel Butler's more mellifluous rewording in prose,

> For though Chineses go to bed,
> And lye in, in their Ladies staid,
> And for the pains they took before,
> Are nurs'd, and pamper'd to do more. ([1677] 1967, 211)

Contemporary ethnography shows that couvade remains common around the world. Anthropologists have documented male pregnancy ritual in Asia, Africa, the Pacific Islands, and the Americas. In fact, in a survey of eighty-four cultures, over two-thirds mandated "significant couvade restrictions or proscriptions." Over a quarter of the societies surveyed demanded that dad deviate from his normal activities for more than half his time (Munroe, Munroe, and Whiting 1973).

Imitative birth has been performed by fathers in all corners of the globe, and probably throughout the full range of human history. Do American men do it? Yes, of course they do, although they are unaware of it. Men might not take to the birthing bed, but they do less conspicuous things: they gain weight, suffer morning sickness, and experience the fatigue of pregnancy. As many as two-thirds of American men experience what we call the "couvade syndrome." But rather than consider these imitative reactions as normal, Americans tend to think of them as unimportant or even inappropriate. Unlike their brethren around the world, American fathers are supposed to be isolated from pregnancy and birthing.

As biomedicine has defined how we think about and enact birth, it has shaped our misunderstanding of our own couvade. The last chapter pointed out that the medical model denies the importance of the mother's place in birthing; this chapter argues that it is even less concerned with that of the father. In the medical definition of pregnancy, family, friends, feelings, and especially fathers are thought to be irrelevant. Medical thinking perceives pregnancy as a physical abnormality of female bodies; fathers' experience of the event can only be understood as an even worse deviance.

Why would fathers act out birth? Rather than considering couvade an aberrant activity of individuals, an anthropological perspective suggests that social convention demands that fathers perform the ritual. Understanding couvade as ritual highlights its role in transforming men into fathers. The following surveys the ritual aspects of imitative birth in South America and around the world. Exploring couvade as it has been practiced across cultures and through time helps us to understand our own practices, and points to their function in forging the role of a father and his relationships with his new child, his partner, and society.

Couvade

Male birthing activities were first called "couvade" in a nineteenth-century study of Basque peasants (Michel 1857). The Basques of northern Spain and southwestern France have long been considered the vestiges of early European tribes. The French were fascinated by reports that Basque men took to the birthing bed to rest, as new mothers cared for them, the newborn, and the household. The word probably derives from the Old French term *couver* or *couvement*, which is what a hen does with her body when she broods a clutch of eggs. It draws a simple parallel between the attentive hen and the husband who takes on gestation and birthing. Once created, the concept moved quickly through the literature. The word was picked by J. J. Bachofen (1861, 17) and popularized in Sir Edward Tylor's classic, *Primitive Culture* ([1865] 1975), just eight years after its introduction. By the first decades of the twentieth century, couvade was a standard concept in the anthropological literature. (The term "couvade" also comes to us with a certain amount of moral baggage. Before it was used for men in birth, the term was in common use in French as "faire la couvade," referring to those fainthearted men who "sit cowering and skolking within dores," and "lurke in the campe when Gallants are at the battell" [Cotgrave 1611]).

Although the image of Basque men acting out birth captured the imagination of nineteenth-century scholars, the word "couvade" has also been used for a variety of less imitative forms of birthing ritual (see especially Klein 1991 and Trethowan 1972). In many societies, men avoid certain foods and often are prohibited from work or travel. In some South American forest groups, all of a mother's lovers will observe some restrictions while she is pregnant (for examples, see Beckerman and Valentine 2002). In the nineteenth century, James Mooney (1887, 146) reported a form of couvade in rural Ireland in which a birthing woman could wear her husband's undershirt as a means of passing the pain of childbirth onto him.[1] Likewise, in his *Dictionaire des Superstitions*, Chesnel de la Charbouclais, a French physician, reports in 1856 the French belief that a birthing woman should don her husband's clothes to relieve the pain. In the Canary Islands, the husband's hat was placed on the woman's head to relieve labor pains; in Salamanca, a woman wore her husband's shirt; or, in Cariño, his waistcoat (Foster 1960, 116). The term has even been used at times to refer to ritual prohibitions on women's behavior (Fock 1963). Rather than imitation, these aspects of couvade emphasize the affinity, the sympathetic tie, of the mother and baby to father, family, and friends.

The variety of past uses for the word "couvade" provides the opportunity to adapt the term to our own purposes. Here, I will use the concept of couvade to refer to fathers' subjective participation in pregnancy and birth. This recognizes that a father, too, takes gestation and birth into his body. Rather than being outsiders, fathers are essential to the process. Instead of emphasizing the empathic relation with the mother, it focuses attention on the direct tie between father and child. Thus, the Guaraní father who carries the new baby's soul in a sling for forty days is analogous to the mother who carried the baby's body for nine months. This highlights the ritual aspects of these activities, actions that constitute a rite of passage from manhood to fatherhood. In addition to recognizing men's participation in the biological process (such as impregnation or cutting the cord), this acknowledges men's personal experience in the birth of a new member of the community.

Couvade Across Time . . .

Couvade has been evident from the earliest European history. Apollonius's
reports from the Argonauts were followed by other descriptions. Writing very
early in the Christian era, Strabo quotes Posidonius's lost texts (135–151 BC)
observing couvade in Bern of the Pyrenees. Iberian women "till the ground, and
after parturition, having put their husbands instead of themselves to bed, they
wait upon them" ([AD 18–23] 1903, 247). Diordus Siculus writes that in Corsica
in 60 BC, "If a woman has borne a child in the island of Cyrnos, no attention is
paid to the woman in childbed. But the man lies down, as if he were ill and
remains for a definite number of days in childbed" (Licht 1932, 522–523). Even
the oral tradition of pre-Christian Ireland remembers that when Maev, Queen of
Connacht, invaded Ulster, she discovered that all the men had taken to bed in
labor as part of their annual fertility rites (Wood-Martin 1902, 40).

Early English playwrights treated couvade as a fact of life among common
people. Wilkins, in 1617, wrote in *The Miseries of Enforced Marriage,*

> I have got thee with child in my conscience and,
> like a kind husband, methinks I breed it for thee.
> For I am already sick at my stomache and long extremely.

Forty years later, Beaumont and Fletcher wrote in their *A Wife for a Month,*

> As 'tis the nature of those loving Husbands,
> That sympathize their wives paines, and their throwes
> When they are breeding (and 'tis usuall too,
> We have it by experience). (Bowers 1977, 399)

In 1675, Wycherly writes in the fourth act of *The Country Wife,*

> How's ere the kind Wife's Belly comes to swell.
> The Husband breeds for her, and the first is ill. (Weales 1967, 114)

This dramaturgical interest in couvade may seem strange, but it must be
remembered that theater in seventeenth-century Europe served as a venue for
a variety of social dialogues, one of which is extremely important: gender identity. On one hand, social transformation fascinated earlier Shakespearean society, especially if it involved gender. One could not spend much time in a
Renaissance theater without confronting the hilarious confusions as characters
took on the guise of the other, be it the prince exchanging places with the pau-

per, the lover with the wife, or the husband with his friend. The cultural historian Stephen Greenblatt (1988, 73–93) points out that these role reversals pale beside transformations of sexual identity, which we assume to be the most immutable natural attribute of the human body. Cross-dressing men and women challenged the artifice of decorum in theatrical farce, and in doing so, made the audience all the more aware of the importance and cultural construction of gender. What could be a more powerful heuristic method for the seventeenth-century mind wrestling with concepts of male and female and the roles man and woman, than a father taking to bed for childbirth?

A second line of reasoning suggests that couvade provided seventeenth-century social critics a forum for appealing to antireligious and antiscientific sentiments. The seventeenth century was an era when the cerebral was becoming increasingly understood to be the primary arena for advancing human civilization. Encyclopedias were written to provide repositories of what was considered all valuable human knowledge. Natural philosophers like Francis Bacon (1561–1626) increasingly fought clergy for recognition and access to state power. Science not only contradicted religion, but also conflicted with the knowledge held by the great unwashed masses.

As scientific knowledge achieved increased power in the seventeenth and eighteenth centuries, it not only found detractors among the clergy, but among the arts and literature. The Russian intellectual Mikhail Bakhtin (1984) argues that by their very reference to commoners' lives and the humor of everyday life, these works create a dialogue with the growing hegemony of religious and scientific knowledge. Playwrights gave voice to the peasants and the laborers, whose lot was increasingly overshadowed by the pageantry and power of the clergy and philosophers. The audience laughs at the scatological and Epicurean adventures of Falstaff, a representation that serves as a counterpoint to the dominant narrative of civilization and social control provided by the princely court. Likewise, references to male birthing serve as a statement of both the organic aspect of everyday life, and the power of tradition in the lives of the masses.

The seventeenth-century playwrights used male pregnancy to refer to the common life of the rural folk, contrasting the silliness of peasants with the rationality of the intellectual movement in society. In contrast, the reports of explorers and missionaries played on the exoticism of couvade. Male birthing attracted the imagination of Europeans precisely because it was so uncommon.

Couvade is discussed by the detached observer as a representation of another culture, contrasting highly with the European reader's own "civilization." Explorers and travelers' reports of couvade emphasize the otherness of these people. They intellectually distance the reader from the being-ness of Asians, Africans, indigenous Americans, and Pacific Islanders.

Before returning to study couvade in America, let us first explore the ritual elsewhere. Understanding the commonness of couvade around the world challenges the medical belief that it is both rare and pathological in our own society. Being aware of the social, psychological, and spiritual aspects of birthing fathers in other societies allows us to recognize the multifaceted experience of couvade in our own.

. . . And Around the World

Couvade has been evident in all corners of the globe. As explorers and missionaries sailed into uncharted waters, they returned with reports of exotic birth rituals of men. There were reports of couvade in Melanesia, Africa, and the Americas. One British medical historian and noted Egyptologist, Warren Royal Dawson, devoted decades to cataloguing the cases. The diversity and number of these reports attest to the ubiquity of the practice (and Europeans' fascination with it). In Asia, Dawson finds that among the Ainu of Japan, "a curious custom used to exist amongst this people. As soon as the child was born, the father had to consider himself ill, and had therefore, to stay at home, wrapped by the fire. But the woman, poor creature!, had to stir about as much and as quickly as possible. The idea seems to be that life was passing from the father into his child." In India, he quotes an English observer: "The father is represented as a second mother, and goes through the fiction of a mock-birth, the so-called couvade. He lies in bed for forty days after the birth of his child; and during this period he is fed as an invalid." In Assam, "the husband may not go out of the village or do any work after the birth of a child for six days if the child be a boy, or for five days when the child is a girl" (Dawson 1929, 24).

Although couvade is practiced throughout the world, it seems to have been most common (and best documented) among South American indigenous groups. The practice is ubiquitous, in one or more of its many forms, in almost all lowland indigenous societies. Among the early explorers and missionaries, Yves d'Evreux wrote a classic monograph that documented what came to be called the *classic couvade,* "He [the husband] lies-in instead of his wife who works as usual; then all the women of the village come to see him lying in his bed, consoling him for the trouble and pain he had in producing this child; he is treated as if he were sick and tired without leaving his bed, as women here keep their beds after childbirth when they are visited and taken care of" ([1614] 1864, 89).

In the eighteenth century, Martin Dobrizhoffer (1717–1791), an Austrian missionary, traveled through the scrub deserts of southern South America and related how Abipone fathers did not mimic mothers in birth, but abstained from what were considered dangerous practices. Abipone fathers fasted after birth, lying covered on mats and refrained from shaving their eyebrows, taking tobacco, or swimming. In addition, they avoided riding fast horses or eating carpincho meat or honey from earth that had been trod upon (Metraux 1946, 319).

My own introduction to couvade was in the forests of Paraguay, among the Guaraní with whom I lived early in my work as an anthropologist. I spent my days clearing forest and hunting peccary, tapir, or armadillo with men my age, most of whom were already married with children. When my best friend, a hard-working young man called Rÿguata, discovered that his wife was pregnant, he became uncommonly generous with the deer that he brought back from the hunt. His explanation was simple: "*imembytahína*," his wife was pregnant. Neither of them could eat venison; it was too strong a meat. I gladly accepted the gift, then (recovering my anthropological demeanor) queried him on the topic. He listed a bewildering array of foods and herbs that were now prohibited to them both. The logic of the assortment was never evident; it included a variety of fruits, vegetables, and meats that seemed to have little in common. What was clear was the unquestionable necessity that they both comply with the new diet. What would happen if they broke the taboo? Rÿguata calmly explained, as to a rather slow-learning child, that the baby would get sick and be born weak. I was struck by the proscriptions and the way that they seemed to make the pregnancy a joint project rather than an individual condition.

Only later I discovered that there was a long tradition of anthropological interest in couvade among Indians of the forests of South America. It was reported by the first French colonists in the sixteenth century along the Brazilian coast, was documented in the southern Chaco in the eighteenth century, and continues to attract attention in the Siriono and Bororo discussed below. Anthropologists analyzed these cases and created the template with which we analyze all male birth ritual. These cases are especially useful in our understanding of the variations of couvade in that they do little to suggest a simulated birth by fathers. Guaraní men are not expected to take on mothers' role in birth and Rÿguata received no more attention and care than his wife, Kunakyra. All Amazonian fathers, however, are closely involved with birth and perform extensive ritual before, during, and afterward. Like Rÿguata, fathers join the mother in assuming responsibility for the health of the new child.

One of the most comprehensive and best documented descriptions of couvade comes from the Siriono of the tropical forests of Bolivia. In the early 1940s, Alan Holmberg was one of the first anthropologists to live among these so-called "primitive" people and subsequently wrote his groundbreaking ethnography, *Nomads of the Long Bow* (1950). Despite differences of time and place, the Siriono couvade shares many characteristics with that practiced today by my Paraguayan friend, Rÿguata, and throughout South American indigenous societies.

In the 1940s, few anthropologists had penetrated the deep forests of South America. When Holmberg lived among the Siriono, they were largely isolated from contact with the larger society. Continually moving through the deep tropical forest, they foraged for most of their food, the men hunting and the women gathering vegetables and fruits. Siriono bands usually consisted of kin groups of forty to seventy people. Holmberg joined them in their simple shelters, which were built quickly when needed and abandoned as the group moved on. Then as now, Siriono birthing practice emphasized the importance of fathers for the spiritual birth of the child. While mothers are entrusted to bring the baby's body into the world, fathers have a responsibility to assure that its soul makes a successful transition into the Siriono community.

Siriono men find their lives changed upon discovering that their wives are pregnant. They are restricted from eating the meat of the harpy eagle, anteaters, and howler monkeys. Many foods are presumed to have what anthropologists call a sympathetic effect on the fetus: eating anteater meat might twist the baby's feet and howler monkey meat would make it scream. Fathers, as well as mothers, avoid plants that grow in duplicate, as a double ear of corn or an attached pair of manioc roots—these plants might cause twins to be born. Likewise, Siriono men should avoid eating deformed plants, such as bent or twisted tubers, which might cause the child to be born with a clubfoot. Sex during pregnancy is not only permitted, but also recommended and indulged in until shortly before delivery.

While a mother delivers the child in body, the father must usher the new child's soul into the world. When a woman goes into labor, the father leaves immediately to hunt for the infant's name in the forest. Siriono names are closely connected with the character of the soul, which has an animal nature. Consequently, the father sets out in search of game with characteristics he desires for his child. A powerful animal such as a tapir, peccary, or jaguar makes for a valiant child. Should the father fail to kill a powerful animal, he will settle for whatever game he can capture, perhaps discovering his child's soul in an armadillo or snake. To return empty-handed would leave the child's name unknown and soul undefined. (If the child should be born at night, when it is impossible to set out for a hunt, the soul is sought in game that passes close to the community, such as monkey troops, or perhaps the soul is divined in the newborn's physical resemblance to a wild animal.) The new father also acquires a new name: he is called the "father of" the new baby. If the new child is "Yikína" (owl monkey), dad becomes "Yikína-ndu" (father of owl monkey). Thus, as a man fathers more children, he acquires a variety of names corresponding to the new roles he assumes in the children's lives.

A Siriono woman gives birth largely without assistance, lying in her hammock and using a plaited rope tied to the rafter for support. In the births Holmberg observed, labor was from one to three hours. The baby drops unceremoniously onto the ground and is picked up by the mother, who kneels and cuddles it until the afterbirth comes out. The woman is generally unassisted, but childbirth is nevertheless a public event, with children playing nearby in the dirt and women sitting by and discussing their own births or predicting the sex of the new child. Men—even fathers who are extremely attentive to food and activity taboos—take a studied disinterest in the event.

When the Siriono child has been born, the father is responsible for cutting the umbilical cord. (If the father is hunting, this task will be delayed until his return.) The umbilicus is severed with a sharpened bamboo knife about four inches from the placenta. Then a six-inch section of the remaining cord is cut off and tied to the underside of the mother's hammock. This prevents the child from crying. The remaining cord is left with the child, untied, to dry and eventually fall off. The cutting of the cord is ceremonial, accomplished without speaking, which heightens the theatrical import of the act. The cutting of the cord is a profound statement of paternity, which was important, according to Holmberg, in that the sexual freedom of the Siriono in the 1940s often left physical paternity in doubt. (Other males who might have had sex with a woman, for example a husband's brother, often performed aspects of couvade. Cutting the cord, however, was reserved for the man who would occupy the position of father to the child.)

Once the umbilicus has been cut, the father joins the mother in the observance of more intense ritual prohibitions. These are designed to protect the weak infant during the first critical days when the soul is only tenuously imbedded in the body's physical substance. Fathers and mothers are expected to stay in the house, near their hammock and close to the child, leaving only to go to the bathroom. Relatives take care of them, bringing extra food from the garden or forest and cooking if the couple lacks the interest or the energy. Food restrictions increase after the parturition. Men cannot eat porcupine (*Coendou prehensilis*), or any parrot, toucan, guan (a large fowl in the *Aburria* family), or howler monkey (*Alouatta*). Many foods cause specific debilities for the infant. Meat from the jaguar and coati (*Nasua nasua*) causes skin ulcers; paca (*Agouti paca*) meat will make the child bald; papaya will give the child diarrhea.

Holmberg points out that more important than abstinence from certain foods are other actions that the father must perform after the birth. Scarification is the most striking of these rituals. The day after the birth, the father makes a small baby sling and a necklace of coati teeth. He covers these with red *uruku* paste (made from the brilliant seeds of the annatto tree, *Bixa Orellana*) that has the power to drive evil away. He puts on the necklace and the sling around his shoulders. Then, as he stands by his hammock, his male relatives cut the outside of his legs with sharp paca teeth, leaving shallow but long scratches from his waist to his ankles. This, Holmberg explains, is part of the belief that the old blood carries sickness and needs to be removed so that the child can benefit from the clean blood. After the father has been scarified, he removes the sling and necklace and provides them to the baby's mother, who undergoes the same purification ritual.

On the second day after the birth, the parents are adorned with uruku and feathers. The father is usually decorated first, by one of his other wives or a potential wife (figure from Holmberg 1950, plate 12). Red and yellow feathers from the nape of the toucan are glued around his face and over his brow. Down from a curassow, a large forest bird of the *Cracidae* family, is covered with uruku and affixed in his hair over his ears. Tufts of breast down from the harpy eagle are also smeared with red dye and glued to the back of his head. Cotton string is then covered with uruku and tied around his arms above the elbows, around his legs above the knees and around his neck. Uruku is finally smeared on his face, arms, and legs, completing the decoration.

On the third and final day of intense couvade, the parents are once again decorated with uruku, this time with necklaces of hawk feathers. The mother takes a calabash of water, gathers a small basket of ash, and places the child, for the first time, in the new shoulder sling. The father picks up his bow and arrows and the three head into the forest, accompanied by any other children that they have. They sprinkle ash behind them on the trail, thus purifying it as they go. After about five minutes the little group stops. The father brings the mother a palm leaf to weave into a basket as he forages for firewood. After the basket is woven and filled with wood, the party retraces their steps. They stop short of the community and leave the basket hanging beside the trail, removing the firewood. Finally, they enter their house, build a fire with the wood that they have brought, and wash the child with the water that the mother carried into and out of the woods. This closes off the most intense time of couvade ritual.

Two things stand out about the Siriono couvade. First, fathers' activities are primarily devoted to the child's spiritual journey during and after birth. Although fathers are expected to follow several basic pregnancy taboos, they are far less restrictive than those of mothers. In fact, the foods that are prohibited for fathers are generally considered unsuitable for any but the older members of the band. Fathers are superfluous to labor and delivery, but once the child's body has arrived, fathers are to stay close to assure the safe arrival of the child's spirit. They travel through the forest to bring the new soul back to the child, and on the third day make the ritual journey again to assure that the spirit is safely settled in its new home.

Second, Siriono fathers do not undergo labor and delivery; ritual focuses on their transformation into new fathers. Men's transitional status is marked by both ornament and action. New fathers are decorated with uruku and bird down, scarified with sharp teeth, and bound in cotton thread. The transformation is perhaps most clear in the father's finding a name for his child and then himself being renamed in reference to his newborn.

The Siriono couvade is one example of a more general type of birthing ritual that is found in all indigenous societies throughout lowland South America. Rather than simple imitative ritual where dads lay in their hammocks and groan, these groups impose a wide variety of prescriptions and proscriptions on fathers' activities from early pregnancy until after birth. We can group these activities into five general types: food, work, space, body adornment, and sex. Analyzing these practices as ritual helps us understand the similar (yet more mundane) behaviors of pregnant men in contemporary American society.

Food taboos are the most common couvade restriction imposed on fathers in South American indigenous society. Many foods, such as certain meats, honey, beans, and big fish are thought of as powerful, and therefore prohibited for new parents. Eating them creates disruption that might harm the newborn soul. On the other hand, vegetables and fruits that are well formed rarely cause problems, although as in the case of the Siriono, fathers are cautioned against eating deformed items that could affect infants' physical development.

While all meats are powerful, fathers are often cautioned to avoid meats that are particularly strong. For example, jaguars are often associated with the supernatural, and pregnant men are usually admonished to avoid them. Among some South American groups, fathers may not eat bird flesh, as birdcalls portend death and would kill the fetus. Many animals have sympathetic relations with the developing fetus. For Garifuna fathers of Belize and Honduras (the descendents of indigenous Caribbean people and Black slaves), eating turtle meat might produce a child who is heavy and without a brain; parrot would give the infant a long nose; crab would cause long legs. Not all food restrictions are based on sympathetic associations: venison is usually proscribed simply because of the strength of its taste. Blander meats, such as the flesh of the peccary, are rarely prohibited.

New fathers are even restricted from going near prohibited foods. Biet observed this among the Tupi-Guaraní in the seventeenth century and the same taboos were evident three centuries later (Meggars and Evans 1957, 577). Among the Xavante, fathers are kept away from large fish (Maybury-Lewis 1960, 64) and among the Cubeo, they avoid manatee, turtles, and larger fish, believing that the soul of the new child might enter the sea creature (Goldman 1963, 169).

Second, indigenous fathers in lowland South American are also commonly restricted from specific work activities in the months leading up to the birth. Most common are prohibitions against touching sharp instruments. Guaraní men, for example, may not touch arrows, axes, or knives while their wives are pregnant. Yuquí men, of an ethnic group similar to the Siriono, were to avoid making arrows for fear that the child would be cut and bleed to death in utero (Stearman 1989, 88). Care with sharp objects extends to fingernails, as the

Arawak restrict the father from scratching himself (Crocker 1985, 53), and thorns, as Garifuna men are prohibited from walking where they might scratch their skin (Lowie 1948, 36). Men are also prohibited from tying knots, for fear that the child will become entangled in the cord and not be able to pass through the birth canal. Among the Guaraní, the proscription on tying knots goes so far as to restrict the father from killing monkeys, as the tails of the quarry, when in their death throes, might affix themselves to tree limbs and hinder the birth. Some societies have more general taboos on activities that would cause men to sweat. The Bororo suggest that the odor or essence of sweat might leave both father and child debilitated (Crocker 1985, 53).

In most lowland South American societies, a father also finds his movement limited when his partner is pregnant and his baby is new. The restrictions begin in the later stages of pregnancy, when fathers are often prohibited from entering the forest to hunt. The forest itself is often considered a powerful spiritual arena, populated by malevolent forces that take the form of jaguars or anacondas. Because association with these forces could harm the child, men are expected to stay out of the forest at night when these animals roam freely and away from areas that they frequent. As the birth draws close, men stay near. In fact, in the final days of the pregnancy, fathers are sometimes restricted from leaving their hearth altogether, with little to do but rest quietly in the hammock as birth approaches.

Given the American interest in having fathers present at birth, it is noteworthy that lowland Indian fathers, who are very involved with pregnancy, are often restricted from birth itself (Goldman 1963, 168–169; Crocker 1990, 112). Either the mother is moved to a more secluded area (often with her female relatives) or the father is expected to leave the house until the afterbirth has passed (Maybury-Lewis 1960, 64). In the large communal houses of the lowland forests, where up to two hundred people might live in one large thatch shelter, this privacy is maintained by the fathers who take studied indifference to the process. In other cases, a plaited screen separates the father and mother.

After the birth, fathers are often in seclusion, isolated in their homes and away from normal social discourse. This is especially true in the matrifocal households of indigenous lowland South America. When residences include people connected only through female relatives, where sisters continue to share a common living space after marriage, fathers often find themselves with few close relatives in their own homes. For example, Bill Crocker of the Smithsonian

Institution, whose life work has been with the Canela of Brazil, notes that a new father is treated as a stranger in the house of his wife, her baby, and family. He is not allowed to stay in the house until the birth is completed, and then must sleep separated by a partition from his wife and baby, take directions from her kin "and scarcely converses with his wife except to understand and obey directions" (1990, 112).

After the birth, as in the pregnancy period, men's movements in the forest are often clearly defined. Among the Canela, for example, a father is called on to leave the house and hunt for meat to feed his wife and child both physically and spiritually (Crocker 1990, 112). On the other hand, it is not uncommon for men to be restricted from entering their hunting grounds. Guaraní and Siriono men are expected to stay close, so that the danger to the spirit of the father does not endanger that of the child, a practice that is accompanied by a parallel prohibition that women not enter the family garden.

In addition, couvade in lowland South America often involves transformation of the body, ranging from daubing the face with paint and wearing amulets to permanently scarring the skin. Many societies ask fathers to paint themselves with red uruku paste after the births of their children. The French ethnologist, Alfred Metraux, surveyed a variety of societies in the 1930s and 1940s, and noted that Guarayu fathers, closely related to the Siriono, paint their feet with the red dye and that Guaques fathers, who occupy forests in southern Colombia, smear themselves with ashes and juice made from the crushed genipap berry (*Genipa americana*) (Metraux 1946, 372).

Men often decorate themselves with woven strings or other accouterments after the birth. For example, among the Garifuna, fathers tie a string around themselves and a second around the waist of the child to protect and strengthen it (Taylor 1951, 91). In other cases, as among the Guaraní, men commonly wear small bows and carry arrows or wear miniature baby slings when they go into the forest. These are for the benefit of the child's soul, which accompanies the father during the first weeks of life (Metraux 1948, 115).

Among the most striking couvade activities are scarification rites that signal the end of the intense couvade, such as those reported previously by Holmberg. The seventeenth-century reports of Rochefort (1665, 50) and du Tertre (1667–1671, 2:371) were among the first, and documented the practice in societies of the Caribbean, the Guianas, and far northern Brazil. According to their records, after a period of restriction to his house on a diet of cassava (*Manihot esculenta*), a father scratched and then cut his shoulders, sides, arms, and legs using the sharpened teeth of the agouti (*Agouti paca*). He was called upon to withstand the process with stoicism to assure the valor of his child. In a bit of theater that seems to reaffirm the link between the father and child, the blood that flowed from his wounds was smeared on the child's face (Roth 1915, 321).

Finally, South American couvade also involves social restrictions, the most common of which is on erotic activity. Prospective fathers and mothers are usually restricted from sex with each other or anyone else. This begins with pregnancy and sometimes extends for as many as three years after birth. In the case of the Bororo of western Brazil, the mother and all her sexual partners must abstain from sex from the first sign of pregnancy until the child has achieved a social persona at the age of between six months and a year. Usually, however, prohibitions begin in the final phase of the pregnancy and extend into the first month postpartum. This takes on additional importance since most lowland South American societies take a somewhat relaxed attitude toward sexual conduct, placing relatively few limitations on sexual behavior of both men and women at other times.

Couvade in lowland South American indigenous societies is striking for its variety and ubiquity. Through pregnancy, birth, and the postpartum period, fathers perform ritualized actions and observances that assure the safety of the child. Even without simulated labor and delivery, the diversity of these practices shows the creativity of the human imagination and speaks for the cultural basis of fathers' involvement in birth. Couvade is not defined by biology, but demanded by culture and society. These groups recognize that fathers are biologically necessary for conception, and rather than believing that they fade from importance during pregnancy, consider them necessary during the gestation of the newborn as well. Rather than superfluous, the involved father is responsible for accompanying the new being in its psychological, social, and spiritual development.

Couvade as Riddle

Couvade has been one of the great riddles of anthropology. Just as it captured the attention of explorers and missionaries, it has challenged anthropologists to explain its existence and meaning. In each generation, the pillars of the profession have tried to answer the sphinx; Edward Tylor, Bronislaw Malinowski, and even Claude Lévi-Strauss have taken turns. In the nineteenth century, anthropologists sought its historical roots and its evolutionary logic; in the early twentieth century, the debate raged between diffusionists and functionalists; more recently, psychoanalysts and structuralists have faced off over this seemingly arcane ritual.

Although inconclusive, the theoretical debates have been productive. Like different lenses turned on the same object, each argument highlights unique aspects of couvade. Each gives a new understanding of the ritual's importance to fathers, babies, mothers, and the larger society. The goal of anthropology is not simply to explain other people's lives, but rather to use our information about others to better understand our own culture. We will see below that as anthropology wrestles with the issues of paternal ritual, it provides some of the keys to understand the meanings and messages of our own childbirth rituals.

Evolutionary Models

The reports of male birthing ritual made by early explorers and missionaries piqued the interest of social philosophers again in the middle decades of the nineteenth century. At a time when Darwin's theories were revolutionizing natural history, anthropologists used evolution to explain the diversity of human culture and society. Published just two years after Charles Darwin proposed his theory, J. J. Bachofen's work incorporated his ideas of couvade into his evolutionary history of the human race. In *Das Mutterrecht* (1861), he considered the "arcane custom of male birth ritual" important in the transformation of society from anarchy through matriarchy to patriarchy. In a book that details the stage of social development characterized by "mother right," he suggested that couvade marked a transitional stage from mother-centered to father-dominated societies.[2] It developed in matriarchal societies where rights over children were established through maternal ties of descent. As these societies evolved and power shifted to men, activities that allowed men to mimic birth allowed fathers to ritually establish claims of paternity over children. Thus, couvade was a means for fathers to fortify lineage claims that were inherently weaker than mothers'.

In the decade after Bachofen's work, Tylor (1873) applied his interest in the evolution of magic and religion to understand the existence of couvade. Tylor documented the existence of couvade in a variety of corners of the world, drawing on Marco Polo and classical historians, as well as contemporary ethnographies that were then filtering back from the New World. Tylor's work focused on the evolutionary stages of religion and specifically, the development of the concept of soul. Tylor suggested that in so-called "primitive" cultures, which could be identified by their lack of theistic religion, people imagined a spiritual aspect of the world that they then invested in material objects. Spiritual and supernatural phenomena necessarily had their mundane aspect and vice versa: mundane physical entities could have a spiritual presence. Couvade, he suggested, expressed the spiritual aspect of the physical bond between father and child. Why were they still present in societies like the Chinese, related by Marco Polo? Tylor rationalized the practice of couvade in more advanced societies as a "survival" that was performed after animistic beliefs had lost favor.

Some years later, Tylor ([1888] 1977, 256) embraced Bachofen's evolutionary explanation of couvade. In a careful analysis of 350 cultures, he endeavored to document that a matrilineal stage predated patriarchal societies and that couvade appeared during the transition from one to the other. His comparative analysis uncovered a clear association between the presence of couvade and matrilineal descent and matrilocal residence. He suggested, "This apparently absurd custom . . . proves to be . . . the very sign and record of that vast change . . . from matriarchy to patriarchy" (Tylor [1888] 1977, 259).

In his far-reaching study of world religions, *The Golden Bough* (1890), Sir James Frazer developed Tylor's ideas about couvade and the evolution of human psychology. Frazer's work posited a general development of modes of thought from the magical to the religious and, finally, to the scientific. Couvade, he suggested, asserted magical powers as a result of faulty reasoning. It could be distinguished from religious activities, which appealed to supernatural entities.

The Golden Bough not only established fundamental distinctions between religion and magic, it distinguished the different forms of magic in these (so-called) primitive societies. Contagious magic was what people perform using objects with a natural association to one another. Whatever is done to the one must similarly affect the other. For example, the use of a lock of the victim's hair to evoke love employs contagious magic. A spell cast on the hair would move the heart of the individual from whom it had been clipped. In contrast, imitative magic occurs between objects that are similar in form or fact. This idea that "like produces like" is the basis for Voodoo dolls in the folk tradition of Haiti. Sticking a pin into the belly of the wax figure produces a pain in the stomach of the person who shares the doll's likeness.

The distinction between contagious and imitative magic proved useful in categorizing different forms of couvade. Previous analyses had focused on men's enactment of childbirth. This spectacular form of couvade was imitative magic: it related to the mother through a similarity in form and action. Frazer suggested that ethnographers had exaggerated the similarity of men in birth to their female companions. As noted above, even in the classical literature the accounts were embellished with details that seemed to equate men's actions with birthing women. In societies in which men actually took to childbed, as in those reported by Marco Polo and Strabo, they did so only after the child was born.

On the other hand, Frazer called attention to the vast array of less extreme couvade ritual that was based on principles of contagious magic. Fathers in most non-Western societies practiced some form of postnatal restrictions on behavior and diet: they avoided meat, work, sex, or social life. The power of these restrictions comes through a fundamentally different but extremely important form of ritual magic. As fathers and babies had been in direct contact during gestation, so fathers' actions would affect infants after birth. Men who avoided the forest or sex were acting to protect the children with whom they were associated.

The last search for the historical origins of couvade came not from evolutionists, but rather from anthropologists interested in tracing the diffusion of ideas and behaviors around the world. In 1929, Dawson completed an encyclopedic study of the various couvade rituals around the world, attempting to trace them all back to a common source. The book stands today as a valuable compendium of the universality of the rituals, but fruitless in advancing diffusionist anthropology. Dawson admitted that there was no clear chain of contiguous societies that could be traced to its ancient source. Nevertheless, he falls back into theoretical myopia, suggesting that "the inherent strangeness of couvade makes it impossible to believe that it originated independently in the various places in which it has been recorded" (Dawson 1929, 57–58).

Freud

In the early twentieth century, questions of social evolution were replaced by efforts to find the contemporary reasons for seemingly primitive thought and behavior. A new theory was developed by Sigmund Freud, a Viennese physician whose work continues to shape our understanding of male birthing ritual today. Freud's interest in couvade grew out of his larger attempts to define psychosexual development and its conflicts throughout the world. Anthropological reports gave Freud fascinating material in which to explore the intersection of sexual behavior, gender identity, and family relations. In doing so, Freudians came to understand couvade as pathological reaction to unconscious drives and sexual impulses.

In explaining ritual, Freud directed himself to the psychology of the individual, suggesting that culture masks the unconscious drives that are the basic dynamic in the human psyche. Arcane and seemingly irrational rituals—such as couvade—are inspired when these urges are thwarted by social convention. Thus, Freud proposed that the animals that American Indians revered as relatives and protected as sacred totems grew from men's stifled urges to kill their fathers and sleep with their mothers (Freud, [1913] 1950, 237–239). (In recognition of his debt to anthropology, Freud titled this study *Totem and Taboo*, in direct reference to Frazer's *Totemism and Exogamy* [1910].) The psychoanalytic search for the dynamic behind couvade was taken up by one of Freud's early students, Theodor Reik, who suggested that the process of "pseudo-maternal" couvade could be understood in terms of unconscious sadistic urges against the mother. "The suppression of [malevolent wishes of a sadistic nature] will bring about a relatively increased intensity of the masochistic instinctual components" (Reik [1914] 1946, 53). Thus, a man imposes on himself the pain he wishes for his partner, who in turn symbolizes his mother. Likewise, couvade proscriptions that relate to the infant result from fathers' overcompensation for aggressive urges against their new children.

Early Freudians thought that non-Europeans were dominated by almost uncontrolled primitive impulses. Reik's ethnocentrism speaks for itself, "Let us attempt to represent the mental attitude of the primitive human being who has just become a father. One cannot conceive him having much fatherly tenderness. A strange being has come into his home and he feels no pleasure in supporting the little creature." On the contrary, he feels impelled to kill and devour the child. Restrictions on killing animals, touching weapons, and doing severe work "are substitutive actions for the forbidden realization of this death wish towards the child." With regard to scarification rituals, Reik suggests that "the father should suffer the same torture as he would wish to inflict on his child" (Reik [1914] 1946, 60–61).

Reik provided the first signpost of what later would come to be called the "couvade syndrome" in contemporary Europeans. Once again, his words speak

clearly: "It is clear that the practice of couvade rests upon a psychical identification. We see to-day cases of marked identifications of this kind in the mental
life of hysterics and other psycho-neurotics. Neurotic men sometimes show
a tendency to imitate conditions specifically proper to women" (Reik [1914]
1946, 47–48).

As the twentieth century unfolded, couvade became a common test case for
psychoanalytic theories. Each case reinforced the idea that couvade was pathological. Bruno Bettelheim, a Viennese psychiatrist who fashioned himself
Freud's successor, continued the study of couvade in unconscious terms, suggesting that

> The man wishes to find out how it feels to give birth, or he wishes to
> maintain to himself that he can. In the pretense, he tries to detract from
> the woman's importance, but . . . he copies only the relatively insignifi-
> cant externals and not the essentials, which, indeed, he cannot duplicate.
> Such copying of superficialities emphasizes the more how the real, essen-
> tial powers are envied. Women, emotionally satisfied by having given
> birth and secure in their ability to produce life, can agree to couvade
> which men need to fill the emotional vacuum created by their inability to
> bear children. (Bettelheim 1954, 211)

As psychological anthropology developed in the decades after World War II,
it took close notice of these Freudian theories, introducing into a new generation of anthropology the idea that a cultural construction might be the result of
pathological psychosexual development. In 1961, with a quote that could have
been Reik's some fifty years previously, Melford Spiro stated that couvade avoids
conflict between child and father over the mother by separating a mother from
her offspring after birth. "If we assume that fathers are initially hostile to their
offspring of either sex (because they are competitors for his wife's affection, nur-
turance, and so forth), either repression of hostility or institutionalized avoid-
ance (or some third functional equivalent) would serve to preclude the overt
expression of the motive" (Spiro 1961, 485).

At the same time, the psychoanalytic basis for couvade was being explored
by John Whiting, a Harvard anthropologist. He and his students, Ruth and
Robert Munroe, decided that couvade was understandable in terms of cross-
gender sexual identity deriving from "status envy." Fathers usurped the role of
the mother because they were jealous of her procreative ability. The desire to

imitate the mother arises, they hypothesized, from fathers' conflicted sexual identification. Specifically, societies in which residence was matrilocal—and especially where boys slept with their mothers—produced men who sought to identify with mothers that they perceived to be powerful. The feelings of envy and confusion found their expression during pregnancy, birth, and the postnatal period as mimicry of the woman's activities (Munroe, Munroe, and Whiting 1973).[3]

Malinowski and Couvade

In 1918, Bronislaw Malinowski returned from over two years in the Southern Pacific islands and picked up the riddle of couvade with great enthusiasm. Not only did the Trobrianders practice extensive fathering rituals, but Malinowski's intimate understanding of their culture allowed him to study the practice in situ. Islanders contended that conception was a spiritual process in which men had no involvement; fathers made their contribution to the developing fetus through rituals enacted throughout pregnancy. For example, a father would ritually rub the mother's growing belly with coconut oil to impart his physical likeness to the baby. Malinowski understood Trobrianders to be extremely rational, and he was convinced that there must be a logical reason for ritual.

Malinowski's theoretical contribution to anthropology was in the development of functionalism, proposing that all cultural beliefs and behaviors contribute something to society. In much the same way that Darwin suggested that the body loses physical attributes that no longer confer some advantage (like the human tail or appendix), Malinowski suggested that humans abandon ideas and actions that do not improve the psychological state of individuals, the social life of the members, or the ecological survival of the group. Often, however, people are unaware of the benefit of their behaviors; rituals like couvade have a pragmatic effect of which even the actors are unaware.

Malinowski points out that an infant's chance of survival (and therefore the social reproduction of the group) is greatly enhanced by the presence of both the male and female parents. He postulated that human fathers have a natural drive to protect a new mother and child, and that this drive finds form and meaning in cultural beliefs and ritual. Thus, couvade expresses innate paternal tendencies, "an intimate connection of a mystical nature between father and child" (Malinowski 1927a, 225). It functions by "accentuating the principle of legitimacy, the child's need of a father" (Malinowski 1927a, 189).

Malinowski asserts that couvade behaviors "shape an attitude of protective tenderness on the part of the male towards his pregnant mate and her offspring" (Malinowski 1927b, 220). Couvade promotes paternal relations with the child and, therefore, the formation of the nuclear family and all of its concomitant cultural knowledge.

Lévi-Strauss and the Structure of Couvade

Claude Lévi-Strauss, the grand old man of French anthropology, disagreed with the idea that couvade could be understood through individual psychology. Using logical reasoning to counter the cross-cultural analysis, Lévi-Strauss suggested that fathers' birthing practice was not equivalent to mothers', but rather a mirror image of it. In an observation that recalls Frazer's work at the beginning of the century, Lévi-Strauss points out that "it would be a mistake to suppose that a man is taking the place of the woman in labor. . . . The husband and the wife sometimes have to take the same precautions because they are identified with the child who is subject to the great dangers during the first weeks or months of its life. . . . In neither [gestation or labor] does the father play the part of the mother. He plays the part of the child. Anthropologists are rarely mistaken on the first point; but they yet more rarely grasp the latter" (Lévi-Strauss 1962, 195).

Janet Chernela has recently built on Lévi-Strauss's insight and expanded his criticism of the psychogenic explanation of couvade. She suggests that men in couvade enact a series of roles, but that this is a "dramatization of maleness, not femaleness, and manifests opposition rather than equivalence between genders" (Chernela 1993, 53). Reanalyzing Garifuna society, Chernela points out that the fathers' actions during couvade are not only congruent with the male's role, but reinforce a man's masculine position in society. First, with respect to the child, men are believed to be the primary contributors to a child's fetal development through the accumulation of semen. A man's couvade action is thus congruent with the equivalence that Garifuna society perceives between a man and his children.

Second, with respect to the mother, Chernela suggests that the man's lying in is a replacement, more than an imitation, of his wife in convalescence. The father's actions emphasize his ability to possess the bodily fluids, as he did before conception, which the mother cannot retain. This emphasizes the opposition, more than the equivalence, of the two parents.

Finally, Chernela points out that couvade emphasizes the conflict, and therefore the congruence between, the father and the mother's brother. As the father retreats into couvade restrictions, the mother's brother supplants him as provider for the family. This emphasizes the potential similarity and structural opposition between the two men. Rather than seeing two actors trading places, Chernela asks us to see couvade as four relationships imbedded in conflict and cooperation within a specific cultural context.

Indigenous Explanations

J. Christopher Crocker, an Amazonian ethnologist, worked extensively with the Bororo Indians of the Brazilian border near the Siriono (Crocker 1985). Bororo fathers observe an extensive and intense couvade. Crocker explains this couvade in terms of a more general life force that humans have, known as *raka*. Raka is a nonphysical force that includes energy, passion, and power. It is evident in blood and semen, and expended in work, sex, menstruation, and injury. Raka is creative; we see its effect in the productive power of work, the generative power of conception, and the physical development of fetuses and humans.

Among the Bororo, conception is not a single act in which semen and ovum join. The first insemination only starts a longer process of slow accretion of raka. With more sex and the cessation of menses, raka collects and the fetus takes on the form and vitality of humanness. During pregnancy, the father must protect his raka to strengthen the fetus in utero. Once the fetus begins to grow, he abstains from sex with all lovers, especially his pregnant partner, which would deplete both his and her power. Although essential in the first stage of pregnancy, semen is dangerous to an established pregnancy. Men are prohibited from eating certain foods, such as young, deformed, or bony animals, and ground-dwelling birds, each of which has too much or too little raka.

Crocker's analysis of couvade provides a striking illustration of the interplay of its spiritual, psychological, and social aspects. In identifying raka as the central organizing force in Bororo life, he traces the complex relations between the biological and the spiritual, and between the psychological and the social. Raka is psychic energy that acts as the principle generative force in human society, but that has equal capacity for destruction and degeneration. Raka needs to be carefully controlled to avoid the dangerous effects of its unchecked outpouring, much like European concepts of libido. For the father, raka's generative power is lost in its expression; the accumulation of the infant's life force is directly related to the permanent loss of the father's life force.

The connection between the father and child is not biological or sympathetic, but based in the flow of raka. Semen is both a constructive force and a danger to the developing infant. But it is not the physical aspect of the fluid that engages the two, but rather the psychic energy that semen (and also menstrual blood) impart. Likewise, fathers are to avoid eating deformed animals, not because of any perceived sympathetic relationship with the developing fetus, but because of the level of raka energy maintained. Just as a gestating fetus would be endangered by contact with the intense raka in semen or menstrual fluids, the smell of raka-laden food from the mother's milk or the father's body presents a direct threat to a newborn.

Fathers and Couvade: A New Perspective on New Fathers

What can we learn from the generations of anthropologists who have studied couvade? Although they all offer different explanations, the various perspectives are not necessarily contradictory. Like the blind men and the elephant, each offers valuable information to help understand the behavior. As the anthropological gaze shifts from functionalism to structuralism, psychoanalysis, and even indigenous explanations, each provides new insights and information. The lessons that we draw from this literature help us understand not just fathers at other times and in far off places, but birthing by contemporary men in American hospitals.

First, from the early anthropological analyses, couvade has been recognized as social ritual rather than aberrant behavior of the individual. If a man avoids venison or hunting during pregnancy, it is according to a cultural plan, not a simple response to his personal dislikes. Couvade is also ritual in that it communicates to an audience: rather than being a meaningless artifact of a so-called "primitive" stage of human development, couvade needs to be read for meaning as we would a text or narrative. When a Bororo man refuses sex with his lover, it is understood as a declaration of fatherhood for the baby she will bear. His actions make sense, and only make sense, within the context of that indigenous culture.

Second, the functionalist analyses of couvade show that couvade is performed for a very good reason. Malinowski recognized that father's birth rituals may be based on erroneous beliefs, but they are not irrational. Although Trobriand men might purport that the nightly massage of their lover's belly imparts their looks to the gestating baby, Malinowski recognized that this nightly ritual is far more efficacious in defining the father's role in society and his relations with mother and baby. Some sixty years later, Paige and Paige have explicitly resurrected Malinowski's argument about the functional aspects of men's involvement in childbirth, tying it to paternity and legitimacy. They cast couvade as "a form of psychological warfare, or puffery, used when opportunities for more direct forms of conflict and more direct bargaining are restricted" (Paige and Paige 1981, 48).

Third, anthropologists agree that couvade has a direct effect on fathers who perform it. Malinowski argued that ritual relieves stress by giving the appearance of power over uncontrollable events. Couvade relieves fathers' fears about a baby's dangerous passage into the world. Couvade also serves as a rite of passage for a man into the new identity of father. The attention that functionalism gives to the underlying personal aspects of these behaviors is pertinent whether couvade is a means to alleviate stress or a ritual to facilitate a man's inner changes in becoming a father. In both cases, we must appreciate the positive and necessary force that couvade is in a man's life.

Finally, anthropologists such as Lévi-Strauss call our attention to the network of social relations affected by couvade, which changes a man's relations with his baby, his lover, and the larger society. Although a father's biological connection with his child is hardly evident, carrying a baby-size bow recognizes and legitimizes his social ties to the child. And at a more general level, as men avoid meat or mothers or machetes, they are expressing changes in the fabric of their social ties with their family, their community, and their nation.

American Men and Couvade

Couvade has been amply documented in other societies and even described in the historical literature of our European forebearers, but do we practice couvade in our own society? Do modern fathers act pregnant? Do they enact ritual labor and delivery? Not surprisingly, with a little research we find that American men *do* perform couvade. Although a father may not take to childbed, contemporary American men continue to take the experience of pregnancy and birth into their minds and bodies.

As among the Bororo and Siriono, American fathers enact rites and perform stereotyped absolutions to assure a safe and healthy child. Rather than avoid armadillo meat, our fathers create a safe baby's room, they tune the car, and organize family finances. Fathers even have sympathetic reactions. Weight gain, nausea, and backaches are common, albeit poorly understood, aspects of American men's birthing. Do these activities accomplish the same ends as those performed by the Bororo? As we did with the Siriono, let us first describe these American rituals, then explore how our own society has sought to explain them in contemporary pregnancy and childbirth.

Food

Siriono men avoid armadillo meat and Guaraní men refuse venison, but American men also change their food, drink, and drugs as their baby gestates. While we are well aware of food cravings and aversions that mothers feel—the stereotypical ice cream and pickles—it is worth noting that fathers' appetites change, too. Pregnant fathers experience an increase in appetite and specific food cravings; many find that they are almost always hungry. Rather than pickles and ice cream, fathers are ravenous for French fries, hamburgers, and malted milks—high-calorie foods that give them that full feeling. Or they pare down and bulk up, consciously or unconsciously eating a healthy diet to get themselves in shape for this new chapter in their lives. In a survey of pregnancy and fathers, one study found that 81 percent of men have increased appetites during pregnancy and 71 percent had specific food cravings (Brown 1988, 527–549).

Some of these food changes are driven by reference to scientific research. Mothers have been quick to respond to medical admonitions about the biology of conception. Potential mothers often stop drinking, smoking, and using other drugs and medicines in the weeks surrounding ovulation (Hannigan and Armant 2000, 245). Some recent studies point to a decline in sperm counts of American men. Although the results are disputed (Carlsen et al. 1992; Kolata 1996), potential fathers are admonished that to increase their sperm count they should stop eating junk food, switch to nutritious foods, and stop recreational drug use. The reasons given are invariably biological, that vices cause chromosomal damage that could lead to birth defects. (For more specific information, see Mak et al. 2000, 465; Ribes et al. 1998, 717; and Attia et al. 1989, 47–48.)

If men feel pressure to stop smoking and taking recreational drugs before conception, pregnancy only increases the weight of social expectations. Data show that mothers who do not smoke have healthier babies; recent reports of the dangers of second-hand smoke make men exceedingly aware of the threat that they pose to their developing infants. In a study of four thousand pregnant fathers, the British Health Education Authority discovered that almost a third tried to quit smoking during pregnancy, although only 6 percent were successful (Nelson 1999).

The same happens with other things a man consumes. Vices or pleasures that were previously his own business become dangerous to his loved ones. A father is no longer responsible only for himself when he indulges in alcohol, cannabis, speed, heroin, cocaine; he has the baby to think about. Even when there is no direct effect on the child, dad's activities are often curtailed by the thought that his influence on his pregnant partner will have indirect ramifications. An expectant father who brings cigarettes, drugs, or alcohol home, makes it harder for his partner to be healthy for their baby.

Space: Preparing the Nest

South American fathers are called upon either to go into or stay out of the forest. Likewise, American men are drawn into the home in a kind of procreative preparation for the baby. Rather than search for a forest name or wild honey, American fathers ready the home and the yard for the new infant.

For many of the men I talked to, the baby's room became an important focus of their attention. Walls need painting, shelves hung, and the crib assembled. I am sure that there is more than one man who had never considered infants or their perspective, who has found himself down on hands and knees painting balloons on the wall at crib height. Those who feel "home-improvement challenged" take on new identities as they hang wallpaper and safeguard electrical outlets. Creating a space for the child, even if it is simply a corner of the living room or bedroom, becomes an important symbolic means to make space for the child in the father's life. One father I interviewed, for example, devoted himself to the baby's room. "[The seventh month], that's when we started really decorating the baby's room and buying all the furniture and getting clothes and diapers, changing table, and of course that's really when the showers started happening. All the gifts started coming in. And when you walk in your house and you see on the floor of your unborn child's new room about a hundred gifts, it starts to hit you: we're going to have a baby."

When the baby's room is set, there are myriad other projects that need finishing. Doors need to be fixed, leaks repaired, floors sanded, and workbenches need to be organized. My tendency was to attend to the car while my wife was pregnant. I tuned the engine and rotated the tires—ostensibly to prepare for the ride to the hospital. Looking back, I realize that the work gave me a feeling that was more important than any improvement in the car's performance. For other men, pregnancy is an important time for finishing long-avoided or partially completed jobs around the house and yard: the fence needs to be painted, the garden tilled, or the lawn fertilized. Each of these gives a man the feeling of success and competence. Entering into the new world of fatherhood, a man exerts control where he can and exercises the skills and talents that he has. This seems fitting since a new baby, especially the first baby, signals the start of a new chapter in a man's life.

Work: Double Time for Nine Months

An important aspect of men's nesting involves organizing finances. Men who spent years with a casual attitude toward careers and income find themselves staring at their pay stubs and bank statements with new concern. They often redouble their efforts to earn more. They put in more hours and take on new jobs, although pregnant mothers often resent the added demands that the work imposes. Fathers who never have had wills or insurance plans call lawyers and agents to get their affairs in order.

Men are redefining their role in American life. (The literature on this topic is extensive, but Kimmel 1996 offers a useful introduction.) Pregnant fathers, however, often slip back into stereotypical gender roles. This is especially true where money is concerned. Financial responsibilities are one of the prime concerns of fathers, and a constant theme in discussions with dads-only groups at birthing classes. This is even true in contemporary families where couples often share financial responsibilities. Susan Walzer, in an analysis of men and women's transition to parenthood, points out that as women leave their jobs, men seem to worry more about the bills. They see themselves as the solitary breadwinner and recognize social expectations that they provide for their family (Walzer 1998, 112–119).

Sex: Once Is More than Enough

In a manner similar to my Guaraní friend, Rÿguata, American men begin to act differently when they find that their partner is pregnant. Like many indigenous peoples, sexual taboos are one of the most common of these observances. In their classic study of sexual behavior, William Masters, a gynecologist, and Virginia Johnson, his psychologist colleague, reported that almost half of the men whom they interviewed eschewed sex during pregnancy; this was despite the fact that a majority of the pregnant women often wanted more sex and orgasms. The decrease did not correlate with the attraction of men to their partners; many fathers found pregnancy enhanced their partner's sexual attractiveness (Masters and Johnson 1966). Over three-quarters of the men interviewed in one study experienced a general decrease in libido during their partners' pregnancy (Brown 1988, 535).

Some couples give up sex as it becomes physically uncomfortable for the pregnant woman, but social meanings attached to abstinence give other reasons for restricting sex that would be physically desirable for both partners. Some men express an attitude that sex during pregnancy is both improper and dangerous. One father reported, "We didn't actually discuss this. We never said, 'Look we must stop this now, it's going to be injurious,' for we had read in books that it wasn't. It was almost built-in which said, 'look, don't.' I went off it. She went off it. Possibly because of the first miscarriage, we wanted to do everything right this time. We weren't taking any risks at all" (McKee and O'Brien 1982, 106).

The idea that pregnant sex is unnatural or dangerous is based on social convention, not scientific fact. Rather than sexual abstinence being biologically "natural" for mothers, lovemaking and orgasm in the final months of pregnancy is correlated with easier births (Tolor and di Graza 1976). Like the Guaraní father who refuses to eat venison, American men refuse sex during pregnancy because they consider it dangerous and wrong—not that they have a specific understanding of why it is either of these.

The Body

The seventeenth-century poetry of Robert Heath makes clear that long before the advent of contemporary research, men have suffered physical symptoms with the birth mother. Recent studies of these experiences substantiate the knowledge of previous generations; they show that most American men experience some form of couvade (e.g., Clinton 1985; Lamb and Lipkin 1982). In a survey of pregnant couples, Brown (1988, 533) found that when a couple becomes pregnant, both partners often gain weight, feel nauseated, suffer stomachaches, and experience gastric distress. Accompanying their increased appetites, men gain weight during pregnancy. In one striking example (although not a scientific study), one birthing teacher noted that the men in her class gained an average of eighteen pounds (Heinowitz 1995, 60)!

The fact that this is a sympathetic reaction to pregnancy is expressed clearly by one father in the study mentioned above. "I don't know why I gained all this weight. I know I've been eating more than usual, but there's something else. I never told this to anyone but when I feel the roundness of my stomach, it's as though I've 'taken on' the pregnancy, even though I don't feel anything inside of me. It's a funny thing, feeling pregnant together. I am more aware of us sharing the pregnancy, and that seems to open me up to feeling things more" (Heinowitz 1995, 61).

Men's sympathetic reactions are accompanied by an increase in indigestion, nausea, and vomiting. Almost half of the men experienced both nausea and vomiting, and two-fifths suffered heartburn. It is worth noting that the rates of these reactions in men are not much less than those experienced by pregnant women, two-thirds of whom felt gastric distress.

Expectant fathers experience a wide range of aches and pains. The most common complaint for men is headaches. Almost half of the men who responded to the survey suffered backaches and stomachaches (Brown 1988, 535). About a fifth of the men reported having toothaches during the pregnancy. Sympathetic labor pains are especially common during the latter stages of pregnancy and often reach a peak at about the time a man's partner begins to have contractions. Characteristically, these labor pains cease as soon as childbirth is over.

In addition, men report a great increase in psychological symptoms during their partners' pregnancy. In one study, forty percent reported an increase in anxiety and over half of these complained of other psychological symptoms: depression, tension, insomnia, irritability, weakness, and headaches or stuttering (Brown 1988, 529). In a study of ninety-seven pregnant men, nine in ten experienced at least some physical aspects of couvade during the pregnancy (Strickland 1987, 186) and almost a quarter sought healthcare for the symptoms (Lamb and Lipkin 1982). These are most common during the first and third trimester of the pregnancy, with relatively fewer expressions of couvade in the middle trimester (Clinton 1987, 60).

The data comparing rates of these symptoms in partners of pregnant and nonpregnant women have varied. On one hand, nausea and vomiting, the most common symptoms recorded, occurred twice as often among pregnant as nonpregnant fathers. Also, nearly a quarter of pregnant fathers sampled suffered toothaches, while one-tenth of fathers in a control group reported the symptom (Clinton 1985, 224). Pregnant men often reported toothaches where no biological basis for the pain could be ascertained (Trethowan 1972, 74). Despite the diversity of these reports, one study of eighty-six men over the course of pregnancy found only five behavioral characteristics that differed from those of a control group. Pregnant men experienced significantly more weight gain, insomnia, colds, irritability, and restlessness (Clinton 1987, 66–67).

But Is It Couvade?

Fixing the home and car, working harder, and watching spending are all ways for a father to get ready for the baby. But is this couvade? Where are the ornate bodily decorations of the Siriono, or the food taboos of the Guaraní? Where is the public recognition that fathers have entered into a new and transformative state called "pregnancy"?

First, it is important to see these activities as ritual. Few of these behaviors have a pragmatic effect on the baby. Anthropologists smugly point out that the taboos of Trobriand men are based on superstition, not science. But a similar criticism could be leveled against much of the pregnancy behavior of American men. Our well-meaning behavior is usually based on good intentions, rather than scientific fact. When men drink milk instead of beer or stop having sex, they do so because they consider the former behaviors dangerous or wrong. When men change the tires on the car or take on an extra job, they believe that they are maximizing the safety and health of their babies. In fact, there is little evidence that these activities do much to benefit the baby. Most mothers would prefer that fathers forego the clean car or the second job so that they can spend more relaxed time as a couple. Even recent concerns about behavior and sperm count must be understood as cultural phenomena. It was only a generation ago that men's fertility could not even be questioned, and now we are quick to suggest that its presence or absence is determined by the vices our society abhors.

Although American fathers perform these birthing activities, their couvade lacks the public presence that recognizes the experience of fathers in birthing. Siriono men are decorated with uruku; Bororo men cannot touch their bows; Guaraní are prohibited from the forest. In contrast, American fathers have little social recognition of the liminal period in which they exist during pregnancy and birthing. Many mothers make special arrangements, taking leaves from work and arranging personal schedules to be free to leave for the hospital on a moment's notice. Fathers have at best only a partial hiatus from everyday life. Men may quietly organize their work and affairs to reduce their responsibilities from the due date forward, but rarely stop work before the day—or even afterward. In fact, while there is considerable social support for a woman reducing her everyday responsibilities before the due date, there is little latitude given men to do the same. Even where men are offered paternity leave as part of benefits packages, it is often impossible to use the time prior to the arrival of the child. Men continue to carry out routine responsibilities, distracted by the prospect of this major event, with one ear cocked for the telephone or the pager.[4]

Without public rituals to recognize pregnancy, American men enter an even more subjective state. Fathers exhibit the physical aspects of pregnancy. Quietly, without anticipating it, and often without admitting it, fathers begin to experience couvade in their own bodies. Rather than public painting, men get nauseated, gain weight, feel back or tooth pain, cannot get to sleep (or wake up), and experience almost the full range of symptoms felt by mothers.

In the United States, these private couvade reactions seem to occur irrespective of class or ethnic group. Men of all races, all religions, and all job classifications suffer when their wives get pregnant. If we look around the world, however, more general cultural factors seem to be important in the incidence of couvade experience. Thus, there is an extremely high incidence of couvade among Garifuna fathers. Although only about half of the fathers in the predominantly white American population suffered symptoms of couvade, 92 percent of the Caribbean men felt its effects. Not only did a greater number suffer symptoms; they also suffered a greater number, length, and intensity of complaints (Munroe and Munroe 1971).

Many analysts of couvade rituals emphasize that these behaviors are experienced by first-time fathers, but are less common among men who have already had children. This developmental-crisis theory suggests that the responsibilities of fatherhood trigger a crisis that changes behavior or becomes somatized in physical symptoms. As a matter of fact, the data are inconclusive on this point. Only one study has found that first-time fathers were more likely to seek medical attention for symptoms of couvade (Lamb and Lipkin 1982, 112).

Medical Culture and the American Couvade

How do we understand couvade in American society? It is not surprising that, in the same way that coconut oil massages are given meaning by Trobriand culture, the American couvade is defined by our own cultural attitudes about health and illness. American medicine identifies pregnancy reactions in physiological symptomology, and explains couvade according to its own biomedical model.

After conception, this biological and essentialist model denied fathers a role in procreation. As we developed a medical understanding of the physical nature of mother's reproductive capacities, we lost sight of the social, psychological, and spiritual links to her partner. Rather than recognize men's experience of pregnancy as social and constructive, American society has defined it as individual and aberrant.

The medicalization of fathers' experience began at the very early stages of the development of the medical model. As early as the Jacobean period, English medical practitioners recorded male responses to birth. Unlike theater of that day, which suggested that couvade reactions were normal (if laughable) in peasant life, these suggested that men were misguided or even diseased in their experience. In 1627, Francis Bacon provided the first empirical description of male birthing reactions in Europe.

> There is an Opinion abroad, (whether Idle or no I cannot say,)
>
> That loving and kinde Husbands,
>
> have a Sense of Their Wives Breeding Childe,
>
> by some Accident in their owne Body.
>
> (Hunter and Macalpine 1963, 217)

John Primrose, a Hull physician at a time when physicians had lower social standing than tailors, reported that

> Among very many other Errours, this seems the most worthy to bee laughted at, that the husband is thought to be sick, and troubled with the same symptomes, wherewith a woman with child is wont. . . . I doe not remember that I have read of it at any time, nor heard it observed in any place but in England. . . . It is no new thing for husbands and their wives to bee sick together. But it is a wonder, and heretofore a thing unknown,

that gravidite, or a woman's being with childe is a contagious desase, and that no other women, but men only, whom nature has freed from the travaile, should be infected therewith. (Primrose 1651, 121–124)

Robert Plot explained this "psychiatric conundrum" by referring to the Hippocratic conception of health, suggesting that noxious humors given off by pregnant women debilitated the men in their environment. "In the birth of man it is equally strange that the pang of the woman in the exclusion of the child have sometimes affected the Abdomen of the husband, which yet to such as have experimented the secrecy of sympathies, and understood the subtlety and power of effluviums" (1677, 16).

Medical literature seems to be ignorant of couvade from the seventeenth century until the twentieth century. This ignorance can, in part, be understood as a result of the Cartesian dualism that came to separate science and the practice of medicine from holistic perspectives. In the eighteenth century, as physicians became more thoroughly indoctrinated in the biological perspectives of science, they lost sight of fathers-in-birth. Medical awareness of men's experience of childbirth declined dramatically as science separated the mind from the body, the woman from the man, and the father from the mother. As the microscope focused ever more specifically on the mother's abdomen, fathers disappeared from view.

At the turn of the last century, the work of Sigmund Freud provided a new window through which many physicians could, once again, notice couvade. In doing so, couvade was understood through the lens of the medical model. Freud postulated a link between biological drives and the human mind that did not abandon science or the Cartesian dualism on which it rested. It was logical that Freud take interest in couvade, as conventional medicine offered no means to its understanding. Psychiatry has gone forward to describe, examine, and explain couvade. In the same way that pregnant women are defined as abnormal and in need of a cure called medicine, however, couvade was defined as an illness that demanded treatment. Sympathetic reactions in the partners of pregnant women are not defined as empathy, but as a pathology known as the "couvade syndrome."

Psychiatry first recognized couvade as a theoretical curiosity in other, less advanced, societies. Once described in the medical literature, however, the behavior was rediscovered in contemporary American fathers. Reports came first from military physicians, where soldiers with pregnant wives suffered physical ailments, such as nausea, diarrhea, headache, and dizziness, without an underlying medical pathology. In one of the first published reports, in 1951, a physician by the name of Freeman reported six cases in which pregnancy precipitated "mental illness" in men (Trethowan 1972, 71). Soon after, an American military doctor reported pregnancy reactions in thirty-one of fifty-five expectant fathers (Curtis 1955). Rather than identify the complex psychological and social states of fathers during pregnancy, these studies defined couvade reaction in medical terms and identified the symptoms in biological characteristics. Symptoms were clustered as a reaction, and the reaction was transformed into a syndrome.

The "couvade syndrome" became a medical reality in 1965 when two physicians, Trethowan and Conlon, scientifically studied fathers' pregnancy symptoms. They queried 327 working-class English men during their wives' pregnancies and defined couvade in medical terms. To assure scientific objectivity, they even established a control group of 221 married men whose wives had not given birth. The subjects were asked if they had suffered symptoms that might be associated with pregnancy, including indigestion, appetite changes, diarrhea or constipation, and physical aches or pains. In addition, men were asked about their psychological state and anxiety that they might be feeling about their wives' condition.

Trethowan and Conlon found that 20 percent of the expectant fathers suffered from toothache, nausea, or decreased appetite; over twice as many as the control group. These fathers also suffered more frequent increased appetite, constipation, diarrhea, and backache, although not in statistically significant amounts. In addition to the increased frequency of individual symptoms, expectant fathers suffered a constellation of three or more of the symptoms at twice the rate of the control group. These fathers' symptoms also lasted longer than those of nonexpecting fathers: on average, twice as long.

Subsequent studies by Trethowan (1972) show the specificity and range of couvade reactions. The variety of physical conditions noted included dental abscesses, inflamed knuckles, sties, herpes outbreaks, and nosebleeds. In addition, he expanded the number of categories of psychosomatic illnesses reported by expectant men to include anorexia, chest and abdominal pain, insomnia, cramps, pica (cravings to eat nonfood), and facial neuralgia. Like their partners, men craved chocolate, ice cream, potato chips, and fried eggs. Not surprisingly,

40 percent of the men experienced weight gain, possibly as a result of these food cravings. On the other hand, 6 percent lost weight. In a literal enactment on couvade, one man reported that he felt compelled to incubate and help hatch out a clutch of bantam chickens in the months before the birth of his child (Enoch, Trethowan, and Barker 1967).

Where Freud provided a psychiatric explanation of couvade, Trethowan and Conlon (1965) and Curtis (1955) specified its medical symptomology. Derived from the medical perspective itself, this description focused on the physical symptoms suffered by individuals. They were objective and observable aspects of men's bodies that could be measured and enumerated. They could be analyzed and explained within the framework of conventional medicine. In short, sympathetic birth was "all in the father's head," not in his relations or social world.

Since couvade syndrome is a medical creation, it is not surprising that reports of its incidence vary according to medical author. Estimates of the portion of men who could be defined as experiencing couvade symptoms vary, ranging from 11 percent (Trethowan and Conlon 1965) to 67 percent (Liebenberg 1973). Much of this variance is accounted for by differences in the symptoms used to categorize a father's reaction as couvade. The majority of reports suggest that between 40 and 50 percent of expectant fathers suffer medical symptoms that are related directly to those of their wives' (for example, Dickens and Trethowan [1971]). One in five have a constellation of reactions that could be termed a "couvade syndrome."

Lamb and Lipkin surveyed the recorded medical histories of three hundred men whose wives had recently given birth. They discovered that almost a quarter of these men had sought medical attention for symptoms identified by Trethowan and Conlon as couvade. The rate was even higher for first-time fathers. The number of doctors' visits by these men more than doubled while their wives were pregnant, then returned to the pre-pregnant level after the birth. Men who suffered no couvade symptoms exhibited no increase in medical visits through the process (Lamb and Lipkin 1982).

The prevalence of couvade symptoms in fathers changes dramatically over the course of a pregnancy. In a sample of ninety-one men, 70 percent of the men experienced one or more couvade symptoms during the pregnancy. These symptoms, however, were experienced at different times throughout the course of the pregnancy. Key symptoms that were associated with couvade syndrome occurred in a quarter of the men in the first trimester, almost half the men in the second trimester, and in one in three fathers in the last trimester of the pregnancy (Strickland 1987, 186).

A longitudinal study of eighty-one expectant fathers had contrasting results. This study suggests that couvade symptoms were most pronounced in the first trimester, when expectant fathers experienced physical symptoms of more and longer colds and greater irritability than a group of controls. In the second trimester, however, the symptoms of these fathers were virtually indistinguishable from the controls. Finally, in the third trimester, expectant fathers experienced greater weight gain, insomnia, irritability, and restlessness than the nonexpecting control group (Clinton 1987, 64).

The medical profession was quick to distinguish between neurotic reactions to a partner's pregnancy and what is called "psychotic couvade." Although couvade as a neurosis is characterized by exotic symptoms, couvade reactions are sometimes aspects of psychotic breaks, with hallucinations or delusions. Although neurotic reactions to pregnancy rarely impede the father in day-to-day functioning, psychotic couvade involves the loss of a patient's ability to relate to people in his environment, and often requires medication and institutionalization. Pregnancy is sometimes considered a precipitating factor in a psychotic break in the father, with 2 percent of psychotic breaks associated with fatherhood (Cavenar and Weddington 1979).

A single classic example perhaps best captures the severity of this couvade psychosis. In 1968, a thirty-year-old engineer suffered from insomnia and depression in the second trimester. The psychological problems intensified with the continuation of the pregnancy and he became paranoiac, believing that his wife and mother were plotting against him. He suspected that his mother was attempting to poison him and that his wife had become pregnant in an affair with his best friend. When he first sought medical help, he believed that the doctors and nurses were part of the conspiracy. Hospitalization, medication, and psychotherapy alleviated the symptoms (Tenyi, Trixler, and Jadi 1996).

Once it had defined couvade as aberrant and identified the symptomology, the medical community set out to find the etiology of this illness. Social relations and spiritual experience give couvade its meaning in other societies. But by viewing pregnancy as an abnormal condition of a woman's body, the medical model ignored those factors that make couvade in fathers understandable. Recognizing only the biological underpinnings of birthing behavior, medical studies were forced to declare the practice pathological, understandable only as a weakness or defect of the father.

Anxiety

As medicine looked for the pathological origins of couvade, the culprit was often found in men's inability to withstand the emotional pressure of pregnancy. This labeled pregnancy ritual as an abnormal reaction that men have to the anxiety that they feel for the pregnant mother. In a study of ninety-one expectant fathers, anxiety in fathers was directly related to other physical symptoms that the men suffered during their partners' pregnancies (Strickland 1987, 185). In a study of eighty-one men performed in 1983, sixteen fathers experienced a medically diagnosable couvade syndrome, showing two or more symptoms of the illness only during the pregnancy of their wives. These sixteen men experienced significantly more mental symptoms than the other pregnant fathers and were more commonly handicapped by the symptoms (Bogren 1983).

In addition to anxiety, other factors that often are blamed for couvade syndrome are marital discord, a pregnancy that is unplanned, and economic insecurity (Clinton 1985, 224–225). It is worth noting that although the medical community considers this syndrome pathological, mothers may actually see it as a positive statement of relationship. Pregnant women report a higher rate of couvade reactions in fathers than the men themselves report. This suggests that pregnant women may be seeking the empathy of their partners in the pregnancy process (Dickens and Trethowan 1971, 259–268).

Narcissistic Injury and Sadism

As psychiatry developed as a profession, it created a new means to understand men's pregnancy reactions as medical pathology. Following the early work of Freud on repression and neurosis, analysts suggested another subconscious abnormality that explained couvade. This depended on a husband's sadistic urges toward his wife. In this, the pregnancy creates a wave of jealousy in the father, as he feels displaced in the woman's life by the new child. This "narcissistic injury" not only causes anger at the woman, but the man's guilt over that anger forces him to overcompensate, taking on the injury that he would wish on his partner. In true Freudian fashion, analysts suggested that the man's ego hides the entire injury and reaction from his conscious mind.

Despite the scientific pretensions of psychiatry, these hypotheses of paternal dysfunction are bolstered with anecdotal evidence. In one case in which the father suffered severe abdominal pain after his wife had undergone a cesarean section, the symptoms were explained as a regressive manifestation of the father's narcissistic injury experienced when he lost his favored position with his mother-wife. His rage at his wife was transformed into identification with her surgical pain (Maltbie et al. 1980, 91).

Parturition Envy

Even before couvade became a pathology in American medicine, Freudian psychiatrists were "discovering" its origins in abnormal psychosexual development. One of Freud's contemporaries, Felix Boehm (who also tried to explain cannibalism through psychoanalysis) pointed to a "parturition envy" in boys that parallels penis envy in girls (Boehm 1930, 456). In this, little boys become aware of the mother's procreative capacity and, despite their desire to separate from her, envy her capacity to give birth (Jones 1942, 695). A more common psychoanalytic explanation of couvade syndrome explains it as a neurotic attempt for sons to identify with their mothers, and specifically with her procreative function, and that this envy of women for their ability to bear children is a precipitant of psychosis (Zilboorg 1931).

Fetus Identification

Trethowan, who did much to popularize "couvade as pathology" in the medical literature, suggests that in some cases men might identify with the fetus. He credits this identification to jealousy, which is stimulated as the husband's place in his wife's world is supplanted by the new child. The model came to be called the "fetus as rival" hypothesis (Trethowan 1972, 84–85). Other studies point to sibling rivalry as a possible cause of couvade syndromes. They argue that the feelings evoked in childhood by the birth of a younger sibling and the loss of the mother's attention are a possible contributor to a father's later reaction to the birth of his own child (Cavenar and Butts 1977).

Sexual Identity

Turning couvade into an abnormality to be explained in the defects of the father is not solely the work of psychiatrists, however. Psychological anthropologists have sought to find a link between couvade and confused sexual identity. One study analyzed men's sexual identity and found a relationship between men's

masculinity and the extent to which they suffer couvade reactions. This explanation leans heavily on an analysis of a man's relationship with his own father,
and in turn, on his own feelings toward being a father.

In a study of white American men, the same study found that men who suffered couvade reactions while their wives were pregnant were more likely to display feminine behavior in covert measures. For example, these men enjoyed
television shows favored by women: medical dramas and family westerns. In
overt behavior these men were flagrantly masculine, a stance that was portrayed
by the authors as defensive. Men who experienced couvade symptoms were also
four times more likely to have grown up without fathers at home. This was seen
to suggest that couvade reactions reflect a man's "cross-sex identity," afflicting
men who have failed to develop a strong sense of themselves as men capable of
fulfilling a man's role and responsibilities (Munroe and Munroe 1971).

New Couvade and New Visions

After a century of using anthropology to understand couvade in other societies
and medicine to analyze it in the United States, it is time to use its insights to
show how fathers' pregnancy rituals are not necessarily pathological. Where
anthropology emphasizes the diversity of beliefs and behaviors around the
world, and the medical model defines each instance of what it perceives as
divergence from the normal and healthy, couvade needs to be appreciated as a
means of defining a new identity for a man and a new relationship with his
baby, his partner, and society.

It is clear that the biomedical model determines the diagnosis of "couvade
syndrome" that is offered by a physician, but our more general understandings
of men and pregnancy are influenced by the same meanings as well. Based on a
biomedical model of health and illness that locates the pregnancy in (and only
in) the mother's body, American medicine can only understand couvade reactions of fathers as a pathological state. When a father's symptoms are recognized, they are explained as aspects of his body, without reference to the
changes that are taking place in his partner and his baby. In short, if a father
experiences a subjective involvement in the gestation of his child, he is diagnosed as diseased.

With the same dualism that the biomedical model imposes on other health
matters, pregnancy is defined according to a basic distinction between mind

and body. The biological fact of gestation is isolated from its psychological aspects. Malinowski made clear almost a century ago that fathers are intimately involved in pregnancy—in all its spiritual, emotional, and social facets. Nevertheless, the medical community of today ignores fathers, whose link with the child is not biological. If a man experiences a psychological state of pregnancy, it is considered to have little or no relation to the pregnancy at hand.

Second, the medical assumption of individualism ignores the physical relationship between a father and his gestating child. Medicine does not regard pregnancy as a social phenomenon. Unlike the Trobriand father, who has a responsibility to physically shape the baby in utero, American fathers are perceived to be physically isolated from the developing baby. If a man's relation to the pregnancy stimulates physical reactions such as weight gain or backache, it may be a matter for medical attention. The cause of the reaction is not identified in the pregnancy, but rather in a man's individual attributes: his anxiety, envy, sadism, or sexual identity.

Men's reactions to pregnancy are considered especially aberrant because they take on female characteristics. In addition to mind-body dualism and the reification of the individual, medical models are deeply invested in differences between men and women. The male body has served as the normative model for the construction of the concept of "healthy." Likewise, the socially constructed concept of the masculine psyche has been used for the definition of the "well-adjusted" patient of both sexes (Broverman et al. 1972).

By taking the stereotypical masculine body and mind as the medical norm, pathology can be measured by the divergence from that socially prescribed model. Therefore, the fact that men display atypical gender characteristics makes them vulnerable to medical definitions of pathology. As pregnancy emphasizes the female aspects of the reproductive function, it focuses the attention of the medical eye on aspects of personhood that diverge even more so from the standard definitions. Men's couvade reactions are viewed as more pathological because pregnancy itself is a malady. It is not only aberrant for men, but abnormal for all humans. That pregnancy transforms the body further from the norm of healthiness is of considerable importance for understanding the pathology associated with American men and couvade.

In the medical model, men who experience reactions to pregnancy are understood to suffer from either psychological or biological disturbances. Their experience of pregnancy is defined as pathological somatic reactions and

explained in psychological diagnoses. These men generally are thought to suffer
the same feminine pathologies that are diagnosed in women: they suffer from
hysterical reactions that give evidence of delusion and neurosis. More notice-
able divergence from the norm demands a more extreme diagnosis. Men who
suffer a serious difficulty in maintaining stereotypical role expectations are
diagnosed as psychotic. They are suggested to have undergone a fundamental
break with reality.

So how do we understand couvade? Is it a neurotic attempt to deal with sub-
limated drives, as is suggested by the medical literature, or is it a ritual preparation of the father for his new child? American medical research has limited its
exploration of couvade to its individual expression and its psychological roots.
Thus limited, it explains fathers' reactions as signs of a flawed constitution. If we
understand these activities as a culturally patterned social process, however,
then we uncover a fundamentally different level of meanings. Increasingly, midwives—who reject many of the medical approaches to women's pregnancy—are
becoming aware that fathers share pregnancy and express it in both body and
action (Gaskin 2003; Davis-Floyd and Saint John 1998). Thus, we can see couvade
as a constructive and proactive preparation for the coming of a new child.

Birth is a biological fact, but it is also a social process in which mothers are
joined by fathers (and family, friends, and others). Just as eating is patterned by
myriad diverse cuisines, childbirth is a basic biological activity of humans that
is patterned and defined by culture. Human birth is accomplished with cultural
practices that were developed over millennia of successful reproduction and
that shape even the meaning of birth as a biological and spiritual process. More
than just cultural, birthing is a highly ritualized social event. For generations,
anthropologists have analyzed men's birth ritual used by so-called "primitive
people" as a means to assuage fear, reduce psychological conflict, and assume
their rights and responsibilities as new patresfamilias.

The carefully painted crib gives men the opportunity to commune with the
new child even before its arrival. The increased time at work signals the new
responsibilities they assume. Similar to fathers in indigenous South American
societies, American men change their behaviors to support and protect the
fetus as it develops inside the womb.

In addition, and perhaps not surprisingly, many dads take on the physical
aspects of pregnancy. Men gain weight, they get nauseated, and they suffer back
pain. Anthropology has been fascinated by couvade in other cultures, but we

must also recognize these sympathetic reactions as normal and functional parts of our own reproductive ritual. Medical definitions deem contemporary fathers' couvade pathological, and blame sympathetic reactions on the flaws and failures of the individual psyche.

Perhaps we can learn from South American Indians' rituals of childbirth. First of all, we can learn the importance of the relationship between father and pregnancy. American society is well aware of the magical transformation of women into pregnant mothers, yet we discount the importance of fathers in the pregnancy of their children. In contrast, South American indigenous groups recognize and promote the idea of pregnant fathers. Among the Siriono, the Bororo, and the Guaraní, men are considered to be vital to the health and well being of their children from the moment of conception. While a mother holds the developing child in her womb, the father is charged with protecting the baby's body, caring for the infant's spirit, and shaping the newborn's personality and talents. South American indigenous society sanctions the right and responsibility of a man to have a relationship with his developing child; couvade creates the time and energy to establish it.

3

Standing Vigil

Fathers in the Waiting Room, 1920–1970

Intimacy between two human beings should have its limits . . . , a girl is simply not at her romantic best in the delivery room.

−Dr. J. H. Morton (1966)

The traditional role of fathers in American childbirth is captured in the image of the distraught husband pacing the waiting room floor. For most of the last century, as birthing mothers were admitted to hospitals, delivery room doors swung forcefully closed behind them. Hospital policy and physicians' directives prohibited the father's presence at the birth of his own child. The father of the 1950s was left outside to wring his hands and add yet another cigarette to an overflowing ashtray. He paced anxiously in the maternity waiting room, heard the good news from the doctor, and then rushed out to distribute cigars and drinks to his buddies.

Today, American fathers are not restricted from attendance at childbirth. In family birthing rooms, men accompany their partners through labor, watch the deliveries, and often cut the umbilical cords. Mothers find the joint experience rewarding, fathers are transfixed, and hospital staff report that fathers ease labor and speed delivery. The social and medical success of family birthing raises important questions about the traditional exclusion of fathers from birth. If fathers can be so valuable to the process, why were they previously restricted from birth? If birth is so important to fathers, why did men allow themselves to be excluded from it?

The answers to these questions become clear if we analyze the traditional activities of fathers as ritual, as rites of passage. The admissions process can be seen as ritualized separation of fathers and mothers; pacing the waiting room floor can be understood as vigil; and handing out cigars marks fathers' reincorporation into society with a new identity. Envisioning fathers' activities as ritual points out that they are carried out according to a cultural template. Men were restricted from birth, or excluded themselves, because it seemed normal, right, and appropriate according to the prevailing ideas about fathers, birth, and medicine.

What were the underlying cultural conditions that gave sense to restricting fathers from birth? Anthropology has been long aware that the cultural codes and social framework of society become most apparent during times of change, periods when those beliefs and actions are being questioned. Therefore, to identify the cultural basis of traditional American childbirth, studying the debate that arose as critics advocated change is useful. Throughout most of the twentieth century, medical institutions assumed that fathers were unnecessary to and perhaps uninterested in labor and delivery; their contribution to birth was thought to end at conception. As early as the 1930s, however, "humanist" birthing proponents began to defend fathers' rights and interest in their children's birth. They pointed to fathers' birthing assistance in hospitals, as well as to the importance of fathers in generations of births outside medical settings.

As these perspectives gained popularity, physicians were forced to marshal their own counterarguments. The medical literature of the 1960s provides a clear record of the rationales provided for fathers' restriction from birth. In the magazines and journals of the day, obstetricians argued that fathers should be excluded for the sake of the mother, the child, and the men themselves. They argued that visitors were dangerous to the process, pointing to the biological contamination and institutional inefficiency caused by men. Moreover, physicians posited fathers' own psychological vulnerabilities and prurient interests as reasons to exclude them from delivery.

The explicit arguments to restrict men to waiting rooms conceal an underlying logic—one more concerned with power than with health. Analysis of the power dynamic of traditional American delivery suggests that fathers were excluded because they challenged the ideology and power structure of medical birthing. On one hand, a father's presence in the birthing room reinforces the mother's self-concept as a social being, resisting the medical redefinition of the mother in strictly biological terms. On the other hand, as patriarchs within the family, fathers challenge the dominance of the obstetricians over birthing women.

Restricted from attending the delivery, men constructed their own rituals of birthing. They marked the event in other ways. A script was developed for what

men *should* do while their partners gave birth. They paced the floor, smoked cigarettes, and watched the clock. Not only did men perform these routines, but
these inconsequential activities also took on new meanings. Rather than the
boredom of marking time at the office, clock-watching in the maternity waiting
room became a vigil that fathers kept for birthing mothers. The rituals and
meanings were not developed in a vacuum. They conformed to the medical
model of birth: fathers were unnecessary to the process; they *should* worry.
Moreover, excluding fathers from parturition made sense in traditional American families and society. As providers and protectors, fathers were expected to
buy the best services to keep their women safe—and then retreat to smoke cigarettes and fortify themselves for the news that they would receive. In essence,
in pacing the waiting room floor, men created meaningful rituals to mark the
transformation into fatherhood.

The Way It Was: American Home Birth

There is no single traditional way that American fathers have birthed. In our
short history, fathers have been excluded, invited, restricted, or expected at
birth, according to prevailing social attitudes. The information that we have
about men-in-birth suggests that they were probably restricted from birth in the
eighteenth century, admitted in nineteenth, excluded in the twentieth, and now
are once again a common fixture at their babies' births.

Home birth, which was the most common form of birth in America until
1945, offered men a variety of important roles in birth, even when they were not
participants in the birth chamber. From the diaries of midwives, frontier mothers, and immigrant women, we know that fathers boiled water, brought clean
cloths, and gave emotional and physical support, even if female midwives or
male obstetricians were the principle attendants.

Martha Ballad, whose diary as an eighteenth-century midwife was edited by
Ulrich (1990), offers some of the best notes on fathers in birth in colonial America: the first responsibility of fathers was to inform the midwife or physician of
the impending delivery and often to bring them to the birthing woman.
Accounts of other frontier women often mention that as labor began, the men
hitched up the team or saddled the horse and brought an experienced neighbor
woman, a midwife, or, in the latter part of the nineteenth century, a physician
to attend the birth (Leavitt 1986). Home birth was a social event and, as delivery

drew close, fathers rode to the homes of female friends, neighbors, and relatives, to bring these other women to the birth.

In the close environment of common people's small homes, birth took place behind a makeshift partition or in what was usually the only bedroom. Men were frequently called on to do specific tasks. Children needed to be trundled off to neighbors or relatives; water needed to be boiled; sterile cloths needed to be prepared. While birthing accounts focus on the presence of midwives and physicians, it is clear that men were often present during labor. They comforted, cared for, and attended to their partners' needs. Sometimes husbands served as primary assistants to midwives. Woodcuts of childbirth in early America show husbands performing the heavy work of physically supporting their wives during labor. The husbands moved in and out of these birthing rooms, helping where possible, and absenting themselves to bring the necessary goods and to keep the domestic sphere running. In some cases, husbands were sent out during the final delivery. If all went well, they were brought back in to greet their healthy child and wife after the birth.

Furthermore, in cases where there was neither time nor opportunity to bring in a specialist or a woman, husbands were sometimes the only attendants. Frontier women often gave birth far from other households; even in rural communities, bad roads and poor weather sometimes prohibited another woman's arrival. The husband made the necessary preparations, ministered to the laboring woman, and eased the delivery of their new child. Even under arduous conditions and difficult deliveries, fathers showed themselves able. One frontier woman remembered that when her logger husband returned to their isolated cabin to find her laboring alone with a difficult breech birth, "He came blowing in that night. Said he just had a feeling. I never was so glad to see anyone. He pulled that baby out [feet first]" (Leavitt 1986, 95).

While fathers were usually there to help, birth remained the work of women and specialists. In the normal course of events, husbands did not officiate over the birth or serve as the primary fount of birthing knowledge. In Colonial America, older women gave the birthing mother knowledge, emotional support, and physical assistance. In the nineteenth century, physicians offered whatever technical expertise and comfort they could.

In American home birth, a baby was kept with the parents. A newborn was lifted into the mother's arms and placed on her breast, often while the umbilical cord was still pulsing. Nursing linked mother and child. Fathers, too, were on hand to greet the new arrival. Husbands who had waited outside were called in. As the baby nuzzled its mother's breast, father had the opportunity to caress the baby's brow and place his fingers in the little clasping fist. As the mother prepared to push out the placenta, fathers could hold the infant and let the mother and her birth attendants devote themselves to the final stages of birth. This personal time of fathers and their new children offered the opportunity to begin their relationship. Holding the babies, inspecting their tiny, wrinkled faces allowed men to form an affective link with these new beings. The time also gave babies the chance to smell the bodies of their fathers, pick out their hazy shape, and hear the voice that had been muffled in utero. After the immediate moments, it was often the father's responsibility to introduce the newcomer to the family members waiting outside the bedroom. Looking back at her brother's birth at home in the 1920s, one woman I talked with recounted, "I remember that when my mother started having pains, we called my father, who had gone into town to buy groceries. Then we called my grandmother who came and cooked and took care of us. My father went in and stayed with my mother until my brother was born. Then he came out and showed us our new brother and gave him to my grandmother who sat beside the heater and washed him. Then he took us back in to see our mother."

In traditional home births, babies were integrated directly into a series of relationships. Mother, father, siblings, and grandparents created a social womb to hold the newcomer. Most important here, home birth never separated father and child, providing them the opportunity to form an intimate and important bond from the very first minutes.

It would be a mistake to assume that early American birthing provided a standard role for men in birth. Fathers' experiences varied according to region, class, ethnicity, and religion. Even in the short span of American history, the role for fathers has varied greatly. Fathers' role in delivery increased dramatically throughout the last half of the nineteenth century. Early reports such as Ballard's colonial diary offer images of fathers as secondary and supporting characters, but by the 1890s, fathers-in-birth seem to have moved into the role of the primary auxiliary attendants, especially where doctors were concerned. Medical literature of the nineteenth century mentions fathers in 90 percent of the cases in which birth attendants are mentioned; midwives and females attendants receive far less attention (Suitor 1981).

The increased importance of fathers in birth in the late nineteenth century was due to social factors, not the pragmatic aspects of birth. First, the nineteenth century saw the emergence of greater marital intimacy. The legal and social bond of previous generations was increasingly becoming a companionate marriage in which individuals shared a greater portion of their time and personal selves. As the American workforce became more mobile, nuclear families were forced to move away from friends and families. In the increasingly isolated nuclear family, wives' feelings, hopes, and fears that had previously been shared with female relatives were shared with husbands. Birthing processes followed the norm of the larger society. As mothers lost the support of sisters, mothers, aunts, and friends, they increasingly turned to men for help and solace in birth.

Second, the nineteenth century saw lower rates of fecundity, increasing the importance of children to fathers. Between 1800 and 1900, the average number of children borne by American women dropped from seven to between three and four (Coale and Zelnick 1963). As the rate of first-time births doubled in the century, mothers and fathers would have heightened anxiety and excitement as befits more inexperienced parents. With fewer children to carry the social responsibility of the next generation, each child would receive greater social attention within the family, and specifically from the father at birth.

Finally, as medical practice took a greater role in birth in the nineteenth century, the first tendency was to increase, rather than decrease, fathers' involvement with birth. The popularity of fathers at birth was influenced by the growing use of male physicians to facilitate birth. As physicians acquired greater prominence in surgery, male physicians broke the gender barrier of the birthing room. By asserting themselves as medical specialists, they were able to overcome many of the social barriers that they suffered as men. Once inside, however, male doctors both allowed and necessitated fathers' inclusion in the birthing process. On one hand, if a male doctor could enter, why not a male husband? On the other, the presence of the male obstetrician demanded that the husband be present as chaperone to assure that the physician took no liberties during delivery.

The historical role for fathers in home birth has conformed to and changed with the landscape of American culture. Fathers were offered roles that fit the idea of what men in families did, and adapted to the prevailing birthing practice of midwives and doctors. It is not coincidence that as fathers shifted from eighteenth-century providers and protectors to nineteenth-century companions, their duties expanded from providing for the attendants to ministering to their wives. As birth moved into the hospital in the twentieth century, it brought about yet another shift in fathers' role.

Hospital Birthing

As mothers moved into maternity wards in the twentieth century, fathers were left in the waiting room. This major shift in men's role was evident from early labor, even as fathers transported their wives to birth. Rather than ride circuit to inform women and midwives of the labor, the onset of contractions in contemporary America demanded a man warm up the car, get the suitcase to the car, and take the birthing woman to the hospital. One of a husband's basic (and few) tasks during pregnancy was to gas up the car and be ready to jump in. Tales of laboring couples speeding through the night to the hospitals entered the national mythology, as did the accompanying stories of those families who didn't make it: *New Yorker* cartoons show the frantic husband speeding his laboring wife to the hospital chased by a string of wailing patrol cars. Rather than frontier accounts of fathers' importance in solitary and difficult births, now men became known for their assistance as women delivered too quickly under streetlights beside the road.

It was not the invention of the automobile or even the involvement of doctors that most radically transformed American men's role in childbirth; it was the advent of hospital birthing. In hospitals, physical space, individual activities, and social relations were given new meanings. These little worlds were dominated and defined by the models and ideologies of medicine.

Fathers were given new roles in hospitals as their previous tasks as supporting characters were filled by specialists. Nurses took over the technical roles of preparing the mother for birth, doctors assisted in the actual delivery, and emotional support was considered unnecessary to the biology of parturition. Fathers not only found themselves unnecessary; they were separated from their partners. In their separate domain, they discovered an unwritten script for their own hospital behavior. They paced, they smoked, they worried, and they drank— all the time aware of the danger and importance of the event that was occurring. It is instructive to use the lens of ritual to analyze these fathers' experiences in traditional hospital birth. We can see these rituals as a stereotyped and stylized process that carried symbolic meaning beyond any pragmatic effect of the actions. The hospital created new rituals, with new roles, arenas, and identities.

Admitting Patients; Restricting Visitors

Hospital rituals began as the mother was admitted as a patient. As the couple entered the hospital, they were directed to the admitting room. Set apart from the medical arenas of the hospital, the admitting area usually felt more like a business office than a maternity unit. Desks and filing cabinets defined the space and legal forms were the focus of attention. In fact, it was not uncommon to have admitting areas that resembled bank lobbies, with couples standing in front of glass-fronted windows and speaking through holes, passing forms through slits to receptionists on the other side. (Today, the activity usually takes place in the semiprivacy of an admitting alcove, more like opening a checking account than like cashing a check.)

The stated reason for admissions was to fill out the necessary forms to perform birth in the hospital. The admitting couple was called upon to declare any information that could influence the course of events in the hospital setting. The birthing woman's medical history included a list of allergies, past illnesses, and previous medical interventions. As it elicited information from the woman, the hospital created the medical definition of the woman, the identity that would be used in its subsequent relations with her. While the explicit purpose for hospital admissions seemed to be to ask "who are you?" the underlying actions communicated just the opposite. Hospitals admissions *informed* the laboring couple who they were in the medical setting.

The ramifications of this process on the identity of mother and father are obvious. Instead of viewing a mother as a strong and apprehensive social worker, for example, the medical system might perceive a first-time maternity patient with chronic back pain and an allergy to penicillin. The primary identity for birthing women was that of *patient*, defined first by her pathology (pregnancy) and second by any noteworthy biological attributes that distinguished her from the medical norm of birthing women. Thus, in 1952, a twenty-eight-year-old first-time mother would have been declared high-risk as a *geriatric primipera*. This image then was reflected back to the mother and became who she was in the hospital system.

In contrast, no medical history was taken of the birthing father. His allergies, medication, or illnesses were of no consequence to medical birthing and were ignored in the admissions process. The institution created no medical definition for him, nor did it perceive him as a social, spiritual, and psychological being. Admission constructed an image of the father-as-provider that fit the 1950s model of masculinity. The man's financial situation was of primary interest. What was his occupation? Where did he work? Did he have insurance or income sufficient to cover the costs of the delivery? These allowed the hospital to create a definition of the man that would suit its purposes. The hospital's financial definition of the family was based on criteria that the couple might find inconsequential to the birth of their child, but which became critical to all subsequent interactions between the father and the medical staff.

The admissions process also defined the father in legal terms that determined his rights in the medical setting. Was he the (biological) father? Did he live with the mother? Were they married? These criteria then became the facts that the hospital used to relate to the father, and the elements that defined his relations with the mother and expected child. Woe to the unmarried father who claimed a right to being a partner with the birthing mother. The admissions process redefined a father's legal rights to his wife and child as well. His presence at the admissions window was a public statement of his acceptance of the fact that his wife relinquished her rights in the hospital. As to his progeny, he was forced to sign a form surrendering his own legal rights over the child who will be born to him. (If the admissions process stripped the man of his power as a husband, it verged on emasculation with regard to his child. Before the sex of the child was known, the father was called upon to empower the physician to circumcise a boy.)

Even the organization of physical space in admitting affected the identity of the couple. The glass barrier between the couple and the admitting nurse (when nurses still performed this function) emphasized their identity as outsiders. Fathers and mothers did not yet have a place within the institution of the hospital, and the official held the power to either admit or reject them. (Without the proper qualifications—be those financial, racial, or religious—the birthing couple might well be prohibited entrance.) Moreover, the structure of the admitting window called on parents to act as consumers of services, rather than participants in an event. They behaved as they would at a bank or government office, requesting assistance for which they would gladly pay. In behaving as consumers, they came to see themselves as consumers. To quote William James, "Only act in cold blood as if the thing in question were real and it will become so" (James 1890, 42). Without thinking—but with much meaning—couples learned about their place in hospital birthing.

Leaving the admissions interview, the couple had new identities. As the admitting nurse gathered information, it was analyzed, evaluated, repackaged, and returned to the birthing couple in the form of identities that placed them in the hospital setting. A birthing mother was a patient; the father became a visitor. These differing identities created two differing paths through the birth process. A nurse set the laboring woman in a wheelchair and removed her into the hushed efficiency of the hospital corridor. The words were clear: husbands were not *admitted* into the hospital. The husband watched his wife go, and the swinging doors of the maternity ward fell heavily into place between them. A stern voice and a firm hand directed him to the waiting room.

More than a mere word, the label of *visitor* changed fathers' identity in the hospital setting. First, men's roles as husbands, lovers, fathers, companions, and friends were superseded. The category of visitor lumped fathers in with all other outsiders, denying them any special status as progenitors or partners. The category of visitor subjected fathers to institutional policies that dictate behavior. Specific and clear policies govern visitors' every activity on hospital grounds: where they may walk, what they may wear, when they can be present. Behavior considered right and normal at home, whether it was loud music or a quiet beer, was defined as disruptive in the hospital.

Second, symbolism of dress communicated fathers' peripheral position in birthing ritual. Official participants in the birth had ritual garb that defined their involvement. Over and above any practical benefits, the physician's scrubs implied life-sustaining powers; the technician's lab coat exuded the aura of science; and the nurse in her white uniform radiated sterility. The mother was placed in a short, thin surgical smock, open in the back that emphasized her biological nature, as well as her inferiority and vulnerability. In contrast, fathers wore street clothes, contaminated and unregulated, which conveyed their alien nature in the hospital setting.

Fathers' superfluous role to delivery was especially clear if birth became complicated. Doctors ignored visitors in medical decisions and took whatever action necessary to facilitate delivery. If a cesarean section was deemed advantageous, fathers might be warned by a nurse or might simply see the delivery room doors flung open as their partners were transferred with great rush to surgery. Informing the father, much less discussing the process with him, was considered a social nicety of little importance in the medical world. In the admissions process, he had, after all, given up his rights and turned over responsibility for the care of his wife.

Just as hospitals created a system of authority over women during birth, it is clear that men-in-waiting fell victim to institutional control. Rules were ubiquitous in official signs and enforced by uniformed nurses. Already only tenuously accepted in the hospital environment, men who broke the rules were formally and legally excluded from the limited access that they had to mothers in the process of birthing (Oakley 1984, 214). One father put it this way, "When they wouldn't let me stay with her and I started to make a fuss, they let me know in no uncertain terms that they would call the police if they needed." By definition, all visitors were formally excluded from the inner circle of birthing ritual. Fathers were unimportant to the biological process that was taking place.

Knaves-in-Waiting

Hospital admission not only created new roles for the father and mother, it relegated each to a distinct arena. By defining fathers as visitors, they were restricted to lounges, cafeterias, waiting rooms, and gift shops. Fathers had limited access to labor and recovery rooms and were prohibited from delivery areas. The nursing station controlled the flow of information and people between the areas. Mothers went off to labor rooms, where they were examined, shaved, given an enema, and drugged, then monitored until the doctor needed to be called. The institution justified its restrictions by referring to the biology of the patient: "You must leave now; she needs her sleep"; or alternately to institutional efficiency, "You'll have to leave during shift change"; or to intimacy, "Could you step outside for a minute? We need to check her." Locked in labor rooms, mothers were removed not just from their husbands, but also from any remaining networks of female support. Sisters, mothers, and aunts had no place in the hospital arena either.

During labor and delivery, the place for a birthing father was the waiting room. In most cases these were converted hospital rooms, stripped of beds and bureaus, with few objects that allowed the occupants to fix their location in geographic terms. Men-in-waiting were not at home, at work, or even in a specific town or hospital. Waiting rooms were largely bare of objects that oriented fathers in human relationships. There were no pictures of previous men-in-waiting, nor of the women and children for whom they waited. The impersonal experience of waiting rooms was exacerbated in that fathers usually took no personal effects, unlike their partners who at least carried a small bag with a few belongings.

The world stood still for men in the maternity waiting room. The telephone on the laminated end table was reserved to notify family and friends of the process and outcome of the delivery. The only other links with the conventional world were television and magazines, the latter dog-eared and askew beside the phone, and intended less to inform than to distract the father from the birth he was awaiting.

Understanding the ritual aspects of men's experience highlights the importance of waiting as a transitional, or liminal period, in the rite of passage into fatherhood. Anthropologists from Van Gennep to Turner point out that liminality is marked by disassociation from conventional space, time, and actions. In fact, the word liminal derives from the Latin for "threshold," which signifies its transitional character. As a phase in ritual, the figurative threshold is conceptually elongated to a corridor or tunnel through which the initiate passes. Envisioning this phase as a corridor emphasizes three aspects: the physical space, the distinct time, and the initiate's activity.

First, understanding men's traditional birthing experience as ritual focuses our attention on the physical space of the maternity waiting room. Defined as a distinct arena, maternity waiting areas were developed and decorated according to a prescribed concept of what the room should look like and what its function was. In the early years of hospital birthing, men were provided a simple chair or bench in the maternity ward hall to hold their vigil. As hospital policy became more uniform and rigorous, family members were increasingly restricted from these halls and rooms of the medical areas. It became necessary to create a place where they could be close at hand, yet isolated from the patient and staff. Waiting rooms became the ritual space that held fathers as they experienced birth.

This spatial isolation gave the hospital waiting room a sense of being sacred. The English anthropologist Edmund Leach (1958) pointed out that we attach symbolic significance to ambiguous aspects of our own culture. For example, a church or synagogue acquires its importance not only by association with the spiritual, but in the ambiguity of its character as an element of both the mundane world and the supernatural realm. Likewise, the space of the hospital waiting room is fundamentally ambiguous; it is inside, but not of the hospital. The waiting rooms occupy that ambiguous area between the sterile realm of the medical world, and the contaminated existence outside the hospital. Mediating the purity of the sacred medical world and the polluted nature of the street, waiting rooms take on an aura of sacred territory.

The liminal nature of the waiting room is evident in a new chronology that defines the passage of time. In the waiting room, the conventional clock stands still for the birthing father. Like the distinctions between day and night, work and rest, personal and public, normal ways of figuring time are superseded while the mother is in the throes of labor and delivery. The father becomes disentangled from his regular daily schedule of responsibilities. The clock no longer marks the passing day, but the time since labor began. The sweeping hands count the seconds, minutes, and hours since the mother was admitted as a patient and the father began his enforced vigil.

Third, fathers' activities in waiting rooms can be understood through the lens of ritual action. They were by nature ineffectual. The waiting room isolated men from the distractions and disturbances of the everyday world. Sealed off from the responsibilities of jobs, worries about bills, and all the petty problems of life, fathers could do nothing but focus on the impending birth. But men were also locked out of the immediate process of birth. Explicitly restricted from doing anything but wait, birthing fathers' attentions were oriented to their partners, the hospital, and themselves. Although relieved of their rights and responsibilities in the everyday world, men-in-waiting performed rituals that conformed to the medical model and the policy of the hospital—and their own ideas of what men in families were expected to do.

Foremost, fathers stood vigil for birthing mothers and children. Magazine cartoons of the fifties and sixties provide the stereotype of the husband in the waiting room: he paced the floor with a cigarette or hat in hand, sweat dripping off his brow. Above all, a man-in-waiting was expected to devote himself to his partner's experience, or what he imagined it to be. He was to be stoic as she faced pain and danger. He was to worry about her, but not allow his anxiety to overcome his masculine control of emotion.

Waiting for the delivery was not entirely an individual affair. Close friends and relatives were often included in the vigil. These subsidiary roles in the birth drama were played not by older and experienced women, but by intimates of either the father or mother. Friends of birthing fathers might be admitted to the scene to lend a calming presence or a supportive word. Close female relatives might take up the vigil for the birthing mother herself, wanting to be close to share in the news that eventually spilled from the closed sanctum of the delivery room.

Fathers' second ritual responsibility during childbirth was to fortify themselves and their bodies. This they did in a manner consistent with the stereotype of men in American society. Unlike women, who were required to abstain from food during labor and delivery, men were expected to eat well. Nurses and staff often directed fathers to a nearby restaurant for a good meal to prepare for the difficult task ahead.

Men-in-waiting were also expected to self-medicate themselves. Alcohol was an acceptable means for men to deal with the anxiety of the birthing period. One physician remembered that during his daughter's arduous birth in the 1960s, his wife's obstetrician suggested he step across the street and have a drink to pass the time and calm his fears. "I went across the street and had two martinis, finding that they brought me gradually down to earth" (Wilson 1964, 54). He returned to the maternity waiting room and found that a friend had arrived to help him along with vodka, coffee, and sandwiches. Cartoon characters also make clear that birthing men were expected to smoke. In an age when smoking and masculinity were intimately linked, nicotine helped men maintain themselves during what could be a long and stressful wait.

Getting the News Instead of the Baby

Probably the most remembered and widely reported moment for men in traditional hospital delivery was receiving the news of the delivery. In this highly stylized moment, the physician or nurse would exit the delivery room, still wearing the delivery garb, and present the news to the father. Exuding professional satisfaction, the physician would assure the father of the health of the mother and the sex of the child. If the physician were too busy, a nurse would perform the duty, passing on the joyful news of mom and child.

The arrival of the baby added another participant to the ritual of birth. Delivered by the obstetrician into the waiting arms of the nurse, the child began a series of activities defined by the hospital environment. In effect, the treatment of the new arrival isolated it not only from its mother, but also from the father who had been keeping vigil.

In hospitals, doctors—not fathers or mothers—were the ones to receive babies. Emerging into the bright light of the conventional delivery room, newborns were subjected to poking, pricking, washing, and wiping. Tubes were pushed into their noses and medicine in their eyes. Medical procedures were more important than the desires of the parents and comfort of the infant. In fact, the obstetrician directed the newborn's activities even before delivery.

While the infant was still in the birth canal, the doctor adjusted its shoulders and shifted the body to choreograph its struggle. With rubber gloves and surgical mask in place, the doctor pulled the baby through the final steps of its entry into the outside world. The most telling image of the traditional medical relation between obstetrician and child was the popular, and erroneous, picture of the doctor dangling the newborn's body by the heels in one hand, and slapping it on the rump with the other. Spurred by the doctor, the child was prompted to take its first breath, and in doing so to become a fully human being. Thus, the child's life was credited to the hands of the doctor, rather than the sperm of the father or the body and egg of the mother.

Receiving the baby was not the start of a new relation for the physician, but the termination of a major step in the process of birth. Thus, as the child uttered its first cry, the obstetrician quickly handed it off to the waiting arms of the nurse and turned his attention to what was thought to be the next problem: delivering the placenta. In the arms of the nurse, babies were subjected to a routine that was every bit as structured as that of birthing mothers and fathers, and similarly highly ritualized. The first step in the life of a child in conventional delivery rooms was to define its physical health. Nurses judged its skin color, responsiveness, and breathing. Next babies were weighed and measured, providing more statistical information for the medical definition of the infant.

Once the baby had been defined in terms and ratings used by the medical institution, nurses and nurseries begin the process of transforming the infant to meet medical expectations of what a child should be. First, infants were washed. Terry cloth towels and chlorinated water scrubbed away all vestiges of the *vernix* that protected the child's skin in the womb. Then the medical staff needed to stabilize the infant's temperature. (Removed from parents and wet from scrubbing, it is not surprising that the infant's temperature dropped.) The baby was swaddled in cotton blankets to provide the support and warmth that human touch would have given in a home birth. Finally, when the baby had been evaluated and altered to fit the strictures of official policy, it was placed in the nursery. The swaddled infant was laid in a little bed, surrounded by all the other newborns. Attended by skilled nurses and separated from inept parents, the newborns lived the first hours of their lives in these plastic boxes, under the harsh glare of florescent lights for up to twelve hours.

The conventional treatment of infants had many rationales. First, hospitals suggested that the babies needed to be in the nursery for observation. Nurses would periodically check their color, breathing, and activity level to assure that they were what hospitals considered normal. Their progress was recorded on a chart at the end of their bassinet. Second, postpartum mothers were deemed unfit to care for their newborn. In fact, heavily sedated mothers were often drowsy or asleep and even epidural anesthesia left mothers too unstable on their feet to keep the child with them. Finally, the idea of having dad care for the infant was not even considered. Not only did fathers lack the scientific and technical skills of nurses, they were considered naturally unfit to care for newborns. A father was, by hospital definition, one of the worst possible caretakers for his new child.

Even more than imposing medical procedures on newborns, hospital birthing dramatically altered the relationship between the new child and its parents. New mothers found that their relations with their new children were dictated by hospital policy. Three times each day, babies were brought on schedule for mothers to hold and inspect. If the child was not fed the specified amount of formula in the nursery, mothers were allowed to perform the rite of bottle-feeding. The hospital decided when the child needed to be returned to its bassinet and the routine of the nursery.

The isolation of babies from parents was most extreme in the case of fathers. Confined to a waiting room and informed of the healthy delivery of his child, a man was forced to wait while the infant went through its ritual absolutions in the nursery. In the traditional hospital setting, fathers' status as visitors stripped them of all rights to their new child. They had no power to remove the baby from the nursery, or even touch the infant. In the same way that infants needed to be protected from their mothers, they needed to be defended from the disease and ignorance of their fathers. The father's polluted state made him more than simply ignored; he was considered dangerous to his new child. The hat that he clutched in his hand might harbor bacteria or parasites that would infect the fully controlled environment of the newborn nursery. His breath or hands might harbor some dangerous substance that would attack the object of his ardor. Moreover, fathers were considered inept. Men were clumsy and incompetent in the face of infant needs. Fathers were to provide for and protect their families, not by cuddling their newborns, but by underwriting the medical care that would train mothers to raise healthy children the scientific way.

Hearing the news of the birth closed off the period of tense waiting, but gave fathers new tasks. Fathers became the conduits for information about the birth to the outside world. Parents, siblings, and friends needed to be called and informed of the results of the delivery. Pay telephones were strategically placed in the maternity wards near waiting rooms. Later, fathers roved their workplace and social circle, handing out cigars to celebrate their newly acquired children and identities.

The father was often permitted to visit the mother for short periods in the recovery room. He held her hand as she rested, although she was tired and often drugged. Nursing staff carefully monitored his actions, as if to assure that his presence was not disruptive to the resting woman. If the delivery had been difficult or the recovery room was large, the father was kept away from the mother until she was granted a hospital room some hours later. There they would be reunited, having traveled very different paths to their postdelivery state. Last, with red eyes and trembling legs, he was allowed to view his child from behind the sealed, thick glass of the nursery wall.

Afterglow

Locked out of birthing rooms, defined as dangerous to their new offspring, men found other ways to mark their new social role. Men could not care for their new children in the nursery, or show the little ones off to friends at work or the corner bar, but they could make other ritual displays of fatherhood. The most stereotypical ritual of postpartum fathers in traditional America was handing out cigars. Returning to work after the birth, puffed up with pride over their new progeny, fathers were expected to bring with them a fistful of cigars. These stogies were passed out to each and every member of their social groups—whether they smoked or not.

Tobacco is common in rituals throughout the world. Among the indigenous groups of lowland South America, tobacco had important sacred powers. For example, Tukanoan men smoke tobacco during religious ceremonies to facilitate the flow of spiritual power between the supernatural and the mundane worlds (Jackson 1983, 203). Among the Wanano, the smoke of tobacco was considered the worldly manifestation of the return of dead ancestors to the land of their birth (Chernela 1993, 82). In addition to its sacred powers, tobacco has had important symbolic meanings. Among the Winnebago, tobacco was given as a sacred gift as a powerful means of establishing friendship between families (Barnouw 1950, 162). Similarly, among the Yanomamo, a gift of tobacco was a means of establishing trust and intimacy between two people (Chagnon 1997,

68). Tobacco carries symbolic power in our own culture as well. Tobacco is associated with masculinity, an image that is fostered by tobacco advertising in popular media that relies heavily on its identification with men and male activities. Whether it is the "Marlboro man" or "Joe Camel," corporate advertising reinforces the equivalence between tobacco products and unvarnished masculinity. By smoking, the hurried car salesman can communicate his commonality with rugged cowboys and urbane pool sharks.

As among the Yanomamo, tobacco in American society is also used as a means of linking people. The importance was not lost on John Steinbeck's union organizers of *The Grapes of Wrath* (1939), who casually offered a cigarette to every worker they met, or the 1950s loner who could erect a social barrier by lighting up without offering a cigarette to his compatriots.

Cigars as symbolic objects carry their own highly specific lexicon in American culture. If tobacco communicates maleness, cigars denote wealth, power, and self-indulgent masculinity. Although the vast majority of American cigars are cheap and of poor quality, the imagery of cigar production tells an important myth. The very best leaf is picked by brown-skinned Third World peasants, rolled against the thigh of a beautiful woman, and wrapped with utmost care by an aged craftsman. The cigar as an object reaffirms a man's power over other people as both class and sexual objects.

Probably the most common perception of cigar symbolism is the cigar as phallus. The familiar quote, "Sometimes a cigar is just a cigar," misattributed to Freud, only reaffirms the popular notion that a cigar is never just a cigar. Whatever is working at the level of the subconscious, the cigar in American culture will remain closely and consciously linked to male anatomy.

Smoking places these powerful symbols in a ritual context where their meanings are expressed and accentuated. Lighting and consuming a cigar involves a highly structured and complex series of activities. Cigar aficionado magazines and early James Bond movies document how the true cigar smoker selects, unwraps, clips, and lights a good cigar. Use a match, never a lighter; heat the tobacco, but never allow it to touch the flame; and rotate the cigar to create an even burn. Thus, it is possible to define the powerful and wealthy male by his proper enactment of the appropriate ritual. Little Orphan Annie's "Daddy" Warbucks is the prototypical cigar smoker. Smoking cigars also reaffirms a man's power by establishing himself in space. As the smoke wafts away, it occupies the space that it touches. It defines and dominates the area surrounding the smoker. As Thomas Mann (1955:48) said, "with a good cigar in his mouth a man is perfectly safe, nothing can touch him—literally." In sum, smoking cigars represents and reaffirms a man's place in space and society.

But one could go too far in emphasizing the seriousness of the message carried by cigars. As the new father pulls them out for his friends, the dad and the stogy are received with smiles, laughter, and backslapping. The exuberance and joviality of the ritual allow the group to recognize and share in the happiness and joy of the new father. It gives recognition and vent to the pride, relief, and excitement that men feel as they become fathers and recognize a new one in their midst.

The passing of cigars can be seen as marking the father's reentry into society, complete with his new identity as father. As a rite of passage, it can be understood as the end of his ambiguous liminal state. With the offering of tobacco, men return to their social milieu and reactivate relationships that were suspended during the critical period of birth. Fathers go into ritual seclusion when their babies are being born; they reenter the mundane world with ritual fanfare.

The Medical Reasons for Excluding Fathers

Why were American men excluded from hospital birth? Why did they end up with a cigar, but without the baby? Across cultures and through time, men have been offered a variety of different roles in the birth process, from catching the baby and cutting the cord to studied indifference and separation. Given the array of choices, why did American medicine choose to seclude men in waiting rooms? To understand the logic of traditional American birthing ritual, one must analyze the medical culture that gave rise to maternity waiting rooms, neonatal nurseries, and handfuls of cheap cigars.

The exclusion of men from birth made sense within the biomedical model of parturition. Mothers did not even need to be conscious during the process: they simply needed to provide their bodies to be delivered of the child. Fathers were even less important; neither their minds nor bodies were involved. Further, as males, fathers were antithetical to the female aspect of pregnancy. Fathers had made their singular contribution to the process at conception. As biologically male, fathers' bodies were tailored for tasks other than childbearing. Rather than help birth, fathers were better adapted to supporting and defending their new families. Third, the biomedical model defined childbearing as an aspect of the individual. The mother was pregnant, not her family, kin group, or community. It might have taken a village to raise a child—but birth was an individual matter. Lovers, husbands, and fathers had no part to play in the drama of birth.

When fathers began to ask to come into the birthing room, the medical establishment needed to go beyond simply ignoring men and explain why they were dangerous to birth and their babies. In the medical literature of the 1960s physicians went on record in response to men's requests and in reaction to progressive obstetricians like Bradley and Dick-Read. They provided a variety of reasons for men's exclusion from labor and delivery. In each case the rational makes sense, but only makes sense, within the biomedical definition of birth. These defenses of conventional policy point to sterility, efficiency, modesty, and even men's own vulnerability, in order to rationalize fathers' restriction from birth. Despite the superficial logic of each of the explicit reasons to exclude men from birth, hospital policy rests on medical definitions and practices of birthing. The exclusion derives not from anything natural about men's place in the process, but rather from the medical model that defines our meaning and practice of birth.

Contamination

First, medical staff expressed concern that fathers would carry bacteria into the delivery room that would increase sickness and death in mothers and newborns (Stender 1965). As the birth became defined in medical terms, great emphasis was placed on the antibodies that might contaminate it. For birthing women, this meant that they needed enemas, sterile drapes, and perineal shaves. For men, it meant that they needed to be separated from mothers, sealed in an area where they could do no harm.

The medical establishment has reason to fear contagions in the birthing room, but not from fathers. When physicians began to manage the births of women and before the advent of modern hygiene, doctors were the "Typhoid Marys" of a variety of illnesses. Maternal mortality from puerperal fever followed physicians as they carried infection from patient to patient on their rounds. Medical calls for sterility cannot account for excluding fathers from birth. Although physicians were early identified as carriers of disease between laboring women, fathers were not shown to be vectors. Of 45,050 births with fathers in attendance surveyed by the International Childbirth Education Association in 1965, there were no cases of puerperal infection traced to fathers (Stender 1965, 20). Although explanation of sterility was commonly used in publicly rationalizing partners' exclusion, it was given far less emphasis in physicians' own journals, when debating fathers' involvement in birth (for example Stewart 1968; Morton 1966).

Efficiency

Second, fathers were viewed as an impediment to the smooth operation of the medical machine. At best, fathers were considered redundant to the staff. There were no doctors to fetch or neighbors to gather together. The hospital provided sterile water and linens. Nurses brought water and medicines. The institution provided the physical support that men offered at home. Women were brought food and drink at appointed times, and assisted in going to the bathroom when the staff deemed necessary.

Hospital policy considered the social and emotional support of fathers (or female relatives and friends) intrusive and unnecessary. In essence, as the birth moved out of the domestic sphere, the tasks that had been shouldered by the father at a home birth were performed by hired personnel or considered unnecessary. The husband at the bedside was considered a physical impediment to the flow of hospital work and the nurses' access to the patient. One physician writing in the 1960s reported that "Everyone in the delivery room must have a definite duty to perform and do it as well as he can. Anything or anybody who might divert attention from the mother and baby is intolerable." Another obstetrician observed of fathers, "They are usually nervous, tend to make everyone around them uneasy and they serve no useful purpose, so why should they be there?" (Morton 1966).

Efficiency was rationalized and legitimized by reference to the professionalism and dangers of delivery. Morton continues, "The day we are born is the most dangerous one of our lives. . . . We believe in a strictly professional approach and have ever since the day we saw our first mother die on the table" (Morton 1966, 103).

Despite the superficial rationality of the arguments, medical demands to exclude fathers for the sake of efficiency are also countered by early birthing literature and hospital experience. As early as 1932, the widely read book by Grantly Dick-Read, *Natural Childbirth*, argued that fathers' presence at birth provided additional support personnel. Fathers brought ice chips, adjusted bedclothes, and took care of personal matters that nurses have neither time nor interest in doing. In fact, this was proposed as one of the most salient arguments to doctors and hospitals to admit fathers into the birthing room.

One of the most enduring and popular myths about men in birth is that they faint. The problem is greatly exaggerated. As early as the 1960s, one study pointed out that in over four thousand births with fathers who were prepared for the event, none had gotten sick or in any way interfered in the functioning of the delivery team (Stender 1965, 26). Problems men did suffer can be attributed to birthing procedures, rather than birth itself. Hospitals failed to prepare men for birth and refused to support them during what was often a long and tension-filled process. Bradley, an early medical advocate for birthing fathers, suggested that men's feeling of faintness in traditional birthing rooms was more often a result of hypoglycemia from being "ignored and unfed" through the long labor and delivery (Bradley 1962, 479).

Modesty

Third, fathers were excluded from labor to protect the modesty of their wives. As one woman remembers, "Every time they gave me a shot or an exam, my husband had to go stand in the hall. As if he had never seen me naked." In a clear statement of the superfluous role of fathers, they were even asked to leave the room while the patient was served something to eat (McKee and O'Brien 1982).

This emphasis on modesty has a clear moral component. Medical literature of the 1950s and 1960s stressed that birth was debasing and it was wrong for a man to see his partner thus degraded. Women would feel humiliated and husbands who saw birth would feel less sexual attraction toward their partners. One professor of obstetrics put it this way, "Intimacy between two human beings should have its limits. We believe in this even to the point of hair curlers. A girl is simply not at her romantic best in the delivery room. We must set limits in the interests of those whom we care for" (Morton 1966, 103). Another suggested: "The male attitude to the female genitalia is one of unconscious hostility. To him the charm of a woman is her mystery. It is inconceivable that a normal male watching the delivery of his wife could experience anything but revulsion at the vision of these genitals exhibited under the worst and filthiest conditions" (Stewart 1968, 1066).

This morality was communicated to the father both directly and indirectly. Even when hospital policy permitted father's presence during labor, other participants signaled the inappropriateness of the action. One father remembered his attempt at natural childbirth, "While the doctor examined my wife, I was told to go and stand in the corner, because my presence apparently embarrassed the nurses or somebody. Standing there with my face to the wall like a bad boy, I felt the tension rising within me almost to the breaking point" (Wilson 1964, 54).

During the heyday of drugged birthing in the 1950s and 1960s, physicians suggested that men should not be permitted to observe the effects of medication on their partners. During decades when sodium pentothal was used during delivery, hospital personnel cautioned that men should not be present when this "truth serum" was administered. They might be humiliated to hear untold secrets or see the promiscuous behavior of their pregnant wives under the effects of this "twilight sleep."

In a related and opposite concern, there was the suggestion that men derive some immoral and prurient pleasure from seeing their partner give birth. One man who removed his wife's cumbersome hospital frock and massaged her back was faced with nurses conferring in low voices: "these natural birthers just can't stay away from one another" (Romalis 1981, 112). An obstetrician put it this way, "This room is no place for sentimentality, sightseeing, sex gratification, or salesmanship" (Morton 1966, 103). Thus, men needed to be restricted from the birthing room to inhibit their own personal interests and desires.

Fathers' Vulnerability

Fourth, the medical community suggested that fathers were excluded for their own protection. Physicians asserted that there were many men who could not bear to observe the messy and dangerous process of birth; the sight of the pain, fear, and blood of their birthing wives made husbands a danger to themselves. Men might faint, fall, and hurt themselves, or at the very least, need the assistance of nursing staff who were charged with managing the birth. One nurse reported, "They are nervous and embarrassed; the younger ones are often frightened to death. All of them give the distinct impression that the role of assistant midwife is one they cannot handle and never wanted" (Gittleson 1965, 137).

This danger extended to the emotional well-being of the father. A man might have problems because of "increased responsibility, latent homosexuality, threatened dependency relationships, or unresolved parental attitudes" (Morton 1966, 103). These weaknesses would be exacerbated by the sight of one's partner in the throes of labor and delivery. "I can give many examples of bad behavior, such as attempted assault and fainting at the sight of blood, knocking over equipment and diverting the 110 pound nurse to haul the 180 pound body out of the way" (Morton 1966, 103). Great care needed to be taken to shield men from the reality of their partners' experience.

Moreover, the medical literature suggests that men need to be protected from the sadistic motivations of their partners. Stewart, once again, reports, "It is not fear that motivates a woman who desires her husband to be present during labor and delivery, but only basic sadistic instincts in which she forces him to realize what he has done to her body, and the suffering and tearing of her tissues which she can endure, and thus prove that hers is the superior sex" (Stewart 1968, 1066–1067).

Medical claims that modesty precludes a husband's presence at birth must be understood in light of the medical and physicians' definition of women in birth. The aspects of birthing most couples find humiliating are imposed by medical practice for purposes of efficiency. Few men want to see their partners sedated by pain relievers. One father reported, "[My wife] was doped up to the eyeballs, you know, and that in itself made it sort of a distressing experience for me. Because, [she] was in a very unreal condition and there was nothing much I could do" (McKee and O'Brien 1982, 106). At the extreme, doctors tied a woman immobile in bed and drugged her insensate, then protected the father from observing her in this state.

Physicians' concern with superficial sexual imagery assumes that a man's relation with a woman is based on fantasy. Rather than rooted in self-deception, however, the bond between father and mother is more likely to be based in the complex realities of life together. A partner is especially capable of understanding a mother in all of her spiritual, emotional, sexual, and social attributes. It is not surprising that fathers are most capable of recognizing the wonders and magic of birthing women. Thus, as fathers were admitted to birthing rooms, most found that their partners are "beautiful in childbirth" (Cronenwett and Newmark 1974, 214).

References to the sexuality, sadism, and masochism in birth highlight, once again, attitudes of medical personnel toward birthing women. That physicians considered these feelings central in the mother's relation to the father suggests that they are important in the relationship of the doctor to the birthing woman. Robbie Davis-Floyd points out that birthing can be extremely erotic. She argues that the medical establishment considered as pathological what is a natural and enjoyable aspect of birth. It is notable that the medical establishment organized birth practice to avoid any hint of eroticism between father and mother, yet ignored (or possibly enjoyed) the sexuality reportedly unleashed when birthing women were given sodium pentothal (Davis-Floyd 1992).

As for the need to protect men from their own psychic weaknesses, when fatherhood is reported as a factor in psychotic breaks, attending birth has not been identified as a significant factor (Freeman 1951; Jarvis 1961; Wainwright 1966; Lacoursiere 1970; Cavenar and Weddington 1979). Certainly the modesty of women and the emotional experience of men could be accommodated without excluding fathers from the event.

Men's Exclusion, Technology, and Patriarchy

The illogical reasons for excluding men from birth obscure underlying power conflicts. Men were excluded not for biological necessity, but because their positions as husbands and fathers disturb the structure of medical birth rituals and threaten the power on which these passage rites are based.

First, the partner reinforces the social identities of the birthing mother. A father's awareness of the mother's uniqueness, capabilities, and ideas contradicts the technocratic and biological definitions of women imposed by the medical establishment. A man's recognition that his partner can walk unaided and that she usually wears a nightgown disrupts the dependent and dehumanized images created by the medicine's rituals of childbirth. By mirroring these social realities to a woman in labor, a partner counters the technocratic messages of the American medical establishment.

Second, as men, fathers threaten the medical community's patriarchal authority over women. American social norms sanction men's authority over their wives and children. The husband's presence within the hospital setting competes with the power hierarchy that the medical community establishes over the woman. One physician reported succinctly that doctors think "most of medicine is a power situation, imposing your will on someone else, and medical practice is a system that doctors have created to make the woman dependent" (McKee and O'Brien 1982, 106). Obstetricians were explicit about the power relation, pointing to the need to keep the female patient "below [the doctor] in the pecking order" with all the back up of "nurses and high technology medicine" (McKee and O'Brien 1982, 106–107).

Physicians are well aware that the presence of the father challenges the authority that they wield in the delivery room. As one doctor clearly put it to me, "If an obstetrician wants to do something to speed the delivery, all he needs to say to the mother is that it's for the safety of the baby. It's harder to bullshit the father." Another physician who delivered in the 1950s remembered, "Of course fathers were a problem for us; they watched your every move and made you anxious. Who wants to deliver a baby with some uninvolved stranger breathing down your neck?" (Morton 1966, 103).

The medical community speaks most openly of this challenge in legal terms. When couples began to request fathers at birth in the 1960s, the medical community was quick to point to the legal threat that a father might present to the physician. Physicians warned that his admission into the birthing room provides a dangerous witness for malpractice suits: "The layman witness in the operating room could be the plaintiff-lawyer's dream and a nightmare to the defense" (Morton 1966, 103).

Finally, physicians make the point that fathers threaten the intimate and affective relationship that forms between birthing mothers and obstetricians. Bradley casually states, "All birthing mothers fall in love with their obstetrician" (Bradley 1962, 34). A physician has much to gain from the birthing mother's focus on him, both in ego gratification and in enlisting her cooperation. Fathers threaten this affective bond. The sociologist Georg Simmel (1955) pointed out the instability of three-person groups. Alliances invariably form between two parties that exclude the other, and the extent to which the third member is excluded is directly related to the power of the alliance of the other two. The obstetrician who seeks to ally with a birthing mother will have to contend with a father with whom she has an established relationship. The possibility of displacing the father demands considerable energy on the obstetrician's part and has an unpredictable outcome.

The sexual aspect of childbirth exacerbates the tensions in the triadic relations in the birthing room. Davis-Floyd (1992) argues that male obstetricians assert sexual power over birthing women. To the extent that birth is an erotic experience for mothers, the birth attendant becomes involved in a sexualized relationship. The male obstetrician sitting between the legs of a birthing woman occupies a region reserved for her most intimate partners. One obstetrician suggested that the conflict between doctors and fathers attending birth was as simple as "the natural antipathy between two men interested in the same woman," and likened the exclusion of husbands to King David's banishment of Uriah "as soon as he had gotten a line on Bathsheba" (Hazlett 1967, 4).

Despite its importance and the power that it gives obstetricians over women, the sexual aspect of the relationship needs to be denied in order to assert the technocratic nature of the medical process. Thus, one can understand the medical community's preoccupation with fathers' prurience and self-gratification in terms of male physicians' own attempts to deal with the suppressed sexual aspect of birth and reaction to it. One obstetrician observed succinctly, "When the obstetrician turns down the request [of a father to attend birth], no conflict over the female is involved, no detectable antipathy, no discernible eroticism. Seldom does the obstetrician anger or sputter or flush behind the ears, or display the hackles or betray any other sign that he is reacting instinctively. Instead he uses logical arguments that fail to hold water" (Hazlett 1967, 4).

As Foucault (1973) argues forcefully, the enactment of ritual provides a means for exerting and resisting power. In hospitals, men were disempowered in their relations with the medical institution. Birthing fathers were expected to relinquish their power over their partners, their children, and the birth itself to medical personnel. Fathers' demeanor was expected to express confidence in the institutional efficiency of the hospital and the technical expertise of their wives' doctors. They were to defer to hospital policy, nurses' experience, and physicians' authority. This hospital policy was reinforced by legal and, if necessary, physical power to constrain their actions. In effect, fathers were powerless in the face of and in their relations with the medical institution.

The Waiting Room and Traditional American Fatherhood

How did the isolation of birthing fathers relate to fatherhood in America? In the idealized, *Father Knows Best* world of the twentieth century, men were considered distant and rational providers who were responsible to provide family members with the best of modern technology and services. The rituals of admissions, the waiting room, and the nursery reinforced these traditional values and sent another generation of patresfamilias out to raise children.

First, traditional American men belonged at work, not with the children. The shop or factory floor was isolated from the home and, as such, reinforced distinctions between men's and women's work and responsibilities. The home and the children were feminized as the domestic sphere and isolated from the masculine world of production. What could be more domestic than birth, and what would seem more right and normal than for the father to step out of the event, whether it be at home or in a hospital? In addition, fathers were the sole providers for families, they provisioned the household and protected the family. As a man returned home on Friday afternoon with his check in hand, he offered his family food, shelter, and services. In the same way that a man could buy a home or car, he could hire someone to care for his birthing partner. He could pay to have his child arrive into as sterile and safe an environment as possible, under the watchful direction of a trained specialist.

Not only did the exclusion of fathers from the birth process conform to American norms of husband-as-provider, it fit the identity for fathers as emotionally distant from their families. As men's role was defined around production, it was characterized by the rationality and pragmatism of industry. The nurturing female homemaker satisfied the emotional needs of the family, as the father devoted himself to more muscular (or more cerebral) activities. Dad, after a long day running the press at the mill, had no energy to notice how quiet and withdrawn his son was.

The exclusion of men from birth fit the larger social ideal of twentieth-century modernity. As machines dominated the factory and the farm, they became a metaphor for home and hospital. Modernity valued technology over biology. Surgical intervention in birth was valued because technology itself was good. Fathers who could purchase the very best in technology for their partners were performing the most highly valued service possible. Fathers attended birth by proxy, through the technology and specialists that they paid for.

The social rituals we enact do not simply reflect our society; they act on the structure of our institutions. Foucault pointed out that medical models do not exist in an intellectual vacuum, but are powerful tools in the real world. The medical model imposes its concepts on the world through medical practice—in this case the birth of a child. As medicine engages with the real world, it becomes a tool in the interplay of social forces. It becomes part of shaping the world that we live in. Institutions that control medical practice become players in social conflicts between classes, ethnic groups, and men and women. Thus, in imposing its ritual on birthing partners, the medical model of birthing exerted power over our definitions of ourselves as mothers and fathers, and the relations that we maintain with other members of society.

4

Birthing Revolution

Men to the Barricades

The first cry of the child is shared by both husband and wife in almost
unbelievable ecstasy and relief from tension.

—Grantly Dick-Read (1932)

In 1968, the United States seemed poised on the brink of social revolution. Students demonstrated against war in Vietnam; women organized against patriarchy; and Blacks took to the streets to demand power. These public conflicts were accompanied by a much more private movement to change one of life's most intimate moments—the birth of a child. American couples who had redefined sexual attitudes and rewritten marriage vows now rejected conventional birth. They refused to submit to a sterile surgical event that removed babies from somnolent bodies; they wanted to birth babies with comfort, control, and confidence. These maternity ward radicals wanted to transcend biology and technology to make birth a natural, social, and spiritual event.

The demand for change was met by new methods of childbirth that were developed and promoted by three reformers: Grantly Dick-Read in England, Fernand Lamaze in France, and Robert Bradley in the United States. Between 1930 and 1980 they developed techniques that a generation of parents have used, practices that are popularly known as "natural childbirth." Dick-Read, Lamaze, and Bradley argue that we have created myths about birth being difficult and dangerous. This misinformation causes fear; fear brings on pain; and pain invites intervention. If a woman is prepared for birth as a natural event, her body will return to its primal state and marshal its inherent power. The liberated bodies of these mothers give birth without pain relievers or medical intrusions.

The birth reformers suggest that fathers are important to the process. More than bringing men into the room to experience childbirth, these proponents of prepared childbirth make them part of the birth team. Dad becomes coach, assistant, choreographer, nursing assistant, and companion. Fathers are charged to help the mother during pregnancy, sustain her in labor, and focus her for delivery.

Radical parents fought the establishment, but their hopes for transformation were never fully realized. Although mothers are now awake and dads in attendance, the new practice of birthing fails to recognize birth's spiritual, psychological, or social importance. Prepared birthing suggests that mothers' bodies are capable of giving birth—but remains rooted in a perspective of birthing as a biological event. Fathers do not share the experience; they direct, support, and reassure mothers. Instead of empowering mothers, fathers find themselves allying with hospital staff, following the directives of doctors and reinforcing the inferiority of mothers as patients in a medical world.

The reintegration of fathers into American birthing raises important questions about the meanings of American birthing ritual. How does fathers' assistance transform birthing? How does it change fathers? How was the fathers' role compromised? To understand fathers' integration into hospital birth, and the effect that it had on their identities and relations, we need to look at the ideological roots for these new rituals.

The Biological Concepts Underlying Prepared Birth

Despite the grassroots demand for a revolution, the new models were developed by physician-obstetricians, not parents or midwives or holistic healers. Dick-Read, Lamaze, and Bradley were all medical doctors. Each learned to deliver babies in a hospital setting and had become disenchanted with unnecessary medical intervention. They promoted models of birth with less pain, fear, and technology. But the models implemented in American hospitals do not draw on the spiritual, social, or personal experience of childbirth. The childbirth reformers promoted birth as a biological process that could be accomplished by mothers' bodies alone, without their psyches, their spirits, their families or friends.

Prepared childbirth suggested that, in order to access their biological selves, mothers need help to overcome the erroneous teachings of folk wisdom and popular culture. The problem was created as modern women were removed from direct experience with birth. Without direct experience of birth as a natural event, warnings about the horrors of childbirth from relatives and well-meaning friends become self-fulfilling prophecies. Fear causes the body to tighten around the baby and restricted its passage, creating pain and inviting medical intrusion. Through education and conditioning ("preparation" as it came to be called), women's bodies are to be relieved of the fear, pain, and intervention of conventional birthing.

The prepared childbirth model offers a fundamental critique of the practice of hospital delivery. It argues against unnecessary medical intervention, such as overmedication and forceps. Instead of treating the pregnant patient as a broken machine, the model seeks to define pregnancy and birth as a normal process. As long as a woman's pregnancy, labor, and delivery follow the course defined by expected biological processes, she should be permitted to birth without the intrusion of science and technology.

Despite its criticism of conventional birth practice, the ideology of these obstetrician-reformers remains firmly rooted in the biological thinking that underlies much of conventional hospital birthing. First, prepared childbirth assumes a Cartesian dualism between mind and body. Mothers need to be managed to assure that their ideas and actions do not complicate the biological process of birth. Second, birth is seen as the act of an individual, not the couple. The father is included, not to promote his transition to fatherhood, but to help the mother deliver the child. Third, birth is understood to be a biological process of females' bodies, which men must meet with their equally biological masculinity. Fathers need to be strong, rational, and objective to counteract the inherent weaknesses of the female psyche. Although the three models emphasize the mother's experience of birth, they consider her subjective state to be a potential problem, rather than a vital aspect of the event.

In short, the birthing reforms transform childbirth from a medical to a biological event. It changes the perception of babies in utero, women's role in birth, and doctors' responsibility in delivery, but not the biological model of hospital birthing. Rather than call it "spiritual birthing" or "natural childbirth," the reformers called their strategies "prepared childbirth"—and the differences are telling. Prepared birth trains women to transcend their personal experience, ignore their social milieu, and forget their cultural understandings of birth. Fathers are their principal companions, coaches, and directors in this.

Holistic Birth

The conventional basis of prepared birthing in hospitals is even more apparent when contrasted with holistic birthing practices that were developed by non-physicians. Holistic birthing was performed by midwives and home birth advocates, and organized around a fundamentally different idea of mothers, babies, and birth. Where the reformer obstetricians created new birthing models emphasizing the biological process, the holistic health movement raised awareness of the emotional, spiritual, and social aspects of birth: rather than divorce the body from the mind, birth is an emotional experience; rather than distinguish the mother from her social ties, she is seen as birthing within her social world.

In one of the classic texts of holistic birthing, *Spiritual Midwifery* (1990), Ina Gaskin describes birth as a miraculous process. Bringing a new being into the world is a profoundly spiritual experience, whether in an institutional religion (Gaskin uses the metaphor of Mary and Christ) or in a mother-as-earth-goddess image. Birth is a creative moment in which the world is fundamentally altered when it is transformed by a spiritual energy in accord with the universal order. In holistic birthing models, mothers are to be counseled to accept and embrace the excitement, joy, fear, and confusion intense experiences inevitably involve. Women are provided the support and guidance to give themselves over to the experience, rather than define these feelings as unnecessary or detrimental to the process. (For a fuller discussion of the ideological distinctions of the two models, see Davis-Floyd [1992, 163–165] and Rothman [1982, 169].)

The holistic model is also exceedingly aware of birth's social nature. Childbirth is a mother-centered event, with her subjective experience second only to that of the infant. But women do not birth in social isolation. If natural childbirth suggests the woman's *body* gives birth, the holistic birthing movement proposes that a circle of family and friends are the fundamental unit of birthing. Women are at the core of the experience, giving birth with their babies. From this social core, the birth reaches out and includes fathers, children, grandmothers, and grandfathers, sisters and brothers, and a host of other friends, relatives, and acquaintances. More than having only an emotional connection, these people are often invited to be present at the event. Women give birth in a team composed of partners, midwives, and other female attendants, friends, and relatives.

The differences are especially important to fathers. By emphasizing the spiritual and social aspects of birthing, holistic birth recognizes the magic of fathers in childbearing. Rather than a singular focus on the product of birth, holistic birthing recognizes the importance and uniqueness of each couple's experience in the process. Most importantly, fathers are full partners, joining with midwives, friends, and family in providing mothers with the emotional and physical support required for them to retreat into their subjective state and inner energies.

Competing Models of Prepared Childbirth

Despite the ideological similarities of the three childbirth reformers—Dick-Read, Lamaze, and Bradley—there are significant differences in their proposals. Driven by their pragmatic interest in birthing babies rather than any theoretical coherence, they advocate distinct programs and practices. Most important, the three birth models emphasize different aspects of mothers' experience and fathers' involvement: Dick-Read recognizes the magic of the event; Lamaze, the power of mothers to train their bodies; and Bradley, the importance of fathers' role.

Given the choices in alternative birthing models, both holistic and biological, it is instructive that most hospitals adopted prepared birthing as presented by Fernand Lamaze. Hospital staff, like conventional obstetricians, find the Lamaze model the most adaptable to existing institutional policies. In many cases, it works to hospitals' advantage. Lamaze parents demand fewer resources than unprepared parents and Lamaze birth is as safe, if not safer, than conventional birth (Bing 1994, 11). Lamaze fathers are on hand to quiet patients and bring ice chips. In addition, prepared birth is a good marketing tool. Facing declining birth rates in the 1970s, hospitals played on its popularity and efficiency to remain competitive. Homelike birthing rooms were opened and childbirth classes began to teach Lamaze to millions of soon-to-be parents.

The following analyzes the roles created for fathers in prepared childbirth: Dick-Read's companion, Lamaze's trainer, and Bradley's now famous father-as-coach. Despite their being present, the roles offered men do not conflict with the biological perspective of medicine or the power structure of the delivery room. To the greatest extent, Lamaze fathers cooperate in hospital practice and facilitate the biological process of medical birth.

Father as Companion: Dick-Read

An English obstetrician, Grantly Dick-Read, started the childbirth revolution with two influential books, *Natural Childbirth* (1932) and *Revelation of Childbirth* (1944).[1] Dick-Read suggests that anxiety is the greatest cause of birth pain. Long before reruns of *ER*, childbirth was being portrayed as dangerous and painful in books like *Gone with the Wind* (Mitchell 1936) and *The Good Earth* (Buck 1931). Popular culture creates fears, which in turn make mothers tense, making labor long, slow, and painful.

Dick-Read suggests, however, that the most common sources of fear were well-meaning family members. "Unfortunately, mothers, sisters and husbands are among the worst offenders" (Dick-Read 1959, 84). Mothers who admonish their daughters to bear the pain, create the tension and fear that cause pain. "Mothers, husbands and friends must therefore be recognized as agencies for the production of fear in the minds of the vast majority of young married women" (Dick-Read 1959, 88).

He points the finger of guilt directly at the upper and educated classes. The class aspect of Dick-Read's argument is evident in his discussions of overbearing mothers. These women tend to be "of considerable influence in London society" or "the tyrannical empress of a family of eight, who exercised her sway over half a county from her baronial mansion of her patient husband's ancestors" (Dick-Read 1959, 83). Christianity exacerbated women's fear of labor and delivery. The biblical precept that childbirth is painful becomes a self-fulfilling prophecy. The Bible then rationalizes that pain, suggesting that women's sin brought it on, making painful birth an act of religious atonement.

Despite being a medical doctor, Dick-Read is well aware of the overmedicalization of modern childbirth. The problems created by fear are exacerbated by the intrusions of medical technology. Forceps, episiotomies, and the variety of birthing technologies have the unintended (and ignored) effect of increasing the pain of birthing mothers. To facilitate birth without pain, women must ignore the advice of their mothers, reject intervention, and return to their more primitive selves. Rather than drugs, women need education, training (exercises and breathing), and emotional support to allow them to access their inner strength to bring babies into this world.

Unlike standard medical training, Dick-Read has a profound belief that a woman's body can birth best without medical intervention. He spent much of his early life in the pastoral beauty of East Anglia and he learned about the naturalness of birth by watching animals. The solitary work of the birthing sow shows the natural role and strength of the mother in birth. His observations were reinforced by experience with peasant women. In anecdotes that are repeated so often as to become almost myths, Dick-Reed writes of being rebuffed in his efforts to help rural women in birth. Having seen birth in agricultural life and unfettered by the misperceptions of urban and upper class women, peasants are closer to our own nontechnological past (or nature) and so know how to give birth without medication or intervention.

In contrast to the medical model, which emphasizes the physical autonomy of the pregnant patient, Dick-Read values birth as a momentous social event. Birth is more than biological; birth creates new family bonds between a mother and father and their child; parents greet the new member with love, hopes, and dreams. This recognizes an important role for fathers. In pregnancy, Dick-Read demands that fathers read and exercise with their partners, and share quiet moments of contemplation. This time together allows a father to understand the mother's reality, while reinforcing the good work that she is doing. In birth, the couple share life's most profound experience and deepen their own relationship. His words are eloquent. For a couple to birth is "to be united in the most wonderful, awe-inspiring experience that can possibly fall to the lot of wedded human beings. There is no drama or play-acting in the full recognition of the magnitude of the event to both of them" (Dick-Read 1959, 276).

Although Dick-Read understood the social nature of pregnancy and birth, he was much more conventional in reducing men and women to stereotypical sexist personalities. He suggests that the biology of pregnancy renders women irrational and he demands that fathers assume a typically masculine supportive role. (In fact, Dick-Read thought that women were inherently irrational, a trait that was exacerbated during pregnancy.) Mothers became especially sensitive, aware of every attention or slight on the part of their husbands. In the early months of the pregnancy, the man must provide companionship and understanding for his partner, acting as the safety valve that she needs in order to weather the storms of her emotions. In later stages, he becomes a protector and guide, helping her practice her relaxation and respiration. Throughout the process, she needs "careful understanding, special tolerance and unselfishness on the part of the husband" (1959, 266).

If Dick-Read suggests that pregnant women are less than rational, it is to his credit that he points to changes in a pregnant man's psyche as well. Some changes are positive, as "pregnancy often intensifies his love for his wife, and creates in him an ardent desire to take care of her and attend to her needs and wishes with tenderness and consideration." On the other hand, fathers often react to pregnancy with an irrational desire to assert control. "He may even state dogmatically what is sense and what is nonsense. His urge to take care of his wife, whom he loves very dearly, easily develops into a rigid military-type discipline. Men often formulate domestic principles during their wife's pregnancy, and demand that they be meticulously carried out. Rest, diet, exercise, recreation and even personal hygiene are matters in which they suddenly become expert without absorbing any authoritative teaching on the subject" (1959, 266).

In Dick-Read's view, men's irrationality and authoritarianism during pregnancy and birth derive not from biology, but from the confusion of pride, anxiety, and tenderness. Men are exposed to the same popular culture as their women and develop unnatural fears for the safety of their wives. These fears are mixed with their own concerns about their new responsibilities of fatherhood, as well as the shame and guilt that they feel for having brought danger and pain on their wives. Uninformed (or misinformed) about the biology of pregnancy and birth and not knowing how to help their wives, they sublimate their ignorance in irritability and irrationality. Rather than castigate men, Dick-Read suggests that fathers need "just as much sympathy and help as their wives" (1959, 267).

Dick-Read stresses that the father needs to prepare for birth with the same regime of education as the mother. He must study the biology of pregnancy to overcome his fears. He should learn the stages of labor and delivery to be able to predict and understand the emotional changes his wife will go through during pregnancy.

The couple's relationship could be either a font of strength or a cause for problems. "Well selected couples" develop a firm bond, a "physical and emotional harmony known as love" (1959, 269). This love awakens in the man a desire for children by his wife; in a woman it prepares her physiologically for pregnancy and birth. Thus, men have a responsibility to their wives to join them in the project of bringing a new life into the world and into their family. A poorly developed relationship, on the other hand, is cause for problems. Women who feel unloved and alone in the pregnancy suffer unhappiness and anger, which in turn affects the unborn child.

Dick-Read broke from medicine's strict mind-body separation in recognizing the powerful relation between emotion and pregnancy or birth. He was specific about the physiological benefits to be gained by educating men for birth. Morning sickness, he suggests, was a biological condition brought on by a psychological state of fear. An understanding husband could ameliorate that fear and the morning sickness it brought on (1959, 270).

This awareness allows Dick-Read to identify that men make a physical contribution to the pregnancy long after conception. The father's support of the mother contributes directly to a fetus's physical development. "If she is alone and feels, justly or unjustly, that the baby she longs for is robbed of her husband's love, serious temperamental and emotional states occur which set up local and general reactions within her body. A disturbed mind will upset the circulation of blood to certain organs of the body. It will cause a serious deprivation of oxygen supply and some of the vital substances from the glands within the body, which are essential for the well being of the small fetus in the womb" (1959, 271).

Given his recognition of fathers as protectors and supporters of birthing mothers, it is not surprising that Dick-Read was an early proponent of fathers attending the birth, suggesting that they could actively support the natural childbirth process. In achieving a pain-free birth, a father could be of greater value than the most skilled and patient nurse or obstetrician.

That being said, he offers few directives. In the entire chapter on "The Husband and the Childbirth," only one paragraph deals with men in birth, and only two sentences discuss men's activities in the process of birth, one sentence on early first stage labor and a second sentence on late second stage labor. "I have had many husbands present throughout the whole of their wife's labor. They have stayed with her during the first stage, reminded her of the lessons they learned together, and assisted her to breathe correctly during the succeeding phases of parturition and to relax when relaxation is indicated" (1959, 16).

In a statement that recalls the adage that children should be seen and not heard, Dick-Read places fathers in the corner of the room toward the head of the bed. "At the start of the second stage, when the quiet purposeful atmosphere of the room creates a calm and peaceful expectancy, the father takes his place in the far corner of the labor ward in full view of his wife" (1959, 275). This allows the father to share the experience with his partner, without being alarmed by or an impediment to the final delivery.

Although he has few suggestions for fathers' assistance in labor and delivery, Dick-Read pays considerable attention to what men should *not* do in the birthing room. Fathers should not show excitement; they should be quiet and control their feelings. Men should not misinterpret their wives' reaction to labor. To Dick-Read, what might seem like discomfort is more likely physical effort. Above all, fathers must listen to the injunctions of the obstetrician.

He argues for father's presence at delivery, but Dick-Read also suggests that some fathers have no place in the birthing room. If men cannot overcome their fears and doubts, then they need to be kept out of the delivery room for the sake of their wives. "The totally unprepared father has no place at birth" (Dick-Read 1959, 275). Presence at a birth is earned; it is not an inalienable right. Men who are not interested enough to be informed and educated will become frightened by what they perceive as dangerous pain and pass that fear to their wives. Most important, fathers must be able to attend to the explanations and admonitions of the medical personnel officiating. Dick-Read maintains that obstetricians have the authority to determine who attends and what they do during the birth. (Dick-Read was also clear that some *women* do not deserve to be at the birth of their children. "They are better served by employing an obstetrician and hospital staff to attend and perform the delivery . . . to take a baby from their unfeeling body and nourish it with artificial food from an unfeeling nipple" [1959, 277].)

This logic of exclusion was based not on the possible dangers it poses to the men themselves, but on the ramifications for birthing women. Fathers must be interested enough in the process to learn all that is necessary to make themselves helpful to their wives. They must be able to overcome their own fears enough to impart confidence to the birthing women.

Attending the birth of his child and behaving appropriately is a litmus test of a man entering fatherhood. As parturition exposes a woman's qualities, a husband's behavior shows his affection, his fortitude, and his philosophy. Fathers should also be present for their relation to their wives, their new children, and to help in the formation of their new families. Men benefit from the "the knowledge of [the baby's] sex, the wrapping of the infant in towels and the handing it to a conscious, delighted woman" (Dick-Read 1959, 276).

Dick-Read recognizes the transformative aspects of birth for fathers. He is aware of the importance of the event for structuring and restructuring the father's identity, and his relation with mother, baby, and society. Despite his awareness, he makes clear that the primary reason for a man to attend birth is for the sake of his wife. The father's face and hands can calm a birthing mother's fear and allow her to overcome the pain that tension causes. They can be "helpful to their wives by imparting the confidence they themselves have in the happy result of her labor" (Dick-Read 1959, 276). When all is said and done, father's attendance is not for his own benefit, but for that of his partner.

Father as Trainer: Fernand Lamaze

Throughout the 1940s, the general directions of Dick-Read remained the primary means to prepare mothers to achieve "natural childbirth." By the middle of the 1950s, however, a second physician, Fernand Lamaze, began to advocate for prepared childbirth. Delivering babies in France, Lamaze advocated classical conditioning to help women redefine the pain of childbirth. Where Dick-Read sought to educate mothers to relax and promote their bodies' natural capacity to birth, Lamaze suggested that the woman's body needed to be trained to overcome cultural conditioning and perform effectively.

Lamaze observed "awake and aware" deliveries in the Soviet Union in 1951. Russian women were taught to overcome the pain of childbirth by a process of conditioning. Breathing focused their concentration and exercise relaxed their uterine muscles, allowing the delivery of the child without pain. The Russian practice and the method that Lamaze developed are based on the theories of conditioning developed by Pavlov, a Russian scientist. Similar to dogs that were taught to cringe at the sound of a bell that precedes a lash, ignorance and misinformation condition women to expect and experience pain in childbirth.

To avoid pain, women first need to understand the physiology of childbirth so that they can experience it without fear and confusion. In essence, they need to unlearn some of their conditioned responses to pain and fear. Second, new conditioned reflexes need to be instilled in the woman. The natural reflex of respiration can be reprogrammed to allow a woman to be aware of the sensations of childbirth, without experiencing the pain. Lamaze puts this in scientific terms: behavioral reconditioning limits "the spread and duration of painful cerebral excitation transmitted by the uterine interceptors" (Lamaze [1956] 1970, 32).

As an obstetrician at a maternity hospital in Paris, Lamaze developed a conditioning routine termed "psychoprophylaxis," more generally known as the "Lamaze method." Lamaze provides a clearly defined and highly specific method for avoiding intervention in childbirth. From the sixth month on, pregnant women are taught basic anatomy of pregnancy and birth, and trained in a series of breathing exercises to program the body's reaction to childbirth. Breathing is the primary focus. Depth and rhythm are adjusted to each stage of labor: slow breathing through the first stage; rapid during second; and panting during the final presentation.

Lamaze introduced the technique of psychoprophylaxis in 1956 in the French edition of his now famous book, *Painless Childbirth*. In the United States, the Lamaze method reached the public consciousness in a popular book, *Thank You, Doctor Lamaze*, written by Marjorie Karmel, who discovered Lamaze in Paris during her pregnancy. Karmel joined forces with Elisabeth Bing and founded the American Society for Psychoprophylaxis in Obstetrics (ASPO) to proselytize the Lamaze method directly to pregnant mothers.

In his original work, Lamaze pays scant attention to men and provides little direction for their involvement in the technique. When *Painless Childbirth* was translated into English in 1956, only two sentences related to men's involvement in the process: "A husband versed in the principles of childbirth without pain will offer his wife active support which can increase her chances of success. He will see that she keep regular hours for her meals, goes to bed and gets up regularly; all this taking place in a peaceful atmosphere, without overwork and away from the company of agitated and noisy people" (Lamaze [1956] 1970, 99–100).

In France, a female *monitrice* was provided by the hospital. Ideally, this skilled Lamaze childbirth trainer could "act as a sort of a coach, timing contractions and keeping the women doing the techniques properly, with the husband providing additional support" (Chabon 1966, 108–109). She helped mothers maintain the prescribed breathing patterns and provided emotional support during labor. In the United States, where there were a shortage of trainers and regulations limiting other professionals in the labor room, fathers assumed the role of monitrice. "The job therefore falls to the husband" (Chabon 1966, 108). Nevertheless, early materials in the United States provide little direction for men. In the first *Practical Training Course for the Psychoprophylactic Method of Childbirth* (1961), Bing and her coauthors write only that fathers are important in both training classes and the labor room; it was five years before Vellay offered any direction for Lamaze fathers in birth (Vellay 1966).

The father's role begins in pregnancy. "His help, his sympathy, and understanding are of incalculable value in sustaining the emotional health of his pregnant wife" (Lamaze [1956] 1970, 107). More than a companion, however, the ASPO literature suggests that the father is a trainer for birth. "You will find that even though you study the material together and know exactly the same amount of actual fact and theory, he will be able to assist you much as a swimming coach might, and will point out errors that you will never see by yourself" (Bing, Karmel, and Tanzer 1961, 6).

Men are expected to direct the training process. It is a father's responsibility to "make his wife practice her exercises and control her breathing and neuromuscular relaxation" (Vellay 1966, 28). He is charged with noticing mistakes and criticizing her if she is not getting practical results. The role of trainer suggests that men should be superior to their wives in the practice of birth. "In nearly all cases we found that the man who was reluctant to come [to classes] in the beginning quickly becomes intrigued with the concepts of the method and often acquires a better grasp of them than his wife" (Bing, Karmel, and Tanzer 1961, 6). In addition to superiority, the role of trainer suggests that fathers have power over their pregnant partners. In practice, the father is expected to direct and "command" his wife to relax. Bing, once again, suggests that pregnancy exercises be introduced with the statement "I want you to practice these exercises with your husband, letting him give you the commands that I will give you now. This will help you to develop such good teamwork that if you should become very tense during your labor, your husband's command will automatically cause you to release the tense muscle groups and relax generally. It will be easy for you to follow his commands even under stress, as you will have been conditioned to react by your practice at home" (Bing, Karmel, and Tanzer 1961, 16).

Where Dick-Read suggests that men emphasize their affective bond in birthing, Lamaze stresses the technical aspect of the relation. "[Lamaze] education makes men more sophisticated helpmates to their wives" (Chabon 1966, 107). The father is to act as a trainer, not a companion, for the mother. He is to rub her back, anticipate her needs, and work to fill them. The father times contractions and marks progress in seconds, minutes, and hours. He is to assure that the mother does not get lost in birth, lose touch with reality, or forget the stage that they are in and the progress that they are making.

The responsibility implies that dads have considerable power to see that a woman births correctly. Bing says, "And remember that during your labor it is your husband's job to see that you stay relaxed" (Bing, Karmel, and Tanzer 1961, 23). In *Awake and Aware,* Chabon writes of the father-to-be, "Here is the fellow who will determine to a large extent the ease with which his wife will proceed through her pregnancy" (1966, 107). Elsewhere, Chabon goes so far as to call the father's responsibilities the "most important job" in the labor room (1966, 108). The mother is a secondary and wholly conditioned member of the birthing team.

But fathers are trainers, not participants, in Lamaze birthing. Any paternal involvement in the mechanics of labor is almost an afterthought. Directing himself to mothers, Chabon suggests "If you feel your contractions in the back rather than the front, press your hands as hard as you can against the lower part of your back while breathing (you may try massage or rotating your fists—find what helps you most) or ask your husband to apply pressure on your back."

More specifically, men are to be the choreographers of a sequence of breathing techniques to induce relaxation. It is the father's role to define the stage of labor and prescribe the correct breathing pattern to meet the different types of contractions. Stopwatches are to be used to determine the time between and the length of contractions. With watch in hand, men are to call out each fifteen-minute interval, providing women an auditory touchstone that allows them to remain in control through each seemingly interminable contraction.

In many ways, men are expected to use their detached position to maintain an objective perspective on the birth process. In the physicality of labor, for example, the father is instructed to place his hand on the abdomen of the woman and inform her when a contraction starts and direct her to collect herself in preparation. The father's objectivity is also important to protect the woman from her increasingly subjective experience of birth. A husband cannot share the experience, but his understanding and evaluation can assist his wife in her all too intimate involvement.

Fathers' role in Lamaze has changed little over the course of the subsequent childbirth revolution. In the most recent Bing guide (1994), the part offered fathers in the drama of birth conforms closely to Vellay's original directives, albeit the word "father" now reads "partner" or "coach." Men's job remains to help women feel confident and comfortable early in labor, and later to help them control themselves during the stress of birth.

Current literature does provide more attention to how fathers accomplish this in birth. Photos show fathers accompanying birthing mothers and their role is discussed in each stage of pregnancy, labor, and delivery. They are also provided more specific words to use to stimulate relaxation and directions to see that tension has left the birthing woman's body. Although fathers are still offered little direct participation in labor and delivery, at least they are treated as the first line of help in back labor, rather than as an afterthought. The guide even suggests that mothers remind their partners to bring a sandwich, so men do not leave during the long labor and risk missing the baby's arrival.

If Lamaze training is sometimes ambiguous as to fathers' involvement with mothers, it is careful to detail the relationship between fathers and medical staff. Men are to perform routine duties that otherwise might be done by staff, such as getting water or ice chips and helping laboring women to and from the toilet. As the primary liaison between the birthing woman and the hospital, fathers are expected to move their wives through medical routines as smoothly as possible.

If Lamaze places the father-trainer over the mother-birther, the model also demands that both submit to the obstetrician-god. To achieve a Lamaze birth, both mother and father must cooperate and comply with the obstetrician. For the woman, the physician has the final word on matters of procedure and practice, including the use of medication (Bing, Karmel, and Tanzer 1961, 7). For the father, this demands that he convince his partner to cooperate and comply with the physician's orders. The power of the obstetrician becomes most clear in the final stages of birth. Although the father is important in practice and through the first stage of labor, the physician's role supersedes the position of the father; the obstetrician's entrance reduces dad to a spectator.

It is unmistakable that a father's primary responsibility is to the doctor, not his partner. Vellay, who worked with Lamaze in France, wrote, "He becomes the doctor's active collaborator," assuring that the obstetrician can deliver the baby unimpeded by a woman's subjective needs and desires (1966, 28). This primary relationship begins even during pregnancy, when the father and obstetrician are advised to establish a relationship independent of the mother. "Knowing that her husband can call her doctor, give an accurate description of her uterine contractions or other phenomena, understand the answer, . . . can be a great source of comfort to a pregnant woman" (Chabon 1966, 108).

The medical hierarchy of hospital birthing is not only unchallenged by

Lamaze; it is reinforced. Birthing is best managed by professionals. Patients are to pay obeisance to medical personnel who guide their way. Fathers, in turn, must reinforce the messages of the Lamaze professionals, especially when mothers were noncompliant. In short, fathers are not present to reinforce the subjective, social, and spiritual experience of mothers; fathers are accomplices in imposing the ideology of biological birthing and the power of conventional medical hierarchies over birthing women.

Father as Coach: Robert Bradley

While Lamaze popularized unmedicated childbirth in the United Sates, it was a physician by the name of Robert Bradley who focused attention most closely on fathers. The title of Bradley's book, *Husband-Coached Childbirth* (1965), is self-explanatory. Adopting the athletic metaphor, Bradley provides training rules to help husbands prepare their wives for a medicine-free birth.

Bradley suggests that fathers support women to be their "natural selves." Bradley developed his model after observing the painless births of animals. (In a manner almost parroting Dick-Read's experience of birthing English farmers, Bradley writes of his youth watching natural birth by animals in rural Colorado.) But he notes a critical difference between humans and animal mothers: the latter can rely on instinct to guide them through birth; humans are not as fortunate. "Your wife, lacking [animal] instinct, must be guided, directed and encouraged" (Bradley 1965, 40). Human birthing practice, then, has developed to fill the vacuum created as we evolved beyond our instincts. Where Dick-Read promotes education for relaxation and Lamaze advocates scientific conditioning, Bradley suggests that mothers need support through a confusing and scary process.

Although Bradley was a physician and advocated hospital birth, he suggests that the hustle and glare of conventional birthing is distracting and painful. To birth without pain, mothers need to be physically comfortable, to relax, to close their eyes and turn inward. They need a room that is dimly lit, quiet, and private. They need to breathe as animals breathe, from the abdomen, relax the rest of their bodies, and permit the baby to slide out. Unlike standard medical practice, the role of the obstetrician is not to control the process, but to set the stage for the mother to birth, then retreat to allow nature to take its course.

Fathers have a clear role in the process, accompanying and guiding mothers through the long and complicated process. They are the obvious choice for companion. Fathers are always on hand; they have strong and intimate relations with the mother, and have a direct interest in the birth and its outcome. Bradley originally admitted fathers into the delivery room with little forethought, and discovered that they had an immediate, profound, and positive impact on birth. He remembers, "The husband [usually] sat in the labor room and did nothing and said nothing. I began to awaken to his importance when I noticed how much more calm and cooperative the patient was when her husband was present. If he left the room, even temporarily, the mother became anxious and tense and relaxed poorly with contractions" (Bradley 1965, 16).

The father's supportive role begins in pregnancy. His first task is as a coach in a mother's physical conditioning. Fathers make sure that women perform their training regime, as Bradley thought that women were prone to ignore or forget their workout schedules. *Husband-Coached Childbirth* stresses the importance of daily routine for tightening muscles and practicing strategies.

Fathers must also evaluate mothers' performance of unfamiliar exercises, such as pelvic rocking. Men are sometimes asked to take part. The father can hold his wife's knees while she performs leg exercises; support her back while she exercises her abdominal muscles, or (in a phallocentric moment) use his erect penis to "check" on a woman's progress with the Kegel exercises.

A father also is to help his pregnant partner relax. Although Bradley does not advocate the strict conditioning regime of Lamaze, he suggests that relaxation is a skill that demands practice, the effort of both body and mind. In working with a woman's mind, a father "can achieve results where none other can." The husband's familiar pattern of action is essential to mental disassociation and physical relaxation by his wife. But rather than try this for the first time in the labor room, Bradley suggests that fathers help their wives learn this skill during pregnancy. Men can develop their "own pattern of verbal suggestion in short periods of concentrated relaxation" (Bradley 1965, 106).

Eschewing the universalism of medicine and science, Bradley emphasizes that every woman and every couple is different. Rather than dictate the "correct" strategy of relaxation, he suggests that couples experiment until they discover the unique methods that work for them. After the daily chores are done, with other children in bed and the cat put out, Bradley suggests that a pregnant father give his partner a soothing back rub. The husband should use whatever combination of verbal and physical suggestions help her relax. Once a successful pattern is established, couples should repeat it each night, allowing the woman to become familiar with the positive association and its effects.

Bradley has other practical suggestions and advice for fathers during pregnancy. Men are to divest themselves of any myths about a pregnant woman's fragility in the first trimester. A woman can continue to exercise, have sex, work, or travel as she desires. But Bradley cautioned that a woman's desires might change with the physical and hormonal shifts of pregnancy. In the first trimester, she may want less or more sex, or she may desire odd foods. She may feel nauseated or ravenous. She may lose her sense of humor, be nervous or excitable. Despite his initial sexist tone, Bradley asks fathers to understand their pregnant partners' needs and, if they seem irrational, accept the desires with a good-natured sense of humor. In the second trimester, Bradley suggests that men should attend to the emotional needs of their wives. "Date your wife at least once a week. . . . Make love to her in the car on the way home from the movie. . . . This is the period to focus on building a strong relationship with your partner." Bradley points out that the third trimester is a time of waiting, wondering, and worrying. A father can be a wonderful source of confidence for the insecure mother. If she feels panicky, "Give her a gentle reminder that this feeling has been manifested similarly in all women" (Bradley 1965, 135).

With the same reasoning, Bradley recognizes that birthing women also have a special message to receive from experienced mothers—a message that cannot come from fathers or male obstetricians. "You and I, husband and doctor, can talk until we are blue in the face, but glib as we may be there is a great handicap; we're men and we've never had a baby" (Bradley 1965, 82).

The role of the father as coach takes on new dimensions in labor and delivery. Once a woman has been admitted to the hospital, settled into a room, and been given the standard prep (which in Bradley's time was a shave and an enema), it is up to the father to provide the familiar presence that can help her relax. To do so, the father must draw on the corpus of strategies that he and his wife have developed over the preceding weeks.

The father, as labor coach, first needs to create a subdued ambience in the hospital room. He reduces the lights and works to protect the tranquillity and privacy of the room. He adjusts the mother's pillows and helps her into a comfortable position. He brings ice chips and a moist cloth to cool her brow and moisten her lips. As contractions increase, the man's responsibilities become more direct. He rubs her back and strokes her body with his fingers, using a gentle voice to help her relax each part of her body in turn. These verbal suggestions and touch should diminish in volume and pressure as she relaxes, letting her move increasingly into herself. The music of the partner's voice and presence helps the mother relax and release her body's hold on the baby. The relaxation for childbirth takes mental focusing or concentration, reaching a meditative state in which the woman is completely engaged with her body, and relaxed within it.

The father orchestrates contractions, sensing them and talking the woman through the feelings. A Bradley mother should relax her body as the uterine muscles and dad can help her breathe as animals breathe, "from her belly." The father should remind his partner to bear down and, as the contraction passes, when to exhale. He can even lay a hand lightly on her abdomen and gently nudge her at the start of each contraction, letting his hand "ride the wave" of contraction to be able to correct and encourage the mother as it passes.

Bradley suggested that some women are unnecessarily concerned about releasing their bladder or moving their bowels in labor, and are able to lose these inhibitions more freely with their husbands coaching. The father can also help mom to squat, a more natural position for the descent of the baby. He can lift her and support her as she bears down in a squatting position or adjust pillows under her back to help her sit up in bed. Bradley suggests that couples work as a team in finding the right position, maybe even with the husband crawling onto the bed and holding her under the shoulders.

Although he envisions birth as a biological process, Bradley has several insights and suggestions that contradict conventional medical practice. First he challenges the power dynamic of traditional birth practice. Being an obstetrician himself, Bradley recognizes that many delivery teams were unaware of the benefits of alternative birth. It is fathers' responsibility to mediate between mothers and uninformed hospital staffs. Whereas Lamaze envisions fathers as collaborating with hospital staff, and Dick-Read demands that fathers acquiesce to hospital authorities, Bradley suggests that fathers educate hospital staff about prepared birthing and defend mothers from unnecessary intrusions. Fathers can explain to nurses that most routine exams and tests are counterproductive and, if necessary, convince uninformed physicians to reduce mechanical control over labor and delivery.

Second, Bradley is explicitly aware of the importance of sensuality in birth.

Fathers are to play the role of lover in the birthing room, to provide the tender touch, the knowing look, and the understanding words of a woman's most intimate physical companion. During birth, her partner's hand has a calming presence; the warmth and the sensitivity of the lover's fingers provide the familiarity to comfort her. His voice and words can speak directly to her subconscious self, allowing her to release the baby. To Bradley, birth is like making love—a natural process by which a woman both pulls inside herself and lets go. Her partner is the most experienced in helping enter this physical and emotional space. He suggests that the father, "Play the lover role during the glorious climax to your act of love—the birth of your baby" (Bradley 1965, 60).

Third, Bradley has a clear sense of the power of birth to create and strengthen social relations within the family. Bradley, like Dick-Read, emphasizes that birth reinforces the affective bond between the mother and the father—and points out that the obstetrician traditionally supplants the father in performing his tasks. Bradley recounts how "after a birth by one very attractive girl, she pulled me onto the hospital bed with both arms and kissed me soundly. What on earth was this lovely woman kissing me for?" he asks the reader, while "her young lover sat uselessly in the waiting room, fearful and anxious over his sweetheart's safety . . . deprived by isolation from the most meaningful emotional experience of their lives together. . . . I feel deeply the responsibility, as an obstetrician, to see that the act of bearing a child makes them fall more in love with their husbands" (Bradley 1965, 117–118). (Bradley almost admits that obstetricians want patients' affection and dependence. "Was my ego in such a bad plight that it had to be constantly bolstered by pushing aside a real lover and accepting substitute favors from my patients?" But in the end he doth protest too much, claiming "I am not the least bit interested in having my patients fall in love with me" [1965, 18].)

Fathers can facilitate labor, but Bradley reserves the act of delivery for the obstetrician. The birth of a child is a magical event and, having suffered with their wives through the most painful and difficult part of the process, fathers deserve to be present. Men are exhilarated. They see the fruits of their months of support and years later have pictures to prove to their children that they cared enough to be there. But to continue the athletic metaphor, coaches have no direct part in the scoring of the point. Like Dick-Read, Bradley demands that fathers get back and out of the way during the final delivery of the infant. Rather than the far corner of the room, Bradley designates the anesthesiologist's chair the "daddy's stool." The chair was usually empty, and was placed toward the head of the bed. While the physician takes his place at the foot of the bed to catch the baby, Bradley believes the father is most appropriately positioned at the mother's head to share the experience with her.

Although Bradley goes to great lengths to integrate fathers into the process of birth, he never appreciates fathers' needs. On one hand, they are coaches and not players in the game of birth; they are to use their masculine talents to prepare mothers to perform on the field. On the other, they are managers, not challenging the position of the obstetrician on the delivery team, but using their rational, masculine, and nonpatient status to educate the physician in attendance.

Fathers and Biological Birth

The biological birthing model integrates fathers into the practice of birth, but without conflicting with the existing ideologies of medical birthing. Although a man's birth experience and relation with the mother are considered important, his presence is intended to facilitate the biological process of birth. Even with the dramatic changes offered by Dick-Read, Lamaze, and Bradley, the birthing revolution fails to break out of the central tenants of medical birthing: that childbirth can be reduced to a general biological process performed by individual human bodies. Consequently, although fathers are present and participate, their needs and the important changes that they experience remain unrecognized.

Mind-Body Dualism

First, fathers' subjective experience of birth wins little attention in alternative birthing models. Fathers can be connected and empathic; they can mirror the mother as powerful and capable; but ultimately, fathers' involvement in birth is to facilitate the biological process of parturition. To a large extent, this results from the new models' failure to break free from the conventional distinction between the mind and the birthing body.

The prepared childbirth movement reifies the distinction between mind and body, attempting to transcend the negative effects of the former to set the body free. Dick-Read, Bradley, and Lamaze place the blame for painful and difficult childbirth in women's heads, not women's bodies. Folk stories of danger and pain make women fearful; religious teachings make them feel guilty. The combination causes mothers to tense up and restrict the baby's birth. But if mothers could quiet these fears, they could retreat into their own personal self to discover their innate, biological capacities of giving birth. Relying on their own powers, mothers have easier deliveries and need less medical assistance.

Fathers can be of assistance, because they are removed from the birthing body. Bradley emphasized this, writing that the father is to "see what she is doing wrong and correct it" (Bradley 1965:121). Being outside the body of the woman, he can better observe how well she conforms to the patterns deemed effective by the model.

Prepared birthing models recognize the emotional relation of a father and mother, but its importance is in its biological effect on the fetus and birth. Dick-Read emphasizes that the mind of the woman has great power over the development of the fetus; the unhappy woman may develop circulatory problems and could starve the developing child. Bradley concurs with Dick-Read that the husband needs to nurture his child physically by making sure that his wife is content and relaxed. "Have some intellectual pursuits in common with your wife. . . . She needs to talk and be talked to" (Bradley 1965, 112). Bradley is explicit that the husband's role in pregnancy is constructed around a couple's relationship as lovers. "Charge her storage batteries of love" (Bradley 1965, 130). "Find the time and the money to get away and enjoy one another" (Bradley 1965, 135).

The goal of this emotional connection is not to strengthen the spiritual aspect of birth, but to promote the physical functioning of the mother and child. As Bradley notes, "The mental and physical quality of the infant varies as the direct and indirect influence that [the father] exerts upon his wife during her pregnancy. A high percentage of unnatural births and difficult children are due to the husband's behavior toward his wife during those seven or eight months of development and growth of their baby in her womb" (Bradley 1965, 110).

Individualism

Many couples seek alternative childbirth practice as a means to increase fathers' experience of birth. The models of Dick-Read, Lamaze, and Bradley, however, reinforce a distinction between the mother as birther and the father as observer. She is a subjective participant and he is the objective observer. Fathers, as observers, can affect labor and delivery; they can speed or delay the course of parturition; but they do not give birth. They are to follow events with their eyes and ears, and they may lend a supportive hand or word, but they are no more involved than are the nurses and obstetrician. Rather than being closely identified with the event, or making themselves the center of attention, fathers should control their own (admittedly strong) feelings and allow the obstetrician and mother to do the most important work (Dick-Read 1944, 274–275).

As observers, fathers reinforce the medical model's suggestion that birthing reality derives from the outsider's definition, not from the internal, subjective state of the birthing woman. Thus, for example, when discussing a woman in the midst of a contraction, Bradley suggests that a father could be aware of the mother's body in a way that even she is not. A mother can neither see nor feel the changes in her diaphragm. "Now you as an outsider can see the difference, and if you will lightly place your hand on her abdomen you can also feel the difference. In other words you can tell what she is doing and she can't. Guide her and coach her until you see that she is breathing correctly" (Bradley 1965, 46).

Essentialism

Prepared childbirth models remain rooted in the medical tradition that defines fathers and mothers in terms of their sex. For example, Dick-Read suggests a basic biological distinction between men's and women's psychology. He quotes a friend and "world-famous neurologist" that menstruating women were beset by "dual or multiple personalities" and would remain a mystery to men, as much as they are to themselves. During pregnancy, women develop a third personality, becoming increasingly irrational. Pregnant women are especially sensitive, aware of every attention or slight on the part of their husbands, and "need careful understanding and special tolerance and unselfishness on the part of the husband" (Dick-Read 1959, 265–266).

Dick-Read envisions the pregnant wife as a new individual who appears in the home, whose activities, thoughts, and behavior may be different from her nonpregnant self. Husbands can either develop sensitivity to these new characteristics, or fall victim to their power; "these are not just whims and moods but real mental states based on sound psychological deductions" (Dick-Read 1959, 268). Bradley stated it in a dated and sexist attempt to connect with pregnant fathers: "Let's face it; they're nuttier than a fruitcake!" (Bradley 1965, 108).

Thus, the father's role emphasizes his masculine rationality. In the early months of the pregnancy, he reads about and learns the stages of pregnancy, helping his partner maintain an exercise routine and healthy diet. In later stages, he becomes a protector and guide. He should take over domestic chores and assist her physical preparation, going so far as to join her in respiration and relaxation exercises.

And the Winner Is . . . Lamaze

Of the three models put forth, Lamaze's won the greatest acceptance with physicians and within hospitals. In hospital training and popular parlance, alternative childbirth became known as "Lamaze." Dick-Read, after providing the impetus for women to seek change in the 1940s and 1950s, was quietly reduced to a historical chapter in the birthing movement. Although the Bradley Method finds a following in home birth, it has gained less ground in hospitals.

The differences between the models help explain the variation in popularity. Lamaze is, not coincidentally, most congruent with existing hospital practice. First, more than the other two, Lamaze makes a serious attempt to ground his model in science. Conditioning theory gained academic popularity in the 1950s and 1960s as a quantifiable explanation of human behavior. Lamaze suggests that this research could provide the solution to age-old problems of birth. Bradley and Dick-Read eschew this aura of scientific understanding. They draw their models of birth from the natural world, suggesting that modern birthers have much to learn from both animals and more earthy peasants. Bradley takes aim directly at Lamaze: "But what is the scientific explanation? What is the mechanical and physiological action? I didn't know then and I don't know now, seventeen years later" (Bradley 1965, 12). Elsewhere, he argues, "I'll leave the answer of the 'how' question to the academic doctors—I can't answer it and, as yet, neither can they—but as a clinical doctor, may I strongly point out that animals *do know* and that this observed fact is not weakened in the least by our human ignorance of *how* they know" (Bradley 1965, 24).

Second, Lamaze advocates preparing for birth with extensive practice to reprogram basic reflexes. This model, like standard medical intervention, attempts to control the body and its function. Bradley and Dick-Read seek to educate women to know what to expect, and to find their personal and social powers to prepare for parturition. In contrast, Lamaze advocates a strict regime of exercise and concentration to combat and dominate the pain of birth.

Where Dick-Read emphasizes the emotional aspects of pregnancy and Bradley focuses on the social ties of childbirth, Lamaze stresses the mechanical

aspects of birth. Dick-Read and Bradley point out the beauty and magic of introducing new life into the world; they are aware of the couple's own personal experience of birth as an emotional, spiritual, and social process. Lamaze speaks little
of the magic of birth; for him, parturition depends on Pavlovian conditioning
based in scientific terminology and logic.

In the early years of the childbirth revolution, independent childbirth centers performed most training for pregnant couples. Independent birthing trainers developed originally out of the home-birth movement. These were often
women who had experienced truly alternative birthing in a nonmedical environment. These birthing classes had little standard curriculum and sought their
strategies from a variety of birthing gurus. Midwives worked with birthing parents to develop highly personalized and holistic experiences that were tailored to
the desires and needs of them and their families. The best-known and the best-
loved of these birthing guides grew out of the experiences at a birthing center,
The Farm, in Summertown, Tennessee. The Farm provides birthing experience
for mothers and midwives and popularized its revolutionary message in what has
become the guidebook of alternative birthing, *Spiritual Midwifery* (Gaskin 1990).

As medical institutions asserted themselves over American birthing, controlling the process by which couples develop and negotiate their identities as
birthing parents becomes critical. Over the last three decades, most of this
childbirth training has been incorporated into hospital systems. It stands to reason that the birthing programs that find the greatest acceptance in medical
institutions are those that adhere most directly to conventional medical definitions and practices.

Physicians who sought to integrate aspects of holistic birthing into conventional delivery first promoted alternative birthing. Seeking to educate parents,
they turned to professional trainers to provide the "holistic" element to birthing. Instituting curricula demands standardization, and private physicians seek
the legitimacy of one of the birthing programs that had been developed by an
obstetrician. The first effort to control the information used in birthing was
through certification by one of the international agencies established by proponents of specific techniques. There were two primary agencies in the United
States: the followers of Lamaze founded the American Society for Psychoprophylaxis in Obstetrics (ASPO); Bradley proponents founded the American Academy
of Husband-Coached Childbirth. These agencies provided certification that proposed to legitimize a specific body of birthing knowledge for parents.

Lamaze offers a birthing strategy that promotes parents' active participation in birth, without challenging the physician's power and primacy in the event. As the guardian and gatekeeper of the movement, ASPO monitors Lamaze education and certifies educators. Great care is taken by ASPO to legitimize Lamaze within the medical profession. Although instructors are not required to be mothers (or even women), it is necessary that they be a physician, nurse, or a professional in a related field. Training programs are organized by ASPO and performed at colleges and universities nationwide. In over thirty years of work, over ten thousand educators have been trained, with about four thousand in current practice (Davis-Floyd 1992, 170). Educated within medical institutions, these trainers are best prepared to be respectful of and comfortable with the hierarchy of medical birthing.

Thus, for American hospitals and physicians of the 1960s and 1970s, Lamaze offered a useful compromise. It provided mothers the opportunity for birth without sedation and intervention; it suggested that couples could control the process and pain of birth; and it offered fathers the opportunity to join mothers in the wonder of birth. Nevertheless, the Lamaze model preserves the paramount position of science and biology in the understanding of birth. Birth remains a scientific enterprise to be understood with the intellect, not intuition. Finally, Lamaze protects the power of physicians and staff in the delivery room.

For fathers, this compromise integrates them into delivery teams without attending to their needs as fathers, lovers, and men. Lamaze birthing has little interest in the subjective experience of men; there is no attention paid to their transformation to fatherhood. Fathers are offered the opportunity to join the team as unpaid staff and their effectiveness is defined in terms of the efficiency with which their partners carry out their role. Finally, they are expected to sit down and shut up when the physician approaches the bed. The professional is the one to officiate over the final act of the biological birth. In short, fathers' presence reinforces the biological thinking about birth and the power hierarchy of hospital delivery.

Fathers' Birth Role and American Society

But why do men accept this compromised position in the birthing room? After fighting to be present, why would a father accept a peripheral role in his family's own drama? The answer is simple: prepared birthing fits the way most American men feel about themselves as men, husbands, and fathers. It conforms to men's role in the larger society. More than adapted to the medical setting, the roles fit the idealized image of fathers in the conventional American family. Rather than being an equal partner in the birthing process, fathers are defenders, coaches, and managers of mothers. This is both gratifying to men's egos and congruent with the model that men have (or wish) for themselves.

In analyzing gender and power, anthropologists distinguish between the domestic sphere and the public sphere (Rosaldo 1972, 23). The domestic (or private) sphere revolves around reproduction, primarily the birth and nurturing of children. In American society, this has been accepted as the primary domain of women. The public sphere, in contrast, encompasses the institutions of society that regulate relations between family groups. These include the church, market, and political arena. While women manage domestic concerns, men represent the family in the larger society and mediate relations with public institutions. Where public institutions command considerable power, such as in American society, this provides men considerable power over their wives and children. We can remember that it is only within the last century that American women have had the right to vote, and many religions continue to restrict church leadership to men.

Just as the distinction between public and private spheres empowers men, Sherry Ortner (1996), an anthropologist, suggests that the distinction between nature and culture is important for our perceptions of men and women in birthing. Claude Lévi-Strauss posited that the development of culture set humans apart from other animals, and that the most basic distinction in human understanding was between culture and nature. In opposing nature, humanity defined itself in opposition to the natural world. Nature is biological and irrational; culture is objective and based on reason. Ortner argues that a woman's reproductive capacity places her in a social position that emphasizes her biological and emotional aspects, and renders her ambiguous in the nature/culture dichotomy of the human mind. Men, without the ability to reproduce, are forced to be creative in the external world and become identified with culture and civilization. Thus, the social distinctions between public and private spheres and the perceived distinction between nature and culture shape gender roles in American birthing and American society.

Men as Representatives

First, American men are expected to manage relations between family and society. As the titular head of the family, the father is expected to act as the liaison for and defender of his wife and children. Similarly, in birthing, men are appointed the mediators between birthing mothers and the hospital facility.

When the prepared childbirth movement asks a father to manage the mother's relationship with the hospital, it fits a man's idealized role for himself as the head of the family. It feels right to carry medical information to the mother, translate the mother's demands to the staff and, in addition, defend her from the staff and hospital. The father is the voice for the family, the one who speaks for the needs and desires of the patient. The staff looks to the man, both figuratively and physically, to find out when and what a woman might want for medication, what juice she prefers, and whether she brought a second nightgown. A husband becomes the voice for his wife and in doing so, accepts a conventional role that empowers him at the expense of his partner.

Worse than mute, birthing mothers are expected to be irrational. The biological ideology of the alternative birthing movement recognizes the Cartesian dualism of mind and body. As a mother is equated with her body, a father is expected to take over the function of her mind. Men are expected to maintain their rational relationship with the objective world. As a member of the birthing team, fathers are expected to remain reasonable and pragmatic. The father is expected to provide the medical staff with a logical link to the mother as she sinks into her primal and emotional self.

Men as Defenders

Second, the childbirth revolution gives fathers the role of defenders of their wives. The childbirth revolutionaries consider most conventional birthing interventions unnecessary and dangerous, and recognize that medical convention can only be changed if individual couples advocate for new methods. Mothers are taught to retreat into themselves; fathers are trained to protect them during this vulnerable period.

The distinction between the public and the private, and men's responsibility to mediate the family's relations with society, demands that husbands defend wives and fathers protect children. Since the time of classical Athens, a man's honor has been won in the public sphere, but could be lost if he failed to protect his wife and family in the home. Throughout European history, having conferred power over the family to the patriarch, society demanded that he be the protector (Veyne 1987). In the hospital, the birthing revolution demands that fathers defend their wives against the intrusions of conventional medical practice. To most men, it is a responsibility fitting a loving husband and a new father.

Medical childbirth and institutional policy balances the needs of the patient with the demands of institutional efficiency (as well as legal security and a host of other factors). The father is expected to monitor the mother's conditions and advocate for her needs with a hospital and staff that have myriad other concerns. If hospital staff members bother women during a contraction, Bradley suggests that fathers intercede for mothers and ask nurses to wait until it has passed. Fathers are even expected to shield their spouses from the unnecessary intrusions of the obstetrician. Bradley recounts with great approval one incident where he entered the room of a woman who did not seem to be progressing, only to be told by the father, "Don't worry doc, she does just fine when you're not here" (Bradley 1965, 44).

Men as Managers

Prepared childbirth models demand that mothers submit to power and authority, and that fathers join doctors as "managers" of pregnant women. Dad serves as the enforcer of the birth plan and preparations; he is both superego and superpower. Bradley (1965, 82) suggests that men become "pregnancy policemen" to make sure that women perform the necessary exercises. But fathers, in turn, must relinquish their power to the obstetrician who performs the final delivery of the new baby. Thus, the childbirth revolutionaries assume an authoritarian air when directing themselves to fathers, as when Bradley (1965, 129–130) demands that fathers take time with their pregnant partners, "and don't tell me you can't spare the time. Take the time!"

The hierarchical aspect of the relation is nowhere clearer than in the role created for father as coach or trainer. In cartoons, in birthing manuals, and in the minds of dads-in-training, the father strides into the birthing room with clipboard and stopwatch in hand, exuding an air of control and confidence. His partner, the talented and highly valued performer, is prepared, practiced, and positioned to perform to her greatest potential. The father-as-coach has the responsibility of guiding the birthing mother through the entire labor, from the first contractions through the final transitional phase.

More than a guide, the coach has power over the player. The revolutionaries of childbirth assume and suggest that fathers are husbands and mothers are wives, and that husbands' relation with their partners is inherently powerful. It suggests that it is the man of the house who establishes the rules of behavior for his family. For example, Bradley advises that fathers give pregnant women the right to be motherlike rather than ladylike. A father needs to release his wife from the demands of propriety; he must give her permission to access her natural self. Pregnant women are supposed to be able to sit with their legs apart, never cross them, squat whenever possible, and sleep on their sides, without fear of a husband's disapproval.

The analogy plays explicitly on the superior position provided to coaches in sports competition. The first responsibility of the birthing coach is to keep the big picture in mind. As the mother begins the long road toward birth, she will undoubtedly be concerned about each contraction. It is the responsibility of the father to watch the goal and mark each movement toward the end point. This task becomes increasingly important as the performer increases the intensity of her concentration, the tunnel vision that characterizes more advanced labor. The labor coach needs to provide her with the larger picture so that she can stay directed toward her goal.

Second, the coach needs to remember the game plan. As the birth moves forward, it is the role of the man to keep track of the strategies that the couple will use. Carrying the athletic metaphor further, he must be able to call the correct play. With a stopwatch in hand and the diagrams in his head, he must remember the correct timing of breathing. The father must know the signs for the onset of each stage in the birth and call the appropriate positions. As the mother flags in her energy or experiences discomfort, he must know when to apply the right massages or compresses. He is responsible to have the materials on hand—pillows, ice chips, or towels—and to direct the mother to use them in the prescribed manner. As Bradley put it, the father must "get the train back on the tracks if she tends to lose the rhythm of what she has been doing" (1965, 50).

Finally, fathers-as-coaches are responsible for remembering the rules of the game. As a birthing woman pulls into herself, or begins to slip out of control, it is the father who is needed to keep her in touch with rationality. The role of father as rational actor plays heavily on conventional American concepts of masculinity. Fathers are expected to be in control and in charge. Uncontrolled muscles and adrenaline drive the performer, and her state intensifies as the birth approaches. The father-as-coach needs a clear head and careful eye, making sure that the labor is carried out according to the dictates of the method.

The Father Co-opted

The role given to fathers in alternative childbirth makes sense in hospitals and fits their identity in American society, but it does more; fathers reinforce the power that is central to medical birthing. First, in being men, fathers reproduce and reinforce society's patriarchal domination of laboring women. Their presence provides yet another masculine figure with power over the female patient. Second, despite the fact that men's role is designed to reduce the need for medical intervention, this involvement does not challenge the technocratic messages of American childbirth ritual. Prepared birthing holds intransigently to the need to birth with obstetricians in hospitals.

The new movement makes room for the father in birthing and creates a place for him on the delivery team, but it fails to provide for his needs. There are no notes in the chart about *his* progress; no nurses bringing *him* lunch; no physician's consultations about *his* blood pressure. There is no social support, or even recognition of the fact that he was undergoing one of the most profound events in a father's life.

Anthropology highlights the social aspects of birth and their importance in the ritual transformation of men into fathers. Our awareness of couvade in other societies—and its presence in our own history—makes clear to us that fathers have always had their own ritual experience of pregnancy, labor, and delivery. Among indigenous people of South America, as fathers observe food taboos, go into seclusion, or scarify their bellies with piranha teeth, they are recognized in the drama engulfing their family. This special recognition has been lost in American birthing. Fathers' role in birthing was denied as medicine isolated birthing mothers from home, family, and, in the end, consciousness. The medical model devotes itself to managing the pregnant patient as an isolated, biological object.

The alternative birthing movement sought to reintegrate social relations, psychological experiences, and spiritual awareness back into birth. But when push came to shove, hospitals and physicians opted for biological birth over holistic birthing, and chose Lamaze over Dick-Read and Bradley. This maintains hospital standards of efficiency and effectiveness, without disrupting the practice of birth or the power structure of hospital birthing. Fathers are admitted, but only to facilitate the biological process of birth and empower the existing institution in relations with the patient.

5

Birthing Classes

Training Men to Birth

I don't remember a whole lot from those classes. There was just one thing I remembered that they had, this little model of a pelvis and they told us how the baby needed to come through that and I was like, "Oh, okay, I never thought that the baby had to go through the pelvis."

–Joe

Men in the United States do not learn about birth from their fathers around the campfire, nor do they watch other dads in the delivery room. They do not generally talk about it over beer or basketball. In fact, men are not much of a source of information for birthing fathers. When experienced dads do talk to young fathers about birth, their advice is usually supportive, but perfunctory; as one put it, "The one friend I talked with said my part is to stay on my feet where she can see me."

Mothers and fathers prepare differently for birth. Pregnant women talk to their friends, their mothers, and their coworkers. They read, often becoming veritable libraries of reproductive literature. Women load shelves with books about conceiving, expecting, birthing, naming, and bringing up babies. The men I talked with tend to avoid written sources. As another father confessed, "I don't read the manual and directions for my new computer, do you think I'm going to sit down and read a book about pregnancy?"

Birthing classes, not books or mentors, teach a man about pregnancy and childbirth, usually while he is sitting on the floor with his partner, surrounded by a dozen or so other pregnant couples. Once a week for six to twelve weeks, soon-to-be fathers set aside work and play to retreat into a dimly lit room where they learn the magic and the mysteries of birth. They feel a mixture of anxiety, excitement, boredom, and fear as they are taught about the drama of birth and their part in the program. Men experience the uneasy camaraderie of boot camp, the vulnerability of a consciousness-raising group, and the magic of a séance. Finally, with ceremonial flourish, they complete the last class and are deemed ready to carry out their first great act as a father—the birthing of their babies.

The prepared childbirth movement was based in education. Birthing women need to know about birth, both to dispel the myths that cause pain and to learn the tools to contend with the travails of childbirth. Just as important as preparing mothers, it is deemed essential to inform fathers. Fathers need education to be confident and efficient members of the team. With this in mind, the architects of the childbirth revolution wrote books and developed courses for parents—the sacred books and liturgies of the new birthing culture.

But classes do more than train men for fear-free or pain-free birth; classes develop men's identity as fathers. For women, conception starts a long series of intense experiences that transform them into mothers. Biological changes give pregnant mothers both explicit and unconscious experiences of the new being; other mothers share experiences about the change, and every stranger on the street looks at a pregnant woman with a new eye. This shared and often silent recognition provides a new mother with a mirror to see herself in her developing role. Not so with men, however. Trained as domestic warriors, not caregivers, fathers have fewer venues to try on their new role. They have none of the physical and far less of the social experience of pregnancy. They do not feel the kick of the baby or the understanding of strangers on the street. But they do have birthing classes. Removed from the workaday world, far from their office buddies and baseball diamonds, birthing classes become an important arena in which to learn about themselves as fathers.

Understanding birth classes as ritual highlights how this training functions as a new American couvade. Men are isolated from conventional life in a liminal time and space, stripped of their conventional identities. They submit to formalized and repetitive activities that communicate important aspects of their new role and relationships in the world. As in other forms of couvade, childbirth classes transform the father's identity, and his relations with the baby, mother, and society.

Birthing classes create the time for men to relate directly to the developing baby. In the frantic final days of pregnancy, they have a moment (or evening) of calm to try on their new role as fathers. Birthing classes are held on a weekend or during the evening in a neutral zone, removing men from friends, coworkers, and relatives who demand their attention and assistance in other tasks. During that time, dads do not have to worry about a leaky pipe or a hemorrhaging securities fund. For this brief period, other identities lose importance. Men are no longer soccer stars, computer hacks, or backyard mechanics—they are now pregnant fathers. Other roles and responsibilities are held at bay while a man thinks about the being who is developing.

Classes also offer the chance for a father to discover and redefine his relationship with his partner. American men tend to allow pragmatic actions to mediate their relationships with people. For example, when a husband checks the tires on his wife's car, it is seen as an expression of his love and concern for her safety. Likewise, a man's nesting activity—whether it be overtime work to earn extra money or painting the baby's room—signals support for his companion. In contrast, birthing classes force a man to focus directly on his pregnant partner. He is asked to rub her body and hold her close. He hears about her physical feelings and emotional changes, and is asked to empathize with her experience. For this period, he is told that his relationship is more important than his talents as an accountant or a room painter.

Finally, birthing education introduces a man to his new relations with other members of society. At the most basic level, fathers learn a script to relate to hospital staff and physicians, what to expect and what is permissible. Behind the script, however, are important messages about knowledge, authority, and the hierarchy of power in birthing. As fathers hear about cesarean and vaginal birth, and as they learn about the power of science and medicine, they come to understand more general messages about being a father in American society.

What are the metamessages of birthing classes? Not surprisingly, they are as conflicted as the childbirth theories from which they derive. The alternative birthing movement was demanded by parents who sought control over birth; it was developed by obstetricians who were embedded in a biological model; and it has been institutionalized in hospitals that empower physicians and technicians. Birthing education becomes an arena for the negotiation of discourse about the meaning of birth. Holistic birthers, physicians, childbirth agencies, and hospitals all seek to control how couples become educated for birth. The result has been dissonance between the ideals of the childbirth movement and the realities of birthing in hospitals. Couples are taught that the ideal birth is without pain or medication, yet birthing classes warn them to expect both. They are taught to make informed decisions, and yet are to unquestioningly obey the decrees of their physician. They learn to defend themselves from the interventions of medical technology, but hear that they need the hospital for safety and support.

The conflict inherent in birthing education has ramifications for men in birth. A father is asked to support the mother in birth and defend her from the unnecessary intrusions of the hospital and physician. Yet, he is also taught to acquiesce to the power of technology and cede authority to nurses and the obstetrician. This places fathers in a difficult spot. Men are taught to live out the political conflicts of the birthing movement, while at the same time they are experiencing one of life's greatest and most intimate moments.

The following analysis of the history of fathers' childbirth training makes it easier to understand how childbirth education developed and its effect on men's role in birth and their identity as fathers. Each of the three primary architects of childbirth revolution propose somewhat different programs for educating fathers—as companion, coach, or trainer—but they all emphasize the biological aspect of birth. They prepare a man to minister to a mother's physical needs, and ignore the spiritual, social, and psychological experiences of both parents.

The Recent History of Birthing Education

Educating prospective parents is nothing new. Medical mythology suggests that Hippocrates counseled midwives to train birthing mothers. In the subsequent millennia, mothers, midwives, and medical practitioners prepared women for birth. But when birth moved into hospitals, education became irrelevant. Patients were objects, not actors, and therefore need no information. Medical knowledge was relocated to medical textbooks for the eyes of physicians. A century of women went into labor believing that they simply needed to arrive at the hospital on time and then the obstetrician would do the rest. It was not until the advent of prepared childbirth that practitioners rediscovered the need to train parents for birth. This time, however, only medical professionals taught about birth. Eschewing mothers and midwives as sources, Dick-Read, Lamaze, and Bradley proposed curricula to educate women for birth and to prepare fathers to assist them.

Grantly Dick-Read instituted the first contemporary childbirth classes, leading couples through lectures, exercises, and practice in preparation for birthing their babies. Mothers learned the intimate details of birth in early classes; fathers attended later lectures that focused on labor and delivery. Dick-Read observed that uneducated men suffer during pregnancy and birth. Although pregnancy brings new intensity to a man's love for and desire to protect his wife, it also leaves him confused and scared. He needs to be educated in the physiology and psychology of childbirth in order to transcend these fears. Men need to learn about birth so that they develop confidence in a woman's natural ability to birth babies. They must learn "the art of companionship and care of wives during pregnancy, and understand by reading and discussion with them the training that they undergo." Moving from attitude to action, expectant fathers are also advised to join their partners in practicing birth techniques, and in becoming physically ready along with their wives (Dick-Read 1944, 330, 334).

Fernand Lamaze also proposed that fathers be "versed in the principles of childbirth without pain" (Lamaze [1956]1970, 99) and that they assist mothers in exercises. In France, monitrices—trained female attendants—accompanied birthing mothers, so the Lamaze education program focused almost exclusively on mothers. As lay attendants were restricted from American hospitals, Elisabeth Bing taught American fathers to assume the role. She proposed that fathers assist in classes, at home, and in the labor room. Men learned techniques in lectures, practiced at home, and directed their wives in labor.

In her little book *Practical Training Course for the Psychoprophylactic Method of Childbirth,* published in 1961, Bing provides the model for most early childbirth classes in the United States. Over the last four decades, Bing's publication has reached a worldwide audience under the title *Six Practical Lessons for an Easier Childbirth,* last revised in 1994. Despite long use, the publication remains faithful to the spirit, and often to the letter, of the original plan for childbirth classes.

The first class introduces the couple to birth. The second teaches the couple about first stage labor and provides them with exercises for concentration, relaxation, and muscles. Subsequent classes are devoted to breathing, exercises, and practice. She asserts that if mothers can convince their reluctant husbands to come to the first class, "it will be almost impossible to get rid of them—even if you should want to" (Bing, Karmel, and Tanzer 1961, 6). Men are intrigued with the method and often acquire a better grasp of the process than their wives do. More than simply explaining the mechanics of birth, Bing teaches men to help women avoid pain, including fathers as important partners in training. In fact,

Bing suggests that if a woman cannot find Lamaze classes to attend, she should take the manual and solicit her husband to act as teacher. "I want you to practice these exercises with your husband, letting him give you the commands that I will give you now" (Bing, Karmel, and Tanzer 1961, 15).

Bradley broke new ground for the training of birthing fathers with his classic, *Husband-Coached Childbirth* (1965). Rather than mere attendants, Bradley fathers participate in pregnancy training and birth. They study the materials, practice the exercises, and coach mothers through labor and delivery. Bradley's book details the philosophy of father-coached birthing, but his training program was formalized and institutionalized with the help of others. The American Academy of Husband-Coached Childbirth® was created to promote the Bradley Method with the help of an enterprising young couple who had experienced "Bradley birthing," Marjorie and Jay Hathaway. An accompanying exercise program was written by a Canadian nurse, Rhondda Hartman (Bradley 1965, 199).

To teach Bradley, fathers and mothers alike are often certified by the academy as husband-wife teams. Like the Hathaways, these couples often request to be Bradley trainers because of their own profound birthing experiences. They take equal part in teaching classes and training pregnant couples. Bradley classes begin in the sixth month of pregnancy. The first three sessions offer an introduction, survey the Bradley Method, and explain pregnancy and nutrition. Two classes focus on the coach's role, four on labor and delivery, and one class each on possible complications and postpartum issues. Students, for their part, are expected to attend classes and work as couples. Bradley classes differ from those of other training programs in emphasizing directed study outside of classes. Students read the materials at home, complete worksheets, and write a birth plan to prepare themselves.

As childbirth education moved more into the mainstream of American birthing, it has shifted from the defined models of Lamaze and Bradley and the organized curricula of Bing and the Hathaways. Increasingly, education integrates various strategies into a more eclectic approach. Borrowing from each other, Lamaze educators teach fathers how to coach and Bradley instructors help parents practice breathing. The range of options has become more varied. Although hospitals and physicians continue to sponsor courses that focus on the biology of birth, independent trainers now offer more holistic approaches that recognize birth as a psychological, social, and spiritual experience.

The books to educate fathers and mothers have grown into a diverse literature. The first generation of books, written by Dick-Read, Lamaze, and Bradley, advocated preparing parents. The second generation, penned by Bing, Hartman, and the Hathaways, offered training programs based on the work of the obstetrician-reformers. In contrast, the third generation of this literature provides eclectic birthing plans based on personal experiences, often of the authors themselves. Two popular books, by Peggy Simkin (2001) and Sheila Kitzinger (1996), are directed at parents, rather than at professionals. These friendly guides adopt an informal tone, avoid medical terminology, and are complete with detailed pictures and drawings of pregnant and birthing couples in homey environments. Rather than analyze the underlying logic of prepared birth, these offer a series of strategies to prepare for and perform birth, providing easy-to-follow directions to alleviate pain and problems—without making any pain-free or fear-free promises.

Freed from the dogma of particular childbirth revolutionaries, this literature is more creative and flexible with respect to fathers. Several books have focused specifically on the birthing partners' role, notably Simkin's book, *The Birth Partner* (2001). These books often propose that fathers, rather than acting as coaches or choreographers, be flexible in their birthing activities. They might assist and experience birth, but work in conjunction with a midwife or other birthing attendant, often called a doula, who is the primary assistant to the mother. In this process, the female birthing specialist provides the knowledge and direction to a woman in labor, allowing the father to experience birth as best suits him and his partner.

Just as the popular childbirth literature is increasingly written by experienced, but independent authors, many childbirth instructors are certified by independent educational institutions, such as the International Childbirth Education Association (ICEA) or the Association of Labor Assistants and Childbirth Educators (ALACE). These have no direct relationship to Lamaze International or the American Academy of Husband-Coached Childbirth®. These trainers then organize and administer their own programs, or affiliate with an agency or hospital that uses a prescribed curriculum.[1]

Most programs sponsored by physicians or hospitals are less interested in the underlying logic of a birthing program, and focus on pragmatic techniques to facilitate birth. Rather than adhere to any one of the three birthing models, they draw from all three. Like Dick-Read, these programs teach couples the basic biology of birth; like Lamaze, they provide conditioning to prevent pain; and, like Bradley, they train mothers to relax. The change to independent, eclectic curricula has an institutional payoff for the medical system: the pragmatic character of these training programs allows physicians and hospitals to tailor their content. In these institutionally administered programs, parents are prepared to experience birth as fully as possible, but within the strictures of standard operating procedures. More than training parents in natural or painless or fearless birth, these courses establish the ground rules for hospital birth. They tell parents what to expect during labor and how to relate to nurses and physicians. And when all is said and done, they explain that a medical doctor officiates at delivery, not the father, midwife, or doula.

This training makes sense, but only makes sense, given the assumption that birth is a biological event. The father who hopes to experience the social, psychological, and spiritual aspects of birth receives little support. He has the opportunity to work with his partner in pregnancy and increase his empathy for her experience, but in the final act of the drama, he is expected to follow the directives of the physician and focus on the needs and desires of his partner. He is to attend to the physician, the staff, and his partner, in that order. His own needs and desires, if considered at all, are peripheral to the act of birth that he is attending.

Birthing Class: A Case Study

As a participant and an observer, and as a pregnant father and anthropologist, I attended a variety of different birthing classes taught in hospitals, in independent agencies, and in private homes. Several of the classes were identified as Lamaze and others as Bradley; some claimed no specific forefather. Some classes were held in office buildings; others met in clinics; and still others were in the homes of the trainers. Despite the differences, however, it is possible to define a common experience for men.

One of these courses serves as a fitting example, and provides a window into the more general organization of birthing classes. The course was taught at an independent agency that operates near a group of major hospitals in San Antonio. The agency hires childbirth educators with certification from a variety of national programs, including ASPO (American Society for Psychoprophylaxis in Obstetrics) and ICEA (International Childbirth Education Association). The curriculum was developed by the agency itself, drawing on literature from each of the major childbirth organizations. (This class was composed only of mothers and fathers; many other classes observed had female couples in which a partner, friend, or mother was training to accompany a woman through birth.)

These particular classes were taught by Mary, a slight woman in her forties with long brown hair and snappy eyes. She is an experienced childbirth trainer, mother of four children, and administrator of a school for young children. Mary is also the educator whom my wife and I discovered during our first pregnancy, and I returned to her classes many times over the course of this research. Most other parents, largely middle-class Anglos and Hispanics, are referred by physicians who deliver at the nearby hospitals. The classes usually meet in the evening, in a suite of offices on the first floor of a conventional steel and glass office building. From the first moment a couple enters the birthing classes, they are ushered through a complex series of activities that are defined and dictated by the structure of classes and the models of the prepared childbirth movement.

Leaving the Everyday World Behind

On the first night of birthing classes, couples enter the building through the darkening evening, men with pillows under their arms and women cradling their growing bellies. Arriving at the suite of offices managed by the agency, they peer into the classroom and then enter with an embarrassed formality. Eighteen blue plastic and metal chairs are arranged in a semicircle and the trainer, Mary, sits cross-legged in the center arranging papers. She greets each couple and, after they sit down, hands them a registration form to be filled out; they wait until all eight couples have arrived. She also pulls a folder from a stack of papers and offers each couple a packet of photocopies and brochures with titles like *Eat Well for Your Baby* and *The Epidural: Pros and Cons*. Despite Mary's own eclectic approach, the packet includes an introductory magazine about the Lamaze method from ASPO.

The neophytes sit quietly, looking at the brochures and around the room with detached interest. The room is softly carpeted and painted a muted gray. Pictures of babies hang from the walls and charts of labor progress stand on the floor. The quality of the graphics varies from medical precision to that of an eighth grade science fair. There are drawings of pregnant women, fetuses, simple graphs, and long lists of strange words like "oxytocin." The overhead lights fill the room without being bright or glaring. Sounds from outside are distant and obscured by the steady whir of the institutional air. Blinds are lowered over the windows, closing the room from the darkening evening outside. In essence, the room is cut off from the outside word; indications of time, space, and place are removed in the otherworldly setting of the birthing class. Quietness descends over the room.

At the start of birthing classes, the boundaries between couples are usually exaggerated. Avoiding the eyes of the other people, pairs tend to pull into themselves, exchanging glances and hushed comments. One couple I observed typifies parents' reactions; I will call them Jane and Marion. Jane wore a gray sweat suit, Marion khakis and a golf shirt. They were in their early thirties, about average for these classes. They quietly placed themselves in chairs near the end of the semicircle and began to shuffle through the packet Mary had offered. They were not reading the material, but looking at the pictures and headings with distracted interest. Their eyes did not meet, nor did they relate to the growing group around them. Marion crossed his legs and leaned back—still without lifting his eyes from the papers. His studied indifference suggested that he was extremely aware of the strange surroundings and people.

Mary's voice marks the first break in the embarrassed quiet. Sitting on the floor, with a leg outstretched in a self-conscious position of repose, she welcomes the group and introduces herself. The simple act of introduction gives Mary a certain authority and separates her from her pregnant novitiates. She then calls out each couples' names and checks off those in attendance. Finally, she suggests that students introduce themselves. Moving around the circle, each couple holds the attention of the others, giving their names (usually only their first names), their due date, and the baby's sex if they know it. Women seem to exchange knowing glances that signal their shared experience. Men have less information and experience in common, but begin to make tentative links among themselves. A young man might lightly and publicly chide his pregnant wife for taking so long getting ready to come, linking with the man sitting next to him. She may share her side of the story by rolling her eyes to the second man's wife. Contact is made; impersonal pretensions are briefly dropped, and a special relationship is established that might continue throughout the classes.

The introduction establishes a place for each participant in the group. More than increasing the amount that initiates know of one another, it reduces personal distinctions. Other than the clothes on their backs, first names are perhaps the only element of the larger world that members bring into the special place of the birthing class. Throughout the eight class periods, knowledge of each other's personalities and identities remains simple and basic. Brian has red hair; Karen dresses in pink; James's untied, oversized basketball shoes make him look like a teen father. More important than job or religion or hometown is the event that is bringing them all together—they are all to pass through a portal into another world.

Attendance taken, Mary provides her first directive to the class—to get comfortable. In birthing classes, formality is quickly replaced by the intimacy usually reserved for the privacy of one's own home. By offering couples the chance to sprawl out or lean against one another, the trainer signals that norms of conventional behavior do not apply in birthing classes. It takes very little encouragement for some couples to get down on the floor and, before long, most women are getting relaxed, leaning against or cuddling into the arms of their partners. Jane begins to get a little more expansive as she reaches across and holds Marion's hand. Since he is a man and lacks the physical experience of pregnancy, it seems to be a little harder for him to become informal.

With identities and basic norms of conduct established, Mary sets out to introduce the subject. In a calm and friendly tone, she explains the basic premise of her childbirth classes, which is that education and exercise will allow each couple to prepare for birth. She prefers an eclectic approach, but other trainers and programs stay closer to specific philosophical roots. Lamaze trainers will speak more of reducing pain; Bradley teachers will emphasize a couple's choice of birth plans; teachers of more institutional classes will speak at greater length of the programs of a specific hospital. Many teachers use the first class as an opportunity to focus on the development of the fetus, explaining growth leading up to the last trimester, and briefly outlining what to expect in the last period of pregnancy.

After a basic description of the process, Mary suggests that the group take a short break. With a knowing smile, she notes that some of the ladies, as she calls them, might want to go to the bathroom and points down the hall to the lavatory. A strained hush falls over those left behind, who sit or wander around the room and eye the charts and drawings. The quiet tension of the break period provides incentive for men to begin to form a sense of common experience.

Much of what goes on in birthing classes happens during quiet time before classes begin, during breaks, or after the end of instruction. Few can sit long in the silence, and most make quiet small talk with their partners or wander into the hall for a cup of decaffeinated tea or, perhaps, outside the building for a smoke. The conversation of those men who stay behind, or those who find themselves sharing a cigarette outside, is rarely substantive—but it usually has great symbolic value. Sports and the weather seem to be topics that allow men to connect, without imposing an uncomfortable vulnerability. Two of the men might break out of their shells and make a few quiet comments about the San Antonio Spurs T-shirt one is wearing—a safe, masculine topic in this unfamiliar environment. Standing outside, one might gesture to the grass with a cigarette and offer, "Never seen it so dry," initiating a casual conversation about the weather. New to the world of parturition, and with few markers of similarity or difference, men use the excuse of small talk to find common ground in the birthing experience.

As Mary calls the members back to the class, she signals that the next stage in the class is going to be different. She requests that each couple spread out their blanket and pillow and sit down on the floor. The permission to be casual becomes a firm suggestion. All the women are to move to the floor, and the men should follow them. The participants, with varying levels of agility, lower themselves onto the carpet and get comfortable. Women smile and giggle at their feelings of awkwardness. Men move to help them down and get comfortable. Some men exhibit concerned tenderness as they assist the pregnant women; others are jocular, tickling their wives or laughing at their efforts; a few try to appear impassive, helping without showing emotion.

On the floor, partners create comfortable niches for the women. Men sit behind the women, and extend their arms and legs to define a warm space for the women to move into. Even if a man still resists the request for informality, he might position his knees to support his partner, and puts his hands on her head and shoulders. The blankets on which couples position themselves become islands on the institutional carpet. Handmade afghans and well-worn bedspreads, each with its own story to tell, provide a fitting backdrop to the intimacy of participants' physical positions.

Mary dims the light, closes the door, and asks couples to be quiet and follow her directions. A tape of the ocean plays; the rhythm fills the room without drawing attention to itself. Mary waits several minutes for the couples to absorb the new environment. Then, in a low and clear voice, she asks each couple to close their eyes and relax. "Beginning with your head," she intones, "let the energy and tension flow out of your body." Slowly and methodically, she directs the couples to relax their necks, shoulders, backs, bellies, bottoms, and legs in turn. "I just want you to relax, and let the worries of the day slip away—that frustration from work, traffic, the fight you had with each other on your way here," she suggests. The invocation mimics the cadence and repetition of the waves. "Let go of your body; let go of your arms and legs; let go around the baby."

Responding to her voice, first the women and then the men begin to loosen up, rotating their heads and shoulders to allow the tension and stress of the normal world to dissipate. Some, seeming uncomfortable with the strangeness, take longer than others to settle into the routine, but soon each couple has retreated into a separate space. Students sink their limp bodies into pillows and blankets; some close their eyes; others fall into an unfocused gaze.

When the class has become relaxed and has spent several minutes in this dreamlike state, Mary begins to bring them back. Slowly, she stops her intonations; the sound of waves fades away and, after giving everybody the chance to return, she raises the lights and smiles to the group. With a sense of normalcy and closure, Mary announces the end of class. She tells them all that they have done very well, assures them that they will do well in future classes, and reminds them to come the next week.

Reversing Roles, Acquiring Empathy

Subsequent classes follow the steps laid down in the first evening. The couples arrive each night with pillows and blankets tucked under their arms. Mary welcomes them as she organizes her materials and, in turn, they casually greet one another. By now, Marion and Jane have established friendships with another couple and find seats next to them. Smiles and light teasing mark the growing friendships. Classes fall into a familiar routine: a descriptive lecture, followed by a relaxation period with white sound and dimmed lights. Finally, after a short break, couples use role-playing to learn specific birthing strategies.

Classes do more than create a sense of community. After couples have been removed into the liminal space of birthing classes, they join in learning and practicing for birth. Lectures and exercises give fathers the opportunity to share mothers' experiences and empathize with their pregnant state. Removed from the roles and responsibilities of the rest of their world, men are offered the opportunity to reverse their conventional role and join women in their pregnant state. In content, the lecture portion of classes progresses through labor and delivery. Charts are used to explain the difference between first and second stage labor, transition, and delivery. Despite the disparate approaches of different birthing methodologies, the curricula of most childbirth training programs cover similar basic material. Courses usually range over six basic topics: nutrition; labor and delivery stages; medications; possible problems (e.g., cesarean, transverse presentation); preparations for and signs of labor; and, finally, parenting.

This educative portion of birthing classes is designed to dispel the mystery of birth. The language of the birthing classes conforms to the biological model of the alternative birth movement, without adopting the technocratic language of conventional biomedicine. Pregnancy, labor, and delivery are presented as normal, stages through which the body proceeds toward a final culminating moment when the baby makes its entrance into the world. Medical drawings of fetuses and pregnant women reinforce that this is standard biology. In conventional medical discourse, confusing terminology tends to mystify and disempower the patient. Childbirth educators use respectful yet commonplace language to give parents the confidence of understanding. Where the physician might refer to the "subfecund primiparous female," Mary would call her "a first-time mother who had a hard time conceiving."

For fathers, the lecture portion of classes has a pedagogical style that is familiar in structure, if novel in topic. Rather than emphasize the experiential aspects of pregnancy, these presentations depend on a linear flow of information. Facts are learned, knowledge accumulates, and the lived reality of pregnancy is explained through biology. The result provides men with a clear and concise understanding of pregnancy and birth.

The information is further normalized in that childbirth educators themselves are not defined as medical specialists. This is true even in Lamaze training, where the educator is often a nurse. Despite their knowledge and certification, the primary qualification in the classroom is experience. They are, most importantly, laypeople who have usually experienced birth as mothers, assistants, and observers. In assuming the task of informing parents, educators act as an important model of and for the parents' successful mastery of the intricacies of biology. Mary often refers to her own birthing and carries an air of having seen or done just about everything in birth.

Stretching is a routine part of most birthing courses and usually occurs early in the class period. Couples sit next to one another and are led through activities to limber up. In Mary's classes, fathers and mothers sit on the floor with feet and knees together, then spread and lower their knees toward the floor. They limber up by stretching their spinal columns, twisting their shoulders, and raising their arms. Mary then has them lie on their backs and lift their hips to strengthen their legs. As class progresses, this type of passive relaxation is supplemented by more active and specific techniques to relax their bodies. Mary uses her voice to induce serenity, "Close your eyes and let yourself go. Feel the surroundings, the coolness of the air as you breathe in and out." Thus, relaxation is more than the absence of stress; men and women actively engage in it.

Most birthing classes use visualization and concentration as a means to promote relaxation. Mary suggests that parents find a mental image that allows mothers to pull into their body and "open up" in birth. Another teacher asks students to close their eyes and visualize a flower bud opening, petal by petal. Other teachers are less directive, simply asking students to find an image that gives them peace. "Think about some place you enjoy being or a favorite object you own." Couples find intimacy in this relaxation.

Jane, who had seemed stiff early on, now sinks into Marion's body; he leans into her, wrapping his arms around her waist or holding her shoulders. Some men stroke their partners' faces, lightly kiss them on the head, or rest their faces in the women's neck or hair. For fathers, relaxation exercises offer the chance to empathize in some small way with their pregnant partners. At a time when stress is increasing, when planning and preparations take on new urgency, the act of touching and relaxing together offers the opportunity to join together in the state of pregnancy. Finally, in the same way that Mary opens the special atmosphere for relaxation, she closes off the period of intimacy. When the exercise finishes, the teacher signals the change by standing up, slowly turning up the lights and calling out, "OK, let's move onto the next step."

After relaxation and the break, classes usually involve a period of physical training. Mary works in three areas: timing, massage, and breathing. The primary focus of these activities is the women of the group, but in each case, the "dads," as Mary calls them, are included in the exercise and critical to its successful completion. Although the activities are physical, there is great attention to the cognitive and emotional aspect of each.

Role-playing is the primary activity for this part of the course. Couples begin to rehearse contractions in the second or third class. Acting the part of the father or mother allows the couple to practice the concentration, breathing, and massage that they will use during birth. These lessons are designed to make labor and delivery more familiar and, at the same time, to teach the couple to work together to reduce the pain and problems of birth.

Mary asks dads to sit behind the pregnant women, either on a chair or the floor, with their arms on their partners' shoulders or loosely around their sides. Once the class quietly organizes itself, she suggests that both partners imagine a contraction in early labor. She describes the feeling of the uterus beginning to tighten around the fetus, being careful to avoid the word "pain," referring instead to the hardness and pressure created by taught muscles. She describes the increasing intensity of the contractions, contrasting their power with the mild Braxton Hicks contractions that most women have experienced. Having reached the peak of the contraction, Mary directs the women to relax into it. "Let the contraction flow through your body," she suggests, "Don't fight it. This energy is what is going to birth your baby." She then counts to ten, suggesting that the women let go of the contraction, and imagine the body relaxing to release the baby.

In teaching strategies for contending with contractions, the father is taught to become a vessel to hold the mother. Partners are guided in a manner similar to that offered to mothers. Mary's calm and confident voice directs fathers to support mothers during the contractions. "Ladies, let your bodies go limp; partners, hold her so she is free to relax into the contraction." The father's role is to contain the mother, giving her the space that she needs to act on her internal schedule, protecting her from distraction and disturbance.

As women begin to experience contractions, fathers learn to be choreographers. Fathers are first taught to keep time, calling out each interval through the cycle. "Here one comes. Contraction starting." he calls out, "Getting stronger," then, "fifteen seconds . . . thirty seconds . . . forty-five seconds . . . sixty seconds. . . . OK, you're coming back down. Contraction completed." From that point forward, the cadence of the contractions is kept with precision. This structure allows women to retreat into their bodies and subjective experiences, performing their visualization, relaxation, and breathing. Watching, holding, and counting, fathers learn about contractions as objective observers.

Mary sometimes has the two change places, reversing birthing roles. Mothers sit behind the dads and support their weight; fathers gingerly lean into their pregnant wives. Now, with men breathing hard, mothers squeeze their partners' arms to mimic a contraction and tick off the time on the stopwatch. Dads grunt and groan (and invariably chuckle) in mock labor, as the women massage their shoulders and necks. Men take a turn at practicing relaxed breathing as moms try to imagine what it would feel like to be the birth attendant.

As women rehearse the contractions of birth, partners also learn massage. In strong contractions, it will help women relax. "Partners," Mary suggests (in a class with a female partner), "place your hands on her shoulders and rub her neck. Run your hands down her head and spine; push the tension out of her body." She thus moves through the woman's body, directing the partner to massage her face, back, neck, and legs in turn.

Rather than giving a carefully defined strategy and schedule of massage, most teachers direct partners to find what works with the women they are assisting. "Ladies," Mary prompts, "tell them what feels good." Alternately, "Partners, your job is to explore those areas and kinds of massage that you feel her body respond to." And women respond to the touch by pulling increasingly into themselves. Eyes closed and bodies relaxed, they retreat into meditative states. For their part, partners observe the contraction, responsive to the subjective experience of the mother.

Couples take to massage with various levels of ease and comfort. Some couples are obviously experienced and move quickly to share the physical aspects of labor and birth. Mothers melt into the massaging hands and give their bodies to be manipulated by their partners. Others couples are more reticent. These partners touch the pregnant women with less sensitivity, and the mothers show less response in return. The conceptual distance between these couples often seems to have as much to do with the unfamiliarity of the physicality as with their embarrassment in the semipublic arena. The dimmed lights provide only a modicum of privacy and the blankets are the only mark of personal space in the public room. But as the exercise progresses, most couples relax and join together in sharing the contraction. Even the most disengaged couples find it hard to resist the steady rhythm of the teacher's voice and the social pressure (and permission) to engage in these very personal activities among virtual strangers.

Like the progress of actual birth, role-playing activities move into heavy labor during later classes. Now Mary suggests that the mothers envision the flow of the contraction as a slope of a mountain, going up the steep slope, sitting on the jagged peak, and slowly coming down the other side. Partners provide the physical aspects of the birth by squeezing mothers' arms; this, Mary suggests, simulates the burning sensation of intense contractions. Helping men to respond to feelings that they will never have, she cautions, "Keep your hands away from her belly. Rub her shoulders and arms."

Breathing is the third strategy taught to birthing couples and is increasingly important as labor training progresses. In the fifth class, Mary first describes the different kinds of breathing, such as panting or belly breathing, demonstrating each in turn. Breathing techniques are adopted primarily from Lamaze training. There are distinct types of breathing that are used in various parts of labor and delivery: slow breathing in early labor; rapid in transition; and panting in the final pushing stage. Mary begins by standing in the semicircle of couples, each couple seated on their own blanket island. With chin raised she explains each of the different breathing patterns, pointing to the stomach as the locus of force and the mouth as the focus of attention. Her hands trace the flow of air through the body and out of the mouth.

After an initial demonstration, Mary asks the mothers and fathers to try the deep, abdomen breathing themselves. Called "the cleansing breath," she explains that it marks the start of a contraction. All stand, or get up on their knees and practice lifting their rib cages as they breathe. Next, Mary requests that they take moderate breaths, counting "one" as they inhale through their nose and thinking "two" as they exhale through their mouth. Like the relaxation exercise, men join women in the routine, performing it as if they, too, were giving birth.

Partners' role in the breathing exercises is more ambiguous than in massage. Partners are expected to do breathing exercises so that they will be able to monitor and coach the women during birth. In breathing exercises a partner is a personal trainer, rather than choreographer or companion. Men encourage women and correct their breathing strategy if its depth or cadence is wrong, training them to integrate breathing into other strategies to contend with contractions in labor.

Graduation—Prepared to Begin

As the birthing classes move to the final weeks, trainers use several experiences to signal the end of the classes and the graduation of the parents. One of the most notable and intense of these is showing videos of birth. Watching birth always elicits powerful reactions, even on video. Couples cannot help but be drawn into the drama of the event, and share the anxiety and excitement.

Toward the end of the evening, when couples are relaxed and tired, Mary screens a tape that follows one or several couples through labor and delivery. The videos usually follow a single narrative: a happy couple in early labor sharing a great deal of eye contact and touching; a couple in middle labor, the mother working intently as the father massages and supports her; transition, when mothers are reaching a limit and fathers back off; and the final anxious moments of delivery, when the physician catches the baby for the happy couple. In the closing scenes of the vignette, laughter and tears break the tension. The ecstatic couple hugs as the mother holds the newborn to her breast.

It deserves mention that videos range greatly in their treatment of pain. Some video-births are accomplished with little more than vague intimations of discomfort; others are explicit in their treatment of mothers who really hurt. Mary usually starts with less dramatic births and later videos show women who really hurt. In all videos, however, the final images show parents with baby in arms, satisfied, and recovering from the ordeal.

For fathers, videos offer familiar and immediate access to birth. Videos have largely replaced written material for entertainment, directions for home purchases, and sports training. It seems only normal to curl up with their partners and watch a video to learn about birth. Birthing videos offer role models for men who have not experienced birth or discussed it with their fathers or friends. Rather than offer specific directives, these real-life birthing vignettes offer examples of what men might do. Most birthing videos show couples trying several different strategies, some of which do not work. Dads in the audience pick and choose what they might like to do and what they think would be helpful. Finally, birthing videos offer one of the first glimpses of what birthing dads might themselves experience as fathers. Labor and delivery are the focus of birthing videos, but the end result is usually defined as the creation of new relations. The final scene shifts attention from the mother to the threesome: baby, mother, and father as a single, integrated whole.

The final birthing classes are devoted to the final preparations for birth. Couples have by this time visited the hospital and seen the labor, delivery, and the more homelike birthing rooms. They have often preregistered and packed their hospital bag. Little stands between them and the final scary and exhilarating act of giving birth. The feeling of the final birthing class is in many ways like the tension of a group of first-time skydivers as the plane leaves the ground. There is no more preparation, nothing between the initiate and the door to be stepped through. The liftoff seems interminable, and the seconds tick slowly toward the unimaginable conclusion. Likewise, the final class ushers in a period of nervous expectation, when there is nothing to do but wait—and perhaps wait and wait some more.

The end of birthing classes defines couples as prepared for birth, but it is not an end in itself. Childbirth classes leave parents at the doorway that they must then pass through. Birthing classes do not make men into fathers, they simply get them ready to make the final jump. As Bill Cosby says, "Birthing classes give you a diploma to attend birth—and nothing more!" (Cosby 1986). Leaving birthing classes, the man carries with him a new sense of who he is and what he is to do in society, but he is not reintegrated into conventional society. The father remains in a liminal state, a conceptual nether region more akin to purgatory than normal life. Life proceeds with one eye on his partner's belly. Contractions could start at any time and, until then, he is neither fish nor father.

Birthing Classes as Couvade

Birthing classes provide fathers with much-needed information about birth and their own part in the process. But classes are much more than simple pragmatic education for parturition. They are the ritual preparation for fatherhood. In the same way that Guaraní use ritual proscriptions in becoming fathers, childbirth classes provide the opportunity for American men to practice a contemporary couvade.

For the Guaraní, couvade is a series of food taboos, activity restrictions, and required acts. Avoiding venison, staying out of the forest, and making a small bow mark the pregnancy and a man's ritual preparation for birth and fatherhood. Our exploration of couvade pointed to two mechanisms through which this practice transforms men and their relations. First, the fathers' ritual behavior parallels that of pregnant women. Guaraní men's actions mimic their pregnant wives, who avoid venison and are restricted from working in the garden. This transcends the simple biology of pregnancy, making fathers important participants in pregnancy. Second, couvade provides men with an experience similar to that of the mother. As a Tupi man lies in his hammock and scrapes his skin with agouti teeth, he assumes (if not replicates) the mother's subjective experience. Ritual role-reversal accomplishes the biological impossibility, providing the cultural context for the father to assume the role of the birthing parent.

Although male birth ritual of indigenous Americans may have little influence over the biological aspects of parturition, an anthropological analysis highlights its social and psychological importance. Like Guaraní couvade, birthing classes give American fathers the opportunity to declare their paternity in public and private rituals. It expresses the social relationship with the new member of the community and develops a man's empathic understanding of his partner's travail. At a social level, couvade serves as the marker of a father's new relationships. In terms of his partner, couvade allows him to redefine and reaffirm his relation with his wife. He also has the opportunity to assume the gestation of the fetus into his body, nurture it with his actions, and develop his own connection with it. Finally, ritualized couvade allows a man to internalize his new role as father. He undergoes a transformation of identity as he shifts from one social position to another, assuming the contingent rights and responsibilities.

As American men have been integrated back into birth, classes have created an arena for them to experience the empathic role-reversals of couvade. As in the classic couvade, fathers learn their part and the importance of their actions for successful birth. They are provided with a series of scripted actions that must be carefully followed to assure the safe and healthy delivery of a baby. They engage in role-reversals, exchanging roles with their partners and acting out the part of the pregnant mother in birth. More than being trained in the technical aspects of birth, they are taught to be part of a social and spiritual unit that is welcoming a new being into the world.

Classes teach men how to think about birth. Birthing classes offer men a set of cultural concepts with which to make sense of this bewildering event. The anthropologist's attention to this cultural template highlights the importance of ideology in the socialization of men into fatherhood. Birthing class information derives from the biological model that underlies contemporary attitudes toward birth. Men come to see birth, and their part in it, according to the biological model defined by Bradley, Dick-Read, and Lamaze.

In the same manner that cultural concepts of the self and health dominate the practice of couvade in Guaraní society, American ideology of health and the body dominate the couvade of birthing classes. Men perform rituals that make sense in the context of what they think about birth and biology, and they reinforce and develop those cultural understandings during the course of birth training. The result, then, is a father with a fully acculturated understanding of pregnancy and delivery, and a father prepared to take part in and reinforce that process.

Just as we have come to see birth as ritual with symbolic meanings, it is useful to think of birthing classes as ritual performance. The ritual of birthing classes gives power to the most basic messages about men and birth. Rather than spontaneous and unique meetings between parents and teachers, most birthing classes conform to a ritualized process and structure. The curriculum is dictated by formal and stylized guidelines. As couples attend to the curriculum, the most important messages are embedded in the symbols and relations that provide the context for learning. As Jane and Marion hold hands, they feel the charged environment where everyday actions have special power. As couples focus on breathing and relaxation, classes carry powerful messages about the transformation of men and women into fathers and mothers.

The mundane routine of joining together with a group of other couples quickly takes on the character of a rite of passage. Turner's (1977) emphasis on the liminal state in passage rites highlights the importance of the isolation of parents during childbirth ritual. Birthing classes create a liminal space for this ritual transformation by separating parents from their conventional responsibilities, roles, and relationships.

Establishing the context for this secular rite of passage, the first birthing class creates an environment free from conventional stresses and strains and open to new experiences and information. First, as they enter this nether world of liminality, participants set aside social status in birthing classes. Identities of the outside world are not asserted in classes; more specifically, setting previous social statuses aside establishes the primary importance of the new identities that are being established. Couples learn only the first names of other initiates; professions are unimportant, and the ties to family and friends are left outside the room. This is especially important to men for whom establishing social position provides the primary parameters for social interaction. The authority and respect that an accountant asserts in the business world has little significance to his or her social interactions in the birthing classes. By setting aside social roles that have significance during the rest of their lives, men recognize in each other and themselves their changing identities as fathers.

Second, the space of birthing classes is designed to accentuate the liminal aspect of the ritual performance. The darkness, white noise, and soft pillows of classes like Mary's isolate couples from their conventional lives, putting them in a liminal zone that has no reference to the time of day or location of the class. The walls of the room shelter the couples from the stresses, strains, pressures, and pains of the outside world. Even areas within the birthing class accentuate the liminality of the experience. From the semicircle of chairs, students are drawn down and forward into the most powerful area of the ritual arena where the world stands still and personal differences are inconsequential.

Birthing classes do more than isolate fathers from conventional life. Fathers submit to a highly structured series of ritual actions. As men learn to breathe like birthing women, as they relax their bellies in response to Mary's suggestions, fathers engage in role-reversal. To act out birth is to be a birthing father. This ritual action forces a man to transcend his own role and enter into that of his partner. Birthing fathers are not unlike the Mardi Gras businessman who cross-dresses or the bishop who washes the feet of his parishioners on Maundy Thursday. Role-reversal allows the actor to share the experience of the other, the woman, or the poor church member. In each case, the ritual provides the script in which the impossible is achieved; the actor overcomes his role and takes on that of his opposite. On the other hand, the ritual role-reversal also calls attention to the conventional state of the man. For one brief period, he becomes his opposite. He experiences the pregnancy and shares in his partner's reality. As a father practices breathing, as he learns to breathe from his belly, he takes on the role of his pregnant partner. In doing so, he receives a powerful message about his own role: he emphasizes his own identity as a birthing father and birthing partner.

Birthing Classes and Biological Birth

Like the philosophies of alternative birth themselves, the messages imparted to parents are defined according to biological models of birth. First, birthing classes teach couples to think about birth happening to bodies, not mothers. The mind is considered the primary barrier to effective birthing. Birth training focuses on relaxation to release the body from the mind's control, and education to rewrite the misguided cultural training of lay knowledge. Rather than anecdotal and experiential information, such as "Joan was in the sixth month of pregnancy when she began to feel . . . ," birthing classes provide scientific explanations for changes during pregnancy. Thus, the teacher in a birthing class will explain that the growing fetus presses on a woman's bladder, making it necessary that she go to the bathroom more often.

The classroom emphasis on objective understandings not only conforms to the biological understanding of birth, but provides a means for men to understand. American fathers have only indirect access to the subjective experience of birth. There is no public recognition of couvade and few private experiences with pregnancy. Decades ago, Bradley pointed out that fathers enjoy learning about the mechanics of pregnancy and birth, and often learn the biology more thoroughly than their partners do. The fathers I talked with mirrored this assessment. As Robert, quoted above, remembered, "I just love to learn stuff. So I found this all extremely interesting." This was especially true among parents training with Bradley instructors. Given the emphasis of the Bradley Method on study and practice between classes, fathers took a greater interest. One father put it this way "I said if I last two lessons at Bradley I'd be surprised, but by the eighth class I was 'Come on, we're going to be late. I don't want to miss anything!' And diet and exercise and things like that that people say they hear about but when you actually hear someone say you need to do it, it has more of an impact. So I tried to make sure we did most of that stuff." American men, having grown up in a society where the Cartesian dualism has divorced the subjective mind from the objective body, seem to be comfortable describing the body in mechanical and absolute terms.

Second, birthing classes reinforce the essentialist perspectives of biological models. Gender roles become especially important to men in birthing classes. The gender distinction is evident from the first moment that the couples enter the room. Physically, the pregnant woman is carrying the child; her partner is engaged from the outside. She and the fetus that she carries are the primary focus of attention. As a corollary, birthing classes create a hypermasculine role for men. Rather than being de-emphasized in the ostensibly feminine world, masculine behaviors are emphasized. Joking by fathers often involves poking fun at their partners' foibles. Thus, classmates smile self-consciously as a father lampoons the pregnant maneuvering of his wife getting out of bed. Among themselves, men fall back into stereotypical masculine behavior. Men's conversations focus on safe areas, like weather and sports; men rarely share questions about the pregnancy or birth with their compatriots. As with other topics that show confusion, fear, and vulnerability, fathers save them for their female partners—if they dare to confront them at all.

In training itself, fathers' birthing responsibilities lean heavily on stereotypical gender roles. Fathers are defined as the protectors of women in pregnancy, the responsible adult in training, and the rational thinker in labor. It is suggested that fathers wield the stereotypically masculine power of defending women from themselves and the pain that they would otherwise feel. Most fathers find the role familiar; it builds on the conventional ideas that they have of men and women in the larger society. It provides them with a position in birth that fits their ideals for themselves as men, husbands, and soon-to-be fathers.

Childbirth training classes appeal to men's desire to assert control over pain, birth, medical decisions, and their partners. They offer order for the chaos of the unknown. As the linear flow of biological knowledge categorizes and compartmentalizes gestation, labor, and delivery, the gestalt of reproduction is reduced to being logical, rational, and ordered: the subjective experience is understood as objective reality.

Birthing Classes and Authority

Childbirth training classes impose a model of authority on birthing knowledge and practice. As the couple learns to attend to the mother-in-birth, the rituals carry another message about power and hierarchy: most birthing classes are careful to legitimize the knowledge that they teach by reference to medical authority. They reinforce the position of these authority figures in birth. In much of the literature of birth, the masculinity of the authority figure has been important. The foreword to Elisabeth Bing's book says of Lamaze, "He was a large man, almost elephantine in appearance" (1994, viii), and refers to him as the paterfamilias by noting his fatherly treatment of birthing mothers. The authority of these birthing classes is further reinforced by reference to medical training. The training guides of Bradley, Lamaze, and Dick-Read emphasize that the authors are physicians, and even Elisabeth Bing is careful to note that she is on the teaching faculty of a medical school (1994, 164).

The information imparted in birthing classes carries the weight of the triadic and interrelated authorities of science, medicine, and masculinity. Parents are taught to submit to the direction of the physician—that the physicians who devised training programs and the obstetricians who officiate at birth have the sacred secrets to control pain and assure a successful birth. The result is a powerful message about fathers birthing and fathers in society, a message that they usually find both reassuring and convincing. As one father put it, "It made me feel better just knowing that it wasn't all up to me. The doctor would know what was happening and what to do."

The French social scientist Pierre Bourdieu has forcefully argued in *Outline of a Theory of Practice* (1977) that ritual is a logical fusion of thought and action in and through which human beings negotiate the social relations and practical knowledge of their worlds. Entering birthing classes, men submit to a regime that acts on them and that has powers greater than theirs. As Mary draws her students around her and the couples become quiet to listen, they place themselves in the role of the initiates. More than simply becoming informed, they enter into a larger social discussion over the meaning of birth and parents' place in it. Class becomes an arena for the contestation of power, for the negotiation of men's identity and roles with respect to their partners and their children and society at large.

In sum, what are the metamessages of birthing classes? Not surprisingly, they are as conflicted as the childbirth theories from which they derive, with dissonance between the ideals of the childbirth movement and the realities of birthing in hospitals. Alternative childbirth was demanded by parents who wanted to share the birthing experience, but it was developed by obstetricians who were embedded in a biological model, and it has been institutionalized in hospitals that empower physicians and technicians. Classes become an arena for our discourse about the various possible meanings of birth and, therefore, a negotiation for power over the process. Holistic birthers, physicians, childbirth agencies, and hospitals all wish to have their say. Couples are taught that the ideal birth is without pain or medication, yet birthing classes warn them to expect both. Couples learn that they need to make informed decisions, yet are to unquestioningly obey the decrees of their physician. Couples are taught to take responsibility for their birth experience, but relinquish decision-making to physicians and hospitals.

The conflict inherent in birthing education has ramifications for the roles created for men in birth. Playing on his ideals of masculinity, a father is asked to support and defend a mother in this most vulnerable time. Yet he is to defer to the power of technology and authority of nurses and the obstetrician—also for the mother's comfort and safety. This places fathers in a difficult spot. Men are taught to live out the political conflicts of birthing, while at the same time experiencing one of life's greatest and most intimate moments.

6

Men's Experience of Birth

You feel almost like you went through labor, too, but in a different way. I was wrung out and worn out and tired, but I feel like I had helped her and I had been a part of the process.

–Martin

Mark fought through the grogginess of early morning sleep, responding to a voice that sounded important. Warm flannel sheets conspired against him. Words assembled as images in his mind, even before he understood their meaning. "Mark, wake up." His eyes flew open and he stared at the ceiling. The voice came again: "Wake up, I think she's coming!"

Mary's voice was gritty with anxiety, as if he might curl back under the covers. Mark's mind raced. She was in labor! The baby was coming! There was no way that he could have fallen back to sleep; nor, however, could he move. His body went rigid. The questions tripped over one another: How did she know? Was it intuition or contractions? What was the plan? What should he do? Finally, electrified, he sat up and swung his feet out of bed and his body into action.

Childbirth is a dramatic conclusion to what often seems a very long and slow pregnancy. Over the course of nine months, couples think about the changes that a baby will bring. They study the books and maybe even practice the moves; they fix up a nursery and mull over names. But there is no preparation for labor; nothing to dispel the shock that parents feel as they start down that arduous and unpredictable, unstoppable, and unavoidable pathway of childbirth. As Mark's feet hit the hardwood floor, he felt both the inner quiet of the Buddha and the spinning confusion of Alice tumbling down the rabbit hole into Wonderland.

The childbirth revolution opened birthing room doors to fathers, inviting men to assist their partners through labor and delivery. Birthing couples envisioned a new, easier, and more family-oriented birth, where men would participate in this most important of family events. After three decades, it is time to take stock of that revolution and what the changes mean for men. As more fathers pass through the portals of the delivery room and tell their tale, not surprisingly, it becomes clear that their experiences differ greatly from those of mothers. Every father tells a different story. Each birth becomes its own drama, unique in plot, protagonists, unexpected events, and spectacular denouement.

Underlying these differences are several common themes that deserve note. For one, childbirth is one of a father's most profound experiences, almost invariably electrifying. There is a height of excitement, anxiety, hope, and fear often unequaled in other aspects of life. Rather than render birth mundane, preparation usually intensifies the experience, making the father more aware of how magical labor and delivery are. Phil, a thirty-something contractor, remembered in utmost detail birthing his son Aaron: "It was incredible. I caught the baby and picked him up and the first thing he did, he opened his eyes and saw me face to face." Other men I talked with had similar powerful reactions. Dave, a lawyer, was left speechless: "It was just great. Tears were streaming down. It was exciting. [I was] just very excited and pleased and just really ecstatic and really overcome." No matter what the father's personality or perspective, he was almost always overcome by the power of the event and the arrival of the baby.

Men are more than the audience of birth; they are actors in the drama. Most men feel good about their performance. Many men talked about feeling essential to the process and close to their wives after the birth. Mark, a tall man who worked with computers, reported, "Whenever she talks about me in groups, about me, about the birth and everything, she tells them what a good job I did and how I was supportive in this way and this way and this way." More than one woman has broken into my conversations with fathers to declare "I couldn't have done it without him!"

But there was another theme that surfaced in my interviews. Many men expressed misgivings and talked about problems that they had during childbirth. They talked about the joy of being with their wives and the power of holding their babies, but they also identified problems. Many discovered that coaching did not work as they had been taught; some felt guilty about being powerless to stop the pain; others were pushed away by mothers and nurses or ignored by the doctor. There were almost as many different concerns as there were men. They talked about reservations and regrets, having not done enough or having done the wrong things, or simply how birth could have been different and better. Often the clearly definable problems were less important than diffuse feelings of not having done it right. One father from Seattle, looking back on his experience in the seventies, reported, "I sort of felt like I wasn't necessarily taking charge of the situation. . . . I think the man at birth, part of you wants to be supportive and you want to be ready to sort of take the lead if you're called upon to do so but it's sort of hard to tell, you know, when that moment has arrived. Because it's not your body and you're not the doctor; you're not the midwife or the nurse."

Why are men glad that they were there and like that they helped, yet feel bad about their participation in labor and delivery? Looking at birthing as ritual performance shows that even in the midst of one of life's most magical moments, fathers are caught in a double bind. On one hand, a father is asked to minister to his partner's needs. He manages or coaches or defends his partner; he works to control her fear and pain, and he tries to be her closest companion and unquestioning partner. Over and above all, he struggles to maintain a powerful and intimate connection with her as she moves through the portals of birthing.

On the other hand, fathers are also expected to be a member of the medical birthing team. As a teammate, dad is expected to cooperate and collaborate with nurses and doctors in delivering a healthy baby. He is responsible for keeping mother on the correct path of labor and delivery, as defined by the medical model and promulgated by the hospital institution. Even as he works to form an empathic relationship with his partner, he is expected to respond to the nurses' needs and the physician's directives.

The conflicting roles for birthing fathers make sense—and only make sense—with an understanding of our attitudes about birth and men's place in it. American hospital birthing distinguishes between the biological, social, and psychological aspects of life. Our analysis of the biological underpinnings of the childbirth revolution shows that fathers have been given tasks to facilitate the biological process—but which ignore its social and psychological components. Fathers are expected to alleviate the pain with massage, breathing exercises, and verbal cues. They are to minister to mother's physical needs with ice chips and bedpans. Most important, as coaches, dads are expected to keep their partners on a predetermined and standardized progress toward birth. These responsibilities in birth demand that a father ignore his multifaceted relationship with his wife and his experience of the birth.

The following traces the process of fathers and birth from conception to delivery, focusing on fathers' own stories. The narrative of fathers in American childbirth provides men's own reactions to the script that they enact in the process of childbirth. Fathers voice their enthusiasm and excitement about birth; they share the wonder of pregnancy, the excitement of labor, and the joy in sharing birth with their partners. In addition, however, the discussion that follows suggests that biological thinking increases the conflict experienced by men in helping their partners birth babies. A father's responsibilities often conflict with his experience of birth and institutional demands often abrogate the trust of his partner and child.

The Actors

Although mothers and physicians usually share the limelight, here I would like to focus on fathers as leading actors. The plot is the same, but the emphasis of the script is different—fathers have their own twist on the age-old story of birth. Fathers describe the drama of birth from the start, through missteps and mastery, to the final glorious finish. They suffer through the pleasures and pitfalls of accompanying their wives from the first hesitant days to the final hours of holding that new baby. Although I draw on a variety of voices to illustrate the father's story, I focus on five men: Mark, Kevin, Nicolas, Edward, and Martin, who illustrate the kinds of experiences that men have. Each father's story is unique; some suffered miscarriages, others difficult labors, and two men tell of unexpected c-sections. Although each birth is unique in its details, the stories have much in common. The men enjoyed and suffered through events and emotions that most birthing men find familiar.

Mark

When I met Mark and Mary, they were preparing for their first baby. He had just turned thirty-three and his wife was thirty. They had been married for four years and planned this baby to fit into their careers. When they married, Mark had quit his job as a chef to build a real estate business. The two bought a new home overlooking a rolling golf course, and sold homes in the same subdivision. I first noticed Mark and Mary in birthing classes. They bustled in late, arms overflowing with pillows and pamphlets and cell phones. Mark is a big man, having enjoyed his own cooking "a little too much for a little too long," he said. But his corpulence was more than matched by his energy, and he threw himself into the birthing classes with enthusiastic abandon. He proved remarkably sensitive to the feelings and emotions of Mary's pregnancy and birthing. Even in the classes, he could share freely his concerns and hopes. Also, his cooking proved a hit in the snacks that he often brought to classes. Of the men that I talked to, Mark stood out for his discussion of the magic of birth.

Kevin

Kevin was compact, with a shock of straight blond hair and intense blue eyes. When I met Kevin and Laura, they were expecting their second child. He was a building contractor, and his wife worked as his office manager. Kevin was quiet and waited to be drawn out. But once he began talking, his story was powerful. He talked much about the birth of their first child. It had been painful for both, beginning with serious back labor and ending with an emergency c-section. Both were traumatized by the event and separated soon after. By the time of this second pregnancy, they had struggled through that difficult time, were back together again, and seemed fairly happy. But they approached their second labor with understandable caution. The concern was evident in the care that Kevin took with his wife. Sitting in class, he held his body and arms to create a safe space for Laura. When she talked, he listened, with obvious caring in his eyes. Kevin and Laura were committed to avoiding another c-section (and this time were graced with an easier labor and a vaginal birth).

Nicolas

Nicolas was a sturdy Hispanic man, with a small mustache that added age to his boyish face. At twenty-eight, Nicolas had three children and a wife who stayed home and took care of the household. In our conversations he was gregarious, extending his hand to shake enthusiastically and retelling his story with charm and detail. This personality was well suited to his work as an account manager in a small public relations office. He loved to talk about his birthing experiences and it took us three interviews to get beyond the birth of his first child. Nicolas threw himself into birthing with the same eagerness that drove his conversation. For Nicolas, birthing was a social event, and his most intense memories of the event were of his relations with his wife, the nurses, the doctors, and his new child. He loved being a part of labor and worked hard to do it right.

Edward

Edward was a short thirty-five-year-old, whose compact body and dark complexion showed his Greek parentage. He worked as a social worker in south Texas and supplemented his income by teaching at a local college. His wife, a lawyer, was an inveterate workaholic and stayed in the office until the moment labor started. Having delayed fatherhood until his career was established, Edward seemed eager to start this new grand adventure. As he talked about the birth of his first child, I could see that he had thoroughly enjoyed being a part of the process and felt that the connection with his new baby boy had been profound. But Edward also harbored a deep ambivalence. Like Rob, birthing had seemed to create distance, rather than intimacy, in his relationship with his wife. He walked away from the event feeling that something had been missing or as if somehow they had been cheated.

Martin

Martin was a tall, blond man in his thirties, whose body seemed in full motion all the time. Martin loved conversation and his voice moved with the same energy as his body, rising in volume then plummeting into a secretive whisper. He had an unabashed laugh. He was a computer consultant in everyday life, and carried a take-charge attitude from his professional life into his marriage. I had been introduced originally to Martin by his wife, who talked about his confidence and affability as a birth coach. She had years of experience with Martin's personality and found strength in it. Martin's story was unique in his telling of the father's side of miscarriage. Their first pregnancy ended early. His experience showed how, for a father, the event could be both powerful and invisible. Happily, this time things worked out and they are now parents of a bright-eyed baby girl.

The Drama

The father's story begins long before going to the hospital. Although this chapter opens with Mark hearing the sound of his wife in early labor, our exploration of couvade makes clear that fathers begin their experience of birth long before parturition begins—even before conception. My conversations explored men's experience, beginning from when the idea of getting pregnant became a reality. As Rob remembered, "I didn't start to get ready at any special point. I'd had the idea of this baby, or *a* baby, when I chose to marry Beverly." When men proceed toward birth in this self-conscious and organized fashion, the process unfolds in one extended experience. It develops as a couple plan and talk, gets complicated as they try to get pregnant and perhaps fail, deepens in conception and miscarriage, until finally they maintain a pregnancy to term and have a baby. On the other hand, the process is not always as self-aware and directed; some men have less time to prepare. To set the stage, then, we begin with the first scary and exciting moment when a couple decide to get pregnant.

Setting the Stage

Even after a lifetime of thinking, wondering about, and then planning a baby, the momentous decision to have a baby is often fraught with ambivalence. Introducing a new member into a relationship—or a new child into a family—creates demands and costs that couples are often cautious about incurring. Despite desire, few young couples have an abundance of time or money to devote to such a long-term project.

There is a common perception that a woman's desire drives the final decision to have a child. We think men are not as eager. This idea is taken up in popular culture and contemporary myths: the woman who flushes her birth control pill down the toilet each morning, or the husband who has a secret vasectomy—both taking full and secret control over the decision. In fact, the majority of men I talked with had previously envisioned children in their lives. Rather than a desire that can be reduced to a single drive or variable, the feeling is a diffuse general understanding that permeates a man's life. Sociologist William Marsiglio (1998, 5) calls it a man's "procreative consciousness": men's ideas, perceptions, feelings, and impressions of themselves in reproduction. Although men, like women, want to have children, fathers differ in their ideas about the timing for the start of their family. Many men would delay the arrival of their first child longer than their partners would. To a greater extent, men feel the pressure of financial responsibility as a critical aspect of fatherhood, and try to delay conception until they feel able to support the child emotionally and financially (Marsiglio 1998, 24). As Kevin (the builder) put it in a group discussion with other men in his birthing class, "Laura was ready, but I wanted to make sure my business was stable enough to go ahead and do it."

On the other hand, once the family is started, men desire to move ahead and have additional children more quickly than women do. Men's decision to have that first child is more influenced by the need that they feel to support the family financially. But in a society where mothers shoulder more child-care responsibilities and the career costs of child rearing, not surprisingly, men are more enthused about quickly expanding a family once they have started. As a physician dad wrote to me to announce the conception of his third child in four years, "We've been having so much fun with the first two, we decided to go ahead and add a third!" Another dad, one who waited until he was in his forties to start a family, remembered, "She wouldn't even talk about getting pregnant again unless I promised to be the one to get up and do all the night feedings."

In addition to issues of life stage and stability, the advent of genetic testing inserts a new, biological dimension into a parent's decision to attempt to conceive a child. Like mothers, fathers can be checked for genetic diseases, including Huntington's disease, cystic fibrosis, Tay-Sachs disease, hemophilia A, and even the propensity for cancer. Biomedical advances that map an individual's genetic material become a new measure of adequacy for parenthood.

The fathers interviewed here, though, were generally uninterested in testing for genetic diseases or predispositions. However, tests to define the individual's genetic makeup are becoming increasingly common, and our society continues to stress preference for individuals who conform to widely recognized biological norms. As a result, tomorrow's men will undergo growing pressure to have genetic testing (defining fathers as biological beings) when deciding whether to father a child. As we move into the twenty-first century, we go from defining the "genetically perfect baby" to defining the "genetically perfect parent."

Overtures

In the past, conception seemed to occur without medical intervention. Fertilization could be avoided by diaphragms and condoms, but impregnation was largely left to fate. When Lucy and Ricky got pregnant with Little Ricky, in an episode of the television situation comedy *I Love Lucy* in 1953, it seemed like an act of God. Today, in contrast, conception seems to depend more on the technical advice of doctors and guidebooks. Our increasingly cluttered lives demand that babies happen on schedule. We no longer have "childbearing years"; we attempt to define the month and week in which we want the baby to arrive. If a couple has worked hard for years to avoid conception until the time is "right," there is a sense of power over nature's rhythm. We think that the same medical techniques and technology can initiate pregnancy in a carefully chosen month. Preparing for conception becomes a biological fact and medical condition, not an emotional or spiritual state.

The desire to assert control over conception only increases if couples fail to join egg and sperm in the first months of trying. The timing of sex is determined more by ovulation charts, thermometers, and viscosity tests than by romance and desire. Long after his daughter was a babe in arms, Edward remembered, "After weeks of being told 'No!' to raise my sperm count, I'd get these urgent calls at work or the grocery store to drop everything and rush home." Then, after perfunctory and repeated sex, dad finds himself cast aside like a depleted male spider as his partner pulls inward to wait for the first sign of conception.

If a couple fails to conceive in six months to a year of trying, it raises a series of new medical issues. In the past, attention has focused on mothers' fertility. Men's egos, it was thought, were too vulnerable to focus on them. Even if a man's sperm count or motility might be extremely low, many medical practitioners suggested that calling attention to it might only exacerbate the problem (Marsh and Ronner 1996).

Infertility is more than a personal problem; it becomes a social issue. In American society, the only qualification for fatherhood more important than the ability to financially support a child is the ability to impregnate a partner. Thus, when a man is identified as the cause of infertility, our culture raises issues of masculinity and manhood. One dad remembered, "Rachel and I discovered that actually becoming parents was not a simple matter. Months passed and we were not able to conceive. She became worried; I felt shaken by this threat to my masculine self-esteem. After all, in biological terms the primary male function is to father children, and it seemed to me that becoming a father would serve as a necessary emblem of my own manhood. . . . I shuddered with anxiety when by chance I ran across a newspaper article discussing the supposed decline in the average sperm count of American men" (Bell 1992, 126).

Medical efforts to conceive are complicated and couples seek help from friends and relatives in order to make decisions about options. As the problem becomes increasingly public, a man is forced to present himself to the larger world as unable to fulfill this qualification for masculinity. Where women lean on other women for support, men often retreat into isolation and restrict their opportunities to transcend their feelings of inadequacy. Even in cases where husbands find that their sperm count or motility is not the cause of fertility problems, they are caught between taking care of their spouse and their own fear that they might never conceive. Edward, who later conceived two healthy children, remembered his first failed pregnancy; "I did my best to help her through the ectopic pregnancy and surgery and her recovery, working full-time and all, and then made the mistake of scanning a magazine article about the chances of getting pregnant after an ectopic. I walked around sick for a week." He went forward without ever talking about his fears.

One of the benefits of the medicalization of birth is increasingly to define men's reproductive capabilities in technological terms. Today, we recognize that men's fertility accounts for roughly half the cases of couples that have difficulty conceiving, and this can be explained without questioning a man's "masculinity." In fact, traditionally masculine activities such as drinking alcohol and smoking can reduce fertility in men by affecting either hormone levels or sperm quality. Even prescription drugs, such as ulcer medicines or the antibiotic erythromycin, can lower sperm counts.

Although today's men do not crumble under the medical analysis of their fertility, their thoughts are indelibly changed by tests and numbers and technicians in white coats. Few things transform a man's thinking about his semen more than the biological ratings it receives in numbers, motility, and form.

Men are, of course, more than male ego; infertility extracts other costs from would-be fathers. Specifically, men who desire children have to deal with the fear or reality of not having them. They must face the possibility of not holding that infant, not tossing the ball to that child. In fact, some recent research suggests that the most important psychological burden is not the narcissistic wound of infertility but the frustration of hope invested into the longed-for son or daughter. Men must let go of the baby on whom these unfulfilled aspirations have been projected.

The Curtain Opens

For millennia, mothers' intuition has been the first evidence of conception. One father, Jason, remembered, "She had this dream of sailboats going over the finish line in a race. She woke up and was sure she was pregnant, but she still waited a couple of weeks before she did the test and told me about it. I guess it was good that she had some time to mull it over before I had to start dealing with it." Mothers then waited for the obvious signs of pregnancy: tenderness, fullness, nausea, and finally, the quickening, to establish the fact of conception. Today, a home pregnancy test takes less than five minutes, has a very high degree of certainty, can be accomplished in the comfort and privacy of home— and can include fathers in the discovery.

Just as fathers and mothers share the decision and schedules for getting pregnant, they often share home pregnancy tests. A new private ritual has entered the contemporary birthing scene as a woman and a man watch anxiously for the test strip to change color. The privacy of the information provides a great deal of personal control over the knowledge of the pregnancy. No antiseptic offices, officious nurses, or authoritarian physicians stand between them and their knowledge about their pregnancy.

Moreover, the new pregnancy tests can be performed far earlier than previous laboratory methods. A couple can determine a pregnancy as early as the first day of a missed period. No longer is there the excruciating, yet adaptive, window of time in which a couple can only suspect, hope, or worry about pregnancy. Today's couple has the power to know now, and the speed of home testing allows little ambiguity with which to assimilate the sometimes new idea of pregnancy into their identities and lives. Bart exclaimed, "I was blown away when she came back from the bathroom with the pad and chart, we did it on the first try!" The wondering and wonderment are replaced by scientific evaluations that take precedence over a woman's intuition and the couple's private magic.

Unexpected Events

Many men are faced with the fact that they have unintentionally conceived a pregnancy, and their reactions are as diverse as their personal ideologies and life choices. Some experience little and simply look for the solution to the problem; others resort to profound soul-searching. When men looked back on the pregnancies that started without planning, they often remembered having conflicted feelings. For a man who has exerted a great deal of power over his life path, an unintended pregnancy often ushers in a series of problematic choices. One father I interviewed, who found out that he was pregnant after his first date (with his future wife), remembered, "What did I feel? Shock, I guess, but there was also this feeling of excitement. My life had always been pretty well organized and this was totally out of the blue." Personal attitudes toward the immutability

of life and the right to abortion, which had heretofore been abstract and ambivalent, must serve as the means to make a decision of action. But there is little time for ambiguity or ambivalence.

Many men confront unintended pregnancy as a crisis. This is especially true
of men who have not had children, or who have not had children with their
present partner. For them, the prospect of a child means a change in lifestyle.
Becoming the father of a baby often means a dramatic transformation of a man's
daily routine, with greater demands on time, energy, and money. Many men
who find themselves part of an unintended pregnancy, moreover, have made a
specific decision not to father a child—yet. As Edward put it, "I guess I kind of
always pictured myself having kids, but I wasn't there yet and she wasn't the one
I wanted to have them with." These men have not made the long-term plans
necessary to act as the father that they would like to be. Not the least is that they
have organized their financial affairs (or often, left their financial affairs disor-
ganized) without providing for the increased burden of supporting a child. Men
not in a permanent relationship suggest that the financial aspect of the issue is
in some ways primary. Even if they may choose not to be a part of a child's social
life, there is considerable social (and legal) pressure to remain financially
responsible for the baby that they have conceived.

Access to legal and safe abortions has changed men's thinking about unintended pregnancy. Pregnancy has always been a biological, social, legal, and
moral issue and, in our era, has been unusually fraught with ambiguity and con-
troversy. Legal abortions provide a social recognition of the biological nature of
the event. Despite the ambivalence and personal conflict a person might feel,
the choice to opt for an abortion is, in many ways, to define the pregnancy as a
biological fact.

Little is known about men's perspectives on abortion and their role in the
decision to terminate a pregnancy. Of the information available, mostly from
Scandinavia, it is clear that men widely support their partners seeking abortion
as a means of terminating an unintended pregnancy. One Swedish study found
that most partners agreed with the mother's decision to abort: almost 60 percent of the men "felt positive" about the termination of the pregnancy and only
13 percent of the men had predominantly negative feelings (Kero et al. 1995,
2673). Of seventy-five men interviewed, only one wanted his partner to carry the
fetus to term.

Research also points out that men are often deeply affected by a woman's decision to terminate a pregnancy. Despite their own feelings about the morality of the process, they usually recognize that the pregnant woman has the right to make the ultimate decision (Holmberg and Wahlberg 2000, 234). The process was easiest for men who have firm ethical attitudes about the right of a mother to elect an abortion for a fetus. For them, the process may be experienced as less of a personal decision, and more of the living out of a predetermined (or predestined) plan.

Social factors also affect men's attitude. According to a study carried out among American men involved in legal abortions, most men wanted to father children within a functioning family—when they were capable of providing a desired quality of life for the child. In many ways, then, the choice to abort is easiest for men who are in very unstable relationships (Kero and Lalos, 2000, 89). Whatever their level of concern, many men are not involved in the ultimate decision of whether or not they produce a child. One study of 120 women found that almost half of the group made the decision to abort largely on their own (Holmberg and Wahlberg 2000, 232), and sometimes without their partners' knowledge. One study in the United States suggests that one in seven did not consult the father; a sample of Norwegian women placed the figure at almost one in four (Skjeldestad 1986, 230). This is especially common in cases in which the couple has a more unstable relationship. There is little legal recognition of a father's right to make a decision concerning the fetus. In most states, women do not even have a legal responsibility to notify the father of a pregnancy. Studies done with college men point out that the vast majority of young men believe that they do not have the right to force a woman to have an abortion. Nevertheless, they also think that a woman contemplating abortion should consider a man's desires (Rosenwasser, Wright, and Barber 1987).

The decision to carry an unexpected pregnancy to term and to accept the social responsibility of fatherhood ushers in a new series of experiences and emotions for men. Most fathers in this study looked on the transition with profound ambivalence. In part the prospect is joyful and exciting. On a concrete level, men get excited about the novelty of cuddling this new being or warm to the idea of tucking a child into bed. Even as an abstract concept, the ideas of fatherhood provide a wide range of joy—and demand that dad begin the task of transforming himself into a father.

The Lights Go On: Fathers' Realization

Although pregnancy is clinically determined early in the process, men gain a new understanding of their significance when they see the sonograms or listen to the sound of the infants' heartbeats. Fathers seem to take a little time to become personally invested in a pregnancy. Since many pregnancies end naturally in the first trimester, finding out about conception in the first weeks of a fetus' development increases the time that a couple must wait until there is a fair degree of certainty that the baby will be carried to term.

The process is clear in the experience Martin, who talked extensively about it. He did his best to control his early excitement. "I was getting excited probably about the second month but I still was holding back, so that I didn't ride the roller coaster with her if something happened. I wanted to be more a stabilizer." Martin felt the stereotypically masculine demand that he remain unemotional. "She was getting so sky high about it and I was trying to be the mediating force to try not to get too excited about it. And I wouldn't let [her] tell anybody until January, because I didn't want her to get all our hopes up. I was trying to keep it subdued but we were both kind of excited."

Most fathers cannot help but be drawn in when they hear the first heartbeat in the doctor's office. The steady thump-a-thump resonates directly with their own hearts and creates an almost physical empathy. For men, this swooshing sound provides the first physical connection with this new being. The effect can be almost overwhelming. Mark said, "Hearing the baby's heartbeat was a sort of emotional high; I remember crying and being really moved."

While the heartbeat provides an auditory link, sonograms provide the first visual images of the fetus. Over 80 percent of American couples have ultrasound pictures taken of the fetus, usually in the second trimester. Especially for men, who have not had the same physical sensation of pregnancy, the vision of the sonogram is a moving experience (Draper 2002). Mark continued "I'm not the kind to get carried away with something just by virtue of my job. Someone will promise me a huge sale and until I see it on paper and I have the order in house, anything can happen. I usually wait till the final to get excited. I was very, very excited to [see the sonogram]. That's when I finally went loose."

The advent of routine chromosomal testing in the 1970s opened yet another medical window into the womb and provided a profound introduction to the biology of the new being. Previous generations were introduced to the new child with a warm caress of a mother's belly; today's father is often handed a photo of a row of globular Xs (and maybe a Y). The black and white image, with all the heart-warming personality of a biology textbook, offers objective proof of the subjective reality.

These medical developments force couples to contend with a variety of new issues, from decisions about sex information to testing for chromosomal abnormalities. Even for parents who do not seek the genetically perfect baby, individual traits can be determined with the specificity of a scientific test. Disposition to muscular dystrophy, sickle cell anemia, and more than 5,000 other diseases are being tracked to genetic origins. Parents of healthy newborns touch each little finger and marvel at its perfection; today's pregnant parent can pinpoint specific chromosomes to assure that everything is correct.

Medical testing can also identify the sex of the fetus. Even without a preference for girls or boys, gender is important in a father's image of his developing child. Our culture's ideas about sex provide one of the primary definitions of identity, and fathers often find that knowing the baby's sex gives images to go with their abstract ideas about pregnancy. Identifying the sex allows men to fix an identity on the newborn in a way that seems more important to them than for mothers. Nicolas, whose eagerness was present from the first days, remembered, "I found out. I wasn't supposed to but I did. I called the doctor and I found out. Then my wife found out. I got in a lot of trouble. She wanted it to be a surprise but she found out that I circumvented her and found out. I guess [knowing] was more important to me." This is not to say, however, that fathers are primarily concerned with the sex of the new child. In fact, almost all the fathers interviewed in this research offered that they had little or no preference for a girl or a boy. Rather, fathers wanted to know the sex to begin to think of the new baby as a being.

Mothers and fathers, therefore, have different kinds of understandings of early pregnancy. Mothers have experiential clues and intuitive understandings; fathers rely more on medical testing and biological facts: as Janice stares out the window in reverie, lost in the feelings that fill her belly and her body, Dave stares intently at a black and white picture, picking out the heart and hands from the snowy image. From the very beginning, then, fathers develop a biological model of the developing fetus as the primary means of realizing the existence of the developing child. Like the fertility and pregnancy tests, these additional uses of technology provide men with a new window into pregnancy; but it is a biological definition, not a subjective understanding.

Birthing Tragedies

Among the couples who realize that they are pregnant, as many as one in six will miscarry. The loss can be minor or devastating. There has been a great deal of attention to the emotional suffering of women who lose a pregnancy, but less to men (see, for examples, Puddifoot and Johnson 1997 and Murphy 1998, 326). Men's stories suggest that they also can experience the loss of a pregnancy, but are often the silent and unaware partner in the grief. Where women feel a sense of loss, men more often expressed confusion. The men I talked with suggest that this may be because they feel more distance from the fact in the first months of pregnancy. They were less involved with the social, spiritual, and psychological aspects of pregnancy. Since the miscarriage rates are the highest in the first days of conception, sometimes it occurs so early that fathers hardly realize what has happened. Nathan, an older dad, put it this way to me: "She had a miscarriage, but it was one of these things where it happened really, really early on. It was like there was never anything there." This attitude does not suggest that they are insensitive to miscarriage and does not negate that they, too, undergo a process of grieving and change. But without an internal emotional compass or social norms of conduct, they are not sure how to react.

Martin's wife miscarried in her second month. The loss that they felt equaled the joy that they shared before. But it hit Martin's wife harder, in part because Martin thought that he was different, and in part because he felt a need to take care of her. When Martin first started to discuss the miscarriage with me, he referred to his own rational approach to life in how he experienced the loss, and then shifted to explain that his primary responsibility was to care for his wife. "It was just a sad feeling . . . it wasn't tremendous. It wasn't really overwhelming. It was just a sad thing. . . . I had to focus on my wife, try to keep her spirits up, and so it took it away from me having to really deal with it. But on an internal level, I would guess I was sad because I really wanted children."

Martin drew on two conventional masculine characteristics in dealing with his loss. First, he adopted a highly rational attitude. The miscarriage was not "overwhelming" because he was "very practical." In contrast, he saw his wife was emotionally overcome to the point of needing help. A second masculine characteristic that Martin exhibited was feeling the need to protect his wife. He denied his own feelings in order to help her deal with the loss.

Despite his words and actions, Martin's pain was evident and undeniable. He saw the fetus as more than a biological entity, and his reaction was emotional. His memories expose his grief and the failure of others to recognize it. "I did say that if one more person comes up and says there's a reason it happened, I was going to hit them. Kind of like saying your son died for a good cause in Vietnam. And another phrase is 'Haven't you had the baby yet?' You don't want to hear that."

Men internalize society's ignorance of their loss. As friends and family fail to recognize their grief, men loose touch with their own feelings of the event. Martin continued his story. "I was sad, but the guy really is the forgotten one because we're so concerned about our wives. They're so dramatic and immediate that we focus on them almost from the start and you almost forget about yourself." Just as birth affects a father's identity, the miscarriage also changes the way a man looks at himself. Martin put it this way: "And it did add doubts. Can we have children? That was probably stronger than the sadness, or more long-term, if we were going to have children, but then right away we did. And that concern I'm sure both spouses carry but don't talk about it."

Nathan, whose pregnancy terminated so early that he had little experience of the miscarriage, was nonetheless profoundly changed: "In some ways we had a lot more trepidation [with the second pregnancy]. All of a sudden we were members of a club—people who know that these things don't always have happy endings." Fortunately, Martin and Nathan and their partners went on to share other pregnancies and other babies, living and growing through their loss.

The Show Begins: Fathers in Labor and Delivery

When a baby decides to finally make its way into the world, the father relies on preparation, trial and error, personal ingenuity, and his partner—as well as pure adrenaline. But personal acts and private experiences are patterned by biomedical ideologies and institutions. As the father proceeds from the first contractions to the final denouement, his experiences are tailored and defined by the larger social and cultural context of western medicine.

As I talked to fathers, I found each man's experience unique, yet also socially prescribed and defined. The power of biomedical ideology and institutions to define men's actions and reactions grows as birth progresses. In early labor men and women often create their own little world for birthing, informed by what they learn in birthing classes, yet tailored to themselves. The time is shared with mothers at home, where fathers feel more like actors than observers. Later labor and the delivery itself are dominated by nurses, doctors, and the medical system. In these stages, fathers increasingly find themselves isolated, alone, and often powerless. The process of shifting emphasis, negotiating, and compromising is clear in men's stories.

The Opening Scene: First Pains at Home

The first contractions herald the onset of labor, and many couples remember this time as intense and magical. Until this event, the end of pregnancy seems as inevitable as it does unreal. Now, they are called upon to start down the road to figure how the fantasy of practice might be wed to the reality of experience. As Mark from the opening of this chapter lay in bed watching the words take meaning in his mind's eye, he stepped through the looking glass into another world.

As in conception, fathers usually learn about the labor after mothers have realized what is happening; and like pregnancy, dads proceed through labor somewhat behind their partners. For men, the onset of labor is more than subjective experience; it brings a new set of responsibilities. In early labor, without medical staff to help and advise, fathers often feel ultimate responsibility for the safety of the partner and child. Jerked out of their everyday existence, they are thrust onto a high wire without a safety net. In fact, they feel that they must be the safety net for the others in the act. Few men feel equal to the task. Kevin, the contractor, remembered his first labor: "All I could think of was okay, she's in the bathtub and she's going to have the baby. I was very uncomfortable with that. She was looking kind of relaxed and she said, 'I think I'm just going to stay here a while.' And I was thinking that she was getting so relaxed that baby was just going to come right out and land in the water."

On the other hand, some couples can place their fears and anxieties aside for the moment, and allow themselves to relax and experience the process. For these couples, early labor can be a period of intimacy and joining. Mark, the chef who brought wonderful snacks to birthing classes, shared a quiet early labor at home with his wife. "We walked all around our neighborhood looking at wildflowers; it was a beautiful time of year, absolutely perfect. . . . We had some good talks and she was joking around a bit. She wasn't anywhere near the serious stage. It was really good time together; really special time for her and me. At home I turned off all the lights, lit candles in the house, and put on some really nice music, some ocean waves and stuff and Mary just lay on the bed and relaxed."

Setting the Stage in the Hospital

Once in the hospital, birthing is transformed from a quiet (or nervous) time of sharing to a more public process defined by the biomedical institution. Today, rather than abandoning his partner to a nurse, a wheelchair, and the cavernous mystery of a maternity ward, the father is more likely to walk with her to the birthing wing. The couple present themselves to the nurses' station and are directed to a room. Once there, they are given a few minutes to settle in. The mother is given her ceremonial garb (the classic hospital gown), which she slips on while her partner places the bags in a closet or cubbyhole. Then, with dad standing aside (or outside), a nurse checks the mother and defines the state of the labor. The power of the medical model to define subjective reality is clear in the technical evaluation of the labor. The words, "You're at three" (or one or . . .) seem to carry the same importance as the original pronouncement of conception.

Once settled in the hospital room, couples often expect that progress will proceed apace. They are usually wrong. Many couples suffer a period that birthing institutions define as "little progress." With the disruption of getting settled into the hospital and being checked by nurses, contractions often become less intense, spacing increases, and dilation slows. This early labor is often spent alone in the labor room, having little contact with nursing staff. Men help their partners get comfortable, fluffing pillows, helping mothers roll over, and arranging the sheets around their pregnant bodies. Dads adjust the temperature of the room and bring ice or water for their partners. They provide caring arms as moms walk the room and corridors to speed the labor's progress. Nicolas, the public relations manager, remembered "We put all the pillows in the right place for her sitting position on the bed. Then we got the medicine ball-looking thing out because that seemed to really relax her; when she was in that position it helped some. I got her comfortable clothes-wise with the gown and everything. We basically put some relaxing music on and just talked. I talked the whole time and tried to think of things, old stories, and something to pass the time."

Looking back on this phase of early hospital labor, fathers remembered feeling in control of the situation. They have time to think about what is happening, and identify the stages that they had learned in classes. Men felt like they could be their best selves. Things were not moving rapidly, nor were they doing a great deal, but fathers felt that they understood where they were in the progress of labor and that there was the time and energy to organize themselves to help.

Early hospital labor is a time for both fathers and mothers to regroup and prepare for what is to come. Men might get a bite to eat at the cafeteria or find the phone and call the families. They run home and take care of final details, check on the dog, get a forgotten brush, or bring a favorite teddy bear. Moms still feel very much in control, and dads work off their excitement (and concern) by attending to details that might have been ignored.

With little change or obvious progress, fathers commonly desire a rest of their own. Some came directly from work; others spent the night waiting and watching contractions at home, where they had primary responsibility. After settling into the hospital, they feel that everything is under control and that they can take a break and get their own needs met. Their partners do not always agree. One dad, Richard, ran home to get a sandwich and was gone for fifteen minutes. "I got back to the room, walked up to her bed and she grabbed me by the lapels, pulling my face within inches of hers. 'Where the hell have you been,' she screamed. 'You've been gone for hours!' I stuck around after that."

Nicolas remembered his own experience. "I left and went home for a couple of hours just to get some sleep because I figured she was very tired and I was very tired. I felt if I could get some sleep, just a couple of hours, I could get back in time. That way I'd be okay. That's still a bone of contention with her that I was able to get away and take some time off. And she's like, 'Oh, you should have been here!' And I said, 'Everything was under control. We talked to your doctor. We talked to your nurses. Contractions were still far apart. You hadn't dilated yet. I needed to get some sleep, because we don't know how long it would be. I needed the time.' And she said, 'Oh, *you* needed it.' She was so upset. She didn't want to cut me any slack." It seems that as mothers lose control of their bodies to the birthing, fathers have a responsibility to abandon *their* own bodies, or at least not to divert attention to satisfy their needs.

As couples become integrated into hospital birthing, institutional policy and practice take increasing control of the labor, the mother, and her body.

Laboring at home is an intensely personal affair; laboring in the hospital is a medical process. Fetal monitors, intravenous drips, and enemas are administered with calm precision. Nurses perform their checks and relay the stage of the labor to the physician. Nurses offer knowledge, experience, comfort, and direction, not to mention the more mundane needs of ice or juice or towels. In many ways, large and small, nurses set the stage for the medical performance of the birth.

The institution's increasing control of labor gives many men the opportunity to retreat somewhat from their immediate concerns for their wives or partners. After the time alone at home and the tension of getting to the hospital, the idea of turning responsibility over to someone else (for at least a while) can be pretty inviting. Many fathers take off the coach's hat and become observers. With the monitors providing their reassuring click, they kick back a bit. Nicolas recalled, "I was watching the monitor, sitting on the bed, kind of taking it easy. It gave me a chance to call everyone, because they knew we were in the hospital and wanted to know how it was going—not that there was much to say." Kevin put it succinctly "There was a recliner in there and I just rested, I just read. I'd look at her and look at the monitors."

Men sometimes raise the role of the father as interested and uninvolved observer to a professional level, documenting the process on film for posterity. Bradley (1965, 86–87) suggested that dads take pictures to prove to their grown children that they were involved from the very start. Fathers' efforts have given generations of families the opportunity to cherish and share the photographs of the birthing experience. The advent of low-light video recording has created a new aspect to this role. Video cameras capture the birth without bothersome lights and cords and confusion. Consequently, today's father confronts the suggestion that he record their entire "birth story" with full sound and color. These homespun birthing movies have their models in the videos viewed by birthing classes, although real-life fathers often confront things that do not show up in birthing movies, like the long slow progress of a first labor or a rude nurse.

Although the idea of the professional observer may offer relief from the boredom or anxiety of birthing, it also has drawbacks. Retreating behind the viewfinder, the father may create unintended distance between himself and his spouse. His relation is to the mother-as-object, rather than with the mother-as-subject. His own perceptions of her are supplanted by the eyes of a detached and invisible audience. This was clear in my interview with one father. I will call him

Tom. Rather than rely on his memories to explain his story, Tom considered the video the best record of the birth. We sat in his living room in silence and watched the miraculous event with rapt attention. Afterward, he found it difficult to talk about his feelings and experiences, and often deferred to the electronic record of what had happened. I suspect that viewing the birth through the viewfinder muted Tom's feelings during the event, denying him the full experience that he might have had otherwise. The eye of the recorder not only captured the images, but his voice in the background as he directs the process: "Look over here, Honey!" and "Hold her up for everybody to see!" Each shrill directive emphasized his disconnection from his partner and their baby.

Many fathers spend a great deal of time watching nurses and learning what they are doing, seeking to master the standard operating procedure of hospital birthing. As nurses check dilation and contractions, men work to learn the medical markers that define the progress of labor (or lack thereof). These markers also provide the father with objective evidence, in numbers and printouts, of the subjective experience that he is biologically unable to have. Nicolas remembers "I asked questions about what was going on, the fetal heart monitor, and the contraction gizmo and found out exactly what they were looking for and all that stuff. And so I found myself being an active participant in that, too. I'd find out, you know, what she was hooked up to, what they were looking for, what we were hoping for, what we were not hoping for. And so I kind of got a nice overview of what was going on at the time and it also gave me a chance to be in the hospital environment inside the labor room and just waiting."

Although it may seem that partners are more interested in the computer readouts than mothers' experience of contractions, this attention gives many men a window of access into labor. A fetal monitor offers an immediate and quantified description of events that otherwise he could only imagine. Timing contractions, monitoring their intensity, and referring back to the charts and stages learned in birthing classes are a diversion from the anxiety (and sometimes the boredom) of early labor. As impersonal as it is, medical intervention provides a new, objective window into the labor process. It allows men to conceptualize and establish their own relationship with the labor, without mediation by mothers or manuals.

Scene Three: Tension Mounts

As early labor moves into active labor, mothers have a more immediate benefit from dads' help. The first exciting minutes in the hospital give way to long and lonely hours of increasingly painful contractions in a strange environment. Mothers need support and fathers are (usually) there to offer it. As women fall quiet during contractions, men begin to search their minds for the breathing patterns and relaxation techniques that they studied. Many fathers move into active coaching, attempting to help their partners take control of the labor. Jim (a math professor) reported, "I stood beside the bed and grabbed her eyes with mine and got her to concentrate. We worked on the breathing and I think it really helped."

Most dads look back to this time and remember that supportive words were among the most powerful tools that they had—and that women responded well to them. One father remembered, "I probably talked more that day than I have in a long time. It was nonstop chatter, chatter, chatter. Just anything I could bring up to engage her in conversation to try to take her mind off having the contractions." Birthing classes that emphasized the importance of other verbal communication have a direct benefit for men in early labor. Joe, a grade-school teacher, remembered, "They said 'Remember to tell your wife this and this.' I memorized a lot of them verbatim, just used those over and over and just tried to keep her relaxed. Yeah. Just a lot of the phrases, a lot of the uplifting phrases." The simple touch of a hand or brushing hair from the mother's eyes becomes a bridge between the two. He went on, "I was just trying to get her comfortable, that's all. Any position that she wanted." And Martin said, "I talked the whole time and tried to think of things, like old stories, to pass the time between contractions. Then of course she squeezed my fingers off one by one during contractions."

Mothers still have the energy and time to respond to their husbands, letting them know what they need and desire. The touching and verbal connection builds an empathy that is lost as women's experience intensifies and their necessity to "pull into themselves" increases. Kevin, whose story introduced this book, remembers "that was probably when we did connect probably better than the whole time before that. Because she was lying there and I was holding her hand and I was telling her it was going to be okay. I made eye contact with her and tried to comfort her."

But as men attempt to assert more control over the labor, they inevitably encounter the limits of their influence over their partner. It is not all sweetness and light. Conflicts often develop. Kevin related that his wife's frustration with the IV and monitor and the labor itself spilled over onto him, creating friction between them and undermining the relationship that he was trying to maintain.

As mothers demand more help and fathers need more support, nurses become increasingly important. Couples are in many ways isolated in their birthing or labor room, and the nurse provides the single point of connection with hospital resources. Perhaps more than anyone else, nurses shape fathers' experience of birth. Martin, whose wife suffered a miscarriage in their first pregnancy, expressed the importance of nurses in the birth of their later child. "The nurse attendant, who is in the room basically watching over you, makes a world of difference. And the one we had for the morning shift was a bummer. She was absolutely no fun at all. More detrimental than assistance. Then the other nurse came on and she was helpful. She said, 'Can I bring you more pillows? Do you want more ice? Can I help you walk? Let me spell you, and [to me] you go get a Coke or something and come back,' and was just as helpful and wonderful as can be. It changed the whole atmosphere in the room."

As labor moves forward, medical professionals become more involved. Nurses are more than support; they become critical members of the birthing team. They are the critical point of engagement between a laboring couple and the institution that will deliver their child. Nurses inform the couple of hospital schedules and policies, answering questions about what will (probably) happen in the labor and delivery. Carrying information in the other direction, nurses perform the checks and tests that define the labor to the institution.

Throughout the long hours of active labor, nurses establish themselves as the key medical professional in the room and exert a powerful influence over fathers. First, the nurse's professional air suggests authority. The precision with which she checks a mother's cervix carries with it a sense of institutional legitimacy. Her neutral tone in asking the father to bring a cup from the bathroom asserts her social standing. The manner in which the nurse ignores dad (and possibly mom) in her routine duties establishes not just her superior place in the birthing team, but their inferior one as well.

Second, nurses establish their power over fathers and mothers in being able to see the future, a vision that few parents (and no first-time birthers) share. Nurses wield the wisdom of having traveled this road many times, and being aware of the possible pitfalls and pleasures. Few fathers can resist the power of the nurse's smile as she reassures him that the end is in sight, or squelch the fear when she suggests, "It'll get a lot worse before it gets better."

Third, the nurse's authority is reinforced by her access to medical knowledge. In a hospital, birthing is defined as a dangerous process, and the role of medical personnel is to guide the patient past possible problems. Fathers quickly learn that the nurse is watching for signs of complications. They realize that she holds the secret repository of information that might identify and avoid their worst fears—or herald a safe and happy culmination. It is of little surprise that fathers provide her the status as omniscient leader in the developing birthing triad.

Finally, nurses bring with them the institutional power of the hospital itself. Hospital policies are enforced through a bureaucratic structure in which patients (much less fathers) have little control. Admonitions carry the weight of law: "We can't let you see the test results until . . ." or "You can't go in there" or "You have to wash before . . ." Few birthing fathers have the energy or interest to buck the system. After all, nurses have the power to force them to leave the hospital. That power is often communicated in subtle ways. Nicolas remembered, "Every once in a while they [the nurses] would say, 'Well, we've got to check something' or 'we've got to check the dilation. Would you mind stepping out?' I'd say, 'No. I'll use that time to go talk to my in-laws.'" Men watch and wait and try to read the signs of these new medical rituals—and usually find themselves becoming more peripheral to the central focus of birth. In talking to men, it was striking how much effort they put into the relationship with the nurses, and how quickly men are drawn into powerful and complicated relationships with nursing staff. Fathers are appreciative and conflicted, but they try to ingratiate themselves and find themselves working on their relationships with nurses. They are reassured if their efforts are noticed. Nicolas deserves extensive quoting.

> The nurses were good. They were very courteous and friendly. I think what kind of helped is that I found myself developing a nice rapport with them and I found them sharing and telling me stuff about what to expect and being very candid, which I like a whole lot. I think they assumed I could take any information they had. I remember one time I found that the monitor wasn't measuring things correctly so I said to the nurse, 'You know I'm checking this monitor that's checking the contractions. I think there's something wrong with it.' Because they had taken it off or something when they were checking my wife and they hadn't hooked it back up right. And I said, 'I apologize, I don't think it's set up right. I don't think you're getting the right information.' They looked at it and said,

'You're right.' And they were like, 'Well, thanks for looking.' I said, 'No problem.' I was paying attention. I think they saw that level of attentiveness on my part.

But the father's relationship with the nurses is more than a vehicle into the birthing team; the father is often expected to mediate the relationship between the birthing mother and the staff. As the hours drag on and the mother becomes more tired and uncomfortable, the father works with the hospital to provide for the mother's needs and demands. While in early labor the father brings ice and juice, as the labor intensifies, the father's role as mediator becomes increasingly focused on medical aspects of birthing. As the nurse scans the tape readout from the fetal monitor, the father has the energy and perhaps the presence to ask about the changing heart rate. The father can go out to the nurses' station and ask the nurses to delay the next check while his partner catches a little bad sleep. The role that he has established with the staff becomes critical to his success in satisfying the mother's requests.

As contractions increase, many dads resort to the strategies taught in birthing classes. For fathers who are interested in actively coaching their partners through the most difficult stages, this is the point when they focus their energies to assist their partners through the pain. They rack their brains to remember the massage techniques (and acupressure points) practiced in classes, and use them to rub mothers' arms and backs. They try to guide their wives through the peaks and valleys as they move toward the next stage of birthing—transition.

Given that birthing classes spend considerable time on fathers' prescribed roles as defined by Lamaze and Bradley, I was interested in how fathers described the strategies that they used. Rather than follow the preprogrammed schedule, most of these fathers cast around for the mix of strategies that might help. Joe, the schoolteacher, illustrates how fathers shift their strategies to react to changes in mothers' conditions and medical interventions. He remembers, "We started trying some different positions. We walked a little bit, lay down a little bit. I'd sit behind her in a chair and rub her shoulders. There's so much that needs to be done and I was counting all that time. I got hoarse. They started [oxytocin] and she actually reacted really fast and she was having some incredible labor pains. Then they thought that maybe they had it too much. Then they backed off on it and slowed the pain. I ended up helping her into the position she wanted to be in and rubbing my fist in her lower back to help her through it."

Despite using strategies offered by birthing classes, many men find it is the emotional connection that feels the most important and does the most good for the mother. Men who do not normally think of themselves as being "sensitive," discover that they can rely on empathy to predict and decide what their partners need. It is often unexpectedly rewarding. Nicolas explained. "I found that she had a lot of doubts and worries and that I was there to reassure her that everything was okay and so I found myself becoming more into it. I guess [I was more of] a participant instead of just being passive. I was being more active and I wanted to be. I was really surprised. I really surprised myself."

Just as fathers relay requests from mothers to nurses, fathers are a means for nurses to communicate with mothers in labor. (This is not surprising, as this is the primary reason that Dick-Read first advocated that fathers enter the labor room.) Whether it is news that the nurses will change shifts at ten, or that the blood tests came back negative, fathers often know how to relay information through the haze of mothers' fatigue and contractions. But as hospital birthing is fraught with power dynamics, a father can be used to assert nurses' power over a mother. Fathers who themselves are seeking to maintain a tenuous tie with the nursing staff have little power in the presence of medical authority. The case of Nicolas, who cultivated these relationships, illustrates this well. "I remember at one o'clock she got so mad. She grabbed my arm and said, 'Tell the nurses to give me the drug now,' and she pushed me toward the door. I mean, literally, I flew across the room. And I went outside and said, 'You've got to give her something. She is upset, she's angry.' And the nurses said, 'We can't give her anything. She hasn't dilated; the baby hasn't fallen far enough yet. It's too early.' So I went back whimpering into the room, 'They can't give you any drugs!' She was just *so* angry."

As labor becomes more difficult and tempers strain, the father sometimes feels compelled to insert himself between nurse and mother, defending his partner from what he sees as insensitive treatment. Joe related his story: "Things were getting bad and Laura was tired and hurting and the nurse came in and, basically she was saying, 'If you don't relax something terrible is going to happen.' How can you relax then? So I was very upset with her. I finally went to the nurses' station and asked that that nurse not come back to our room. Send other nurses. Send any other nurses."

Edward remembered, "The obstetrician said it was fine to leave the monitor off. But then the nurse came in and said, 'You're putting your baby at risk by doing that; and you're taking real chances by using a doctor who would let you do it.' I wanted to get up and just push her out of the room."

As labor intensifies, fathers find that it becomes increasingly difficult to continue with the prescribed birth strategies. Mothers' demands take birthing fathers into uncharted waters, and few dads can do more than simply react to mothers' immediate requests. Many fathers find relief from this confusion in the technological apparatus of the hospital, which they increasingly rely on as a safety blanket. Thus, confused and frustrated fathers abandon their coaching efforts and retreat into the medical system. Kevin put it this way: "I was real stressed out because I just didn't know how to help her, I guess. I kind of felt like there really wasn't very much for me to do because it seemed like it was just all medical."

Scene Four: Conflict and Confusion

As mothers move into their most intense labor, fathers begin the most intense periods of their own travail. Although later reminiscences may be overshadowed by delivery, the last stretch of hard labor before pushing is a time of profound experience that is rarely matched in a man's life. The father who sticks with it is accompanying his lover through (what seems) the most confused, painful, scary, and exhausting hour (or hours) of her life. No man who takes part remains unmoved. A father experiences transition with an intensity that is surpassed only by that of his partner. He confronts extreme contradictions that seem to have no resolution. She cannot do it; she has to do it! We have to stop the pain; it is too late to stop the pain! I have to help her; there is nothing that I can do! As mothers confront the impossible, fathers join them in their own confusion and fear.

First-time fathers cannot help but be tossed into turmoil by transition. The order of early labor and organization (albeit with intensificaiton) of active labor is replaced by chaos. Fathers who have done their best to control the labor and themselves discover that the primary task for both parents is letting go of control. Whether dads like it or not, labor moves into a netherworld in which mere mortals exert little influence. Some men, like Jason, accept the situation philosophically. "We did all this preparation and tried to be trained and ready for everything and at a certain point it was totally out of our control. I think one of the big things that I learned from that experience was that when all is said and done we're just not in control of the really important things that happen in life. You can plan, you can try to influence events and stuff but it's just out of your hands and I guess you can sort of be prepared for that, prepared to accept the fact that at some point you're not really in charge of the situation. Babies have been born come hell or high water for centuries and we just have to be prepared to accept what's on the way."

To a great extent, the father's feelings of confusion and fear revolve around his partner's condition. He worries that she is in too much pain, or too tired; that she won't be able to go on, or that something is wrong. But the father also worries about his baby. Is there enough oxygen? What about the heartbeat? A father can always find evidence to substantiate his worries: the mother's white complexion; the nurse's grimace; or the ping, ping of the empty IV pump. Confusion and fear often heighten a father's anxiety until it becomes almost more than he can endure.

Bradley pointed out almost a half century ago that fathers get no respite in labor, and the same is true today. First, births are slow, even for fathers. As labor moves slowly forward, the father's resources play out. Few dads feel comfortable slipping quietly away from their laboring wives for a bland, impersonal meal in the hospital cafeteria. Even if the opportunity presents itself and mom agrees, few men can set their tension aside to stomach an overcooked cafeteria meal as if there was no drama unfolding upstairs. Men get tired and it becomes almost impossible to get rest. As the sun comes up a second time, the birthing dad realizes that he has somehow missed almost two complete nights of decent sleep, and none is in sight. The reclining chair of the birthing room, where he watched the end of the Lakers game during early labor, sits empty as he stands beside his beleagured wife. Fatigue, hunger, and sleeplessness exacerbate the confusion and anxiety of a man's vigil beside the birthing bed.

One of the most difficult realizations for many men is that they can do little to help during the hardest labor. As contractions peak, many fathers find themselves powerless to diminish the pain of transition. Women need to pull inside themselves, turn inward with all their energy, and massage or coaching is often more distracting than helpful. Several men whom I talked with felt succesful in coaching their wives through transition, and their wives express eternal gratitude. But most men are forced to abandon their efforts and retreat—or pay the penalty if they do not. I know. My own wife looked up at me at this point and

screamed, "Get out of my face!" I did. A good friend of mine almost lost his nose
to his wife's angry teeth. He retreated, clutching his bruised proboscis, to a safer
distance and more passive support. For fathers who are still working on breathing and massage, transition is often the supreme test. Most fail. Fathers like
me—who entered transition believing that they could make all the difference—
discover the limits of what they can and cannot do.

It is not surprising that fathers cannot protect their lovers from the pain of
birthing, but it is useful to explore how men understand the failure. As the men
I talked with looked back on it, they often expressed a quandary, alternately
blaming themselves, their partners, and the hospital. Many men talked about
the failure of the strategies that they had been taught in childbirth classes. Two
fathers had these similar reactions. Nicolas remembered, "I realized a lot of the
stuff they taught at the child-birthing class just really went out the window.
Well, I mean the stuff like the focus point and you know, breathing and talking
in a calm voice, you know, we found a picture that she liked and we put it up
there but she wasn't interested in it. She was in too much pain. I put on music
for her. She didn't want to listen to the music. It irritated her. I found that for
her a lot of the stuff that we learned to calm her down was actually irritating
her." Martin's reaction was much the same: "Well, she was a mess. That's when
the tug starts pulling at your heart, when your wife is trying to have the baby and
she just can't go on. The relaxation wasn't working. She was tensing up. And I'm
not really sure who was failing, my coaching or her ability to relax. Between the
two of us, we weren't doing that good a job. Her concentration level kept going
downhill, the pain was getting more, it was just kind of falling apart in front of
our eyes even though [my wife] and I both knew what we were doing and we
were trying to do the right thing."

Although most men abandon formal birthing strategies, they try to respond
to the needs of their partners, reducing intrusive activities and providing more
quiet support. Many times, the simple presence of a partner helps during the
most severe labor. A father who switched to more passive assistance tended to
stay close to the mother's bed, hold her hand, or provide a calm palm or a cool
cloth on her forehead. For example, Joe says, "I put cold packs on her head and
rubbed her hands and feet and stuff like that. I think we tried a little bit [of
relaxation breathing] and then pretty much threw it out the window. After a little while, we just kind of went with our own instincts."

Not all men can be intuitive in working with their partners; some men find

relief by retreating into the monitors and other technology of the medical setting. The steady stream of paper produced by fetal monitors gives them a focus
for their concentration. Moreover, quantified, objective information sometimes
relieves dads' anxiety. It also suggests things that a father can do to help. Intravenous drips can be checked and timed, fetal monitor printouts can be read,
and blood pressure reports can be watched. Although men are powerless to help
directly, technology allows them to extricate themselves from the confusing
state of their partner and make a different kind of contribution to birth.

As the mother pulls inward to her inner resources of birth, the father seems
to rely increasingly on core aspects of his relationship with his partner. What
role do they play for each other? How do they work to solve other kinds of problems? This relationship offers direction to the most effective strategy to help, be
that coaching, holding her hand, or just observing. The exigencies of birthing
strip away the complexities of intention and planning, leaving most fathers with
the strategies that they have developed elsewhere in their relationship. Several
dads who felt successful about coaching their wives through transition referred
directly back to their relationship. Martin reported, "I guess I've always been the
one who took control when things got tough, and it sure got tough there for
awhile."

Intermission: Pain Medication

Many parents choose to use pain medication during labor. Medication integrates smoothly into the process of hospital birthing, almost mandated by the
routine. Once the decision is made to use it or not, and, if so, whether to have
an epidural or an IV or pills, it defines a specific path for parents. The effect on
mothers' experience is clear, and debated in a massive literature. But men are
also affected by the choice. Some men I talked with found their load lightened;
others found that it complicated matters. In all cases, however, they were clear
that the choice affected their role in birthing.

Fathers generally leave the decision of whether to use pain-reducers up to
their partners. This is one of the very last decisions that the mother will make
over the child in her womb, and fathers seem to think that it is her prerogative.
The options are discussed in birthing classes, and over the months leading up
to parturition, mothers form opinions through their conversations with other
women. One twenty-three-year-old construction worker put it this way, "Hey, I
figured it's my baby, but it's her call. I mean, it's not like I'm going to hurt, is it?"

Even fathers who expressed a preference for a medication-free birth felt that they had little right to impose that decision on their wives. Martin, who went through Bradley training and was concerned about medication, remembered this. "I fully expected to have to sign a [document saying] 'I declare I will not use any medications in the birthing process' after the third class, but that never happened. And while the focus was to avoid medication, the number one idea was to give you the knowledge to make the decision. And a couple of months before the birth she decided she wanted to have a nonmedicated birth. I told her that it was her decision. If she had tried to go the other way, we would have talked."

Analgesics such as Demerol provide some temporary relief for mothers and fathers. Mothers retreat into drowsiness between contractions, getting some much needed rest and allowing fathers to do the same. Dads can abandon breathing and massage (which in any event were probably not giving the relief wanted). But dads find that these pain-reducers are a mixed blessing. As mothers' attention to the pain declines, fathers lose the relationship that has been their primary connection to the birthing process. Drugs, especially narcotics, often make it difficult for fathers to feel that they are connecting with mothers. During the height of the drug's power, the father finds himself trying to relate to a hazy or even intoxicated spouse. The woman with whom he is sharing birth has disappeared into a stupor. At its worst, men become detached observers of the birth that they had expected to share. Kevin remembered his disastrous experience with their first birth: "Her water broke in the middle of the night, so we just packed up the car and went down to the hospital. By the time we got to the hospital she was having some strong back labor and she was in a lot of pain; they got her on the drugs. She was out of it and I was really kind of out of the picture. I just watched TV while she slept through it all."

If the decision is made to use an epidural, the mother stays alert, but the father's role as coach becomes obsolete. As the mother retreats into the relief of the anesthesia, the father is absolved of the responsibility of managing the patient. If the mother is still mobile before the epidural, the medicine makes it difficult for her to continue movement. With the mother increasingly immobile, hospital policy and medical directives more closely define the acceptable behavior of both the mother and the father. For the father, this means that many of the strategies that they had previously used are impossible. She probably cannot walk around, and he cannot climb into bed or massage her back. Often the father finds himself reduced to holding the mother's hand and offering words of quiet encouragement.

For the father who has prepared and looked forward to being a part of a birthing team, this can be disappointing. Edward, who had wanted to be very involved, recalled, "I thought that we had been doing pretty well, but I guess she didn't agree. She thought she had to have it, and I think she could have gone on awhile longer, but the epidural let her lean back and relax and her body take over. For me, I was pushed aside as nurses and doctors took over. They shifted us from the birthing room to the labor room, with one of those weird beds and the whole atmosphere changed. I kind of took my signal and backed off and let the nurses take over. I was there, but I wasn't a part of the birthing any longer."

On the other hand, epidurals are usually administered as mothers find the pain of labor unmanageable (or when their fear of the pain becomes unbearable). Most mothers do not go into labor planning on having an epidural, but request one if they want relief. They are an option for both mothers and fathers to stop using strategies that seem to be failing. For the dad who has faced the task of trying to manage the unmanageable labor, this can be a profound relief (his being second only to that of the mother). He can step back, stop the fight, relax, and become part of the birth in a new way.

Dramatic Conclusions: Delivery

As birth moves toward its conclusion, all three members of the little family get ready. The baby moves into position for that final slow slide into the world of her parents. Mothers, tired from labor, prepare for the hard work of pushing the baby out. As all eyes turn to watch for the baby's head to makes it first appearance, fathers wait with bated breath and try to figure out where they fit in this final chapter of their birthing stories.

The internal changes that signal the start of the final birth are hidden inside the body of the mother, but the external changes in the labor room make it clear to the father that something momentous is about to happen. New nurses show up and begin to prepare with professional efficiency. If they are in a labor room, the mother will be transferred to a delivery room. If they are using a birthing room, the mother will probably be repositioned and a neonatal examining table might be brought in. Nurses check vital signs, lift the stirrups, maybe bringing a mirror so that mom can watch. The low diffuse lights of labor are replaced by bright white spotlights focused on the birthing area. For fathers who have struggled with varying success to understand and help with labor, delivery is a new game—and nobody explains the rules.

When the stage is set for the final drama, the obstetrician is called in to take the lead role. If fathers associate nurses with labor, they associate delivery with physicians. The relationship is more than logical; it is necessary. In the hospital setting, the obstetrician is charged with delivering the baby. Mothers may birth babies, but doctors deliver them. As the doctor strides through the door into the room, the energy changes. New rules of procedure and new relationships take hold. Nurses are supplanted as the primary authority and enforcer of hospital policy. Physicians become the directors of the process, with the power to control the mother, baby, and father.

Just as physicians define the role for mothers during delivery, fathers find their part rewritten by this new director on stage. After spending hours negotiating their rights and responsibilities with nurses, they must now negotiate their relationship with physicians. In recounting their birth stories, many men recall relationships with the physicians that were friendly and inviting. During prenatal checkups, these fathers were greeted by the physicians and included in the discussion. They actually felt invited and welcomed into the birth, and the physicians took the time to explain what they might do at various stages. Other fathers found the physicians to be more formal and businesslike. These men had far less interaction with the physicians. (In fact, these mothers had less contact with physicians as well.) They were also less involved in the final delivery. "All I can remember him saying about me was, 'You stand up by her head and maybe hold her hand. I'll let you know when it's time if you want to cut the cord.'" No men felt that their obstetricians were hostile to them in the birthing room. Doctors gave no quizzical looks, no shrugged shoulders, and showed no animosity. In fact, fathers are even more common than epidurals, and few obstetricians can continue to practice without at least patience for dads-in-birthing.

Despite their acceptance of fathers-in-attendance, most physicians expect each dad to recede into the background. He may stand at the mother's head, or wait in the corner, or sit in the "daddy's chair," but he is to stay away from the area of action. It takes little intuition for a father to realize that he is not the focus of attention, that he is not the object of concern. A father is not a patient, but there is little that he can do to help the physician in his work. This becomes increasingly obvious as the birth reaches its final and most medicalized last act. Few fathers understand the intricacies of medical hierarchies, but all are aware that doctors hold more power than nurses do—and that fathers are at the bottom of the list of important people in the birthing room. To return to the theatrical metaphor, if doctors are directors of delivery, fathers are offered a bit part.

Coming into the delivery room, physicians must establish relationships with all members of the birthing team. Most physicians have working relationships with nurses on the ward, if not always amicable ones. Even when the physician is new to the ward, his power over nurses can be asserted in a few, subtle interactions (Stein 1987). With the mother, the obstetrician usually develops relations of both empathy and superiority during prenatal visits. The father, who has the least previous contact with the physician, is the third, and by far the least important, member of the team. The first few moments of the physician in the delivery room are extremely important for establishing relationships on the birthing team. Fathers watch and wait and wonder what is going to happen and what they should do. Doctors let them know.[1]

Since fathers usually stand outside the glare of the birthing limelight, it is not uncommon for them to be virtually ignored. One older dad noted, "I don't think he even noticed me when he came in to check on her, and then when he was called down for the delivery he was all business. So I don't think there was a word or even a glance until after Cody was born." This in itself can speak volumes to a father: the most powerful person in the room considers him unimportant. If there is something he should or should not be doing, it is usually a nurse who will turn and say something like, "Why don't you stand over there until we get this under control." The quick directive will put him in his place both literally and figuratively. The message is clear: fathers are superfluous; in fact, they are impeding the work of those who are critical to the delivery of the baby.

On the other hand, physicians sometimes reach out to fathers. A handshake, a hello, or simply a calming smile are enough to let most men know that they belong, and where they belong. When doctors extend themselves to fathers, it is more than an invitation; the gesture also emphasizes the doctor's social position in the birthing room. It is the obstetrician, not the father, who makes the first move. The father who rushes forward and grasps the obstetrician's hand is defined as anxious and in need of reassurance. The doctor, on the other hand, is acting with noblesse oblige. The inclusion of fathers into the birthing team is not simply for dad's benefit. As was explored in the third chapter, the relationship between father and mother can either facilitate or obstruct the work of the physician. To be

effective and efficient, the physician must establish the rapport with dad that
allows for complete (or at least unimpeded) access to mom. Thus, the nod and
smile become a means of assuring a father's collaboration.

Some fathers and doctors reach out to one another in a manner that almost
explicitly excludes the mother. Martin remembered:

> He walked in, hands in his pockets, and says, "Oh, how are things going?"
> I said "Fine." He looked and said, "So you graduated from A & M, huh,
> you're an Aggie?" I said, "Yeah." He said, "I've got two sons. One went to
> A & M and he played football." And he wasn't paying attention to my wife
> for the world. He was just talking to me about A & M. "Have you seen that
> big housing development north of the hospital. An Aggie guy's building
> that." And he was just going on and talking to me and all this time I'm
> thinking, "Kook!" I kept interrupting him and saying, "Well, you know
> we've been in second stage for 45 minutes . . ." And he's like, "I don't care.
> It's okay. Everything's fine."

The response by fathers to these overtures is immediate and strong. If
Bradley thought that all mothers fall in love with their obstetricians, he might
also have realized that fathers also have a visceral and powerful appreciation for
the physician who arrives to release them from an exhausted, confusing, pain-
filled, and anxiety-ridden state. The importance implied by the clean scrubs, the
control suggested by the calm voice, and the power communicated in the
nurses' deference assure the nervous father that it will be all right as long as this
doctor stays on hand. It would take a very distant and defiant father to resist the
invitation to join this powerful figure in completing the delivery. Whether
the physician actively includes the father or not, the doctor's first minutes in the
delivery room provide the basis for the relationship that the father has with this
physician-in-charge. Then both doctor and father turn their attention to the
matter at hand.

As doctors and nurses move to direct mothers with pushing, fathers often
find renewed energy. They generally stay close to the beds, often near the head.
Unlike intense labor, when men often find that they can do little to help, pushing seems to create a new (and carefully delimited) place for fathers. They hold
hands, wipe brows, repeat those calming, supportive lines that have previously
helped, and maybe offer verbal cues like "hold that breath." Few women want
the distraction of any more extensive physical contact. Nicolas described find-

ing footing again with his wife: "I could see that she was having a hard time pushing, so I just grabbed her hand and she grabbed my hand. 'I think you've got to do it,' I said. 'This is it.'" Some dads hold and support mothers. In a case reminiscent of eighteenth-century pictures of fathers in birth, Kevin described holding his wife, Laura, as she pushed. He and the nurse stood on either side of her, with the backs of her knees over their arms, holding her legs up so that she could bear down and push, all the while counting to help her breathe.

As the delivery draws near, a new arena grabs dads' attention. Mechanical monitors begin to lose their importance as fathers begin to see the birthing area bulge. Many fathers are torn between sharing the experience of their partners and moving down to observe the progress of the delivery from her feet. Edward, who was watching his second birth, remembered the delivery in three stages. The first was when he got his first real glimpse of the top of his daughter's head as it peeked through the birth opening. "The doctor said, 'There it is, if she can just hold it right there for a couple of more contractions, it will be time.' I moved down over the doctor's shoulder to watch, and this little dark patch started to peep out when she pushed hard. It was top of her head! I couldn't hardly believe it! It appeared and receded as my wife pushed, and he explained how the scalp was crowning, and how she was presenting herself. It was strange when he used those medical terms, because for me it was all magical and wonderful and weird and scary."

Edward remembered the second major step as when his little girl's head "popped" through the birth opening. "There it was, a little head, sitting right there between Sarah's legs where nothing had been a minute ago, all blue and white. After having been at my son's birth, I kind of knew what was happening, but it's still a shock. I was scared that she didn't breathe or cry, but the doctors and nurses were busy suctioning out her mouth and telling Sarah to hold back a bit. They looked pretty calm so I just held my breath and stared." Finally, Edward's daughter slid into the world. "The doctor told Sarah to push hard, and a shoulder and arm popped out; then he told her to wait for what seemed like minutes. Then he said 'All right, give us a big one.' And my daughter came out in a gush. She was all slippery and wet and clean, but skinny and blue. All arms and legs, not like the bunched up ball I expected. And I looked at her, saw she was a girl and that she was all right and looked up to Sarah. I think I said, 'It's a girl!' Sarah was lifting her head trying to see and so the doctor gave her to the nurse who put her into Sarah's arms. I just about died!"

Every father's experience is unique. Some fathers retreat into their own world. Some fathers are more involved with the mother and less focused on the baby. Kevin, whose wife had had a difficult labor, remembered the actual delivery with a quiet satisfaction, "I was by my wife's left hand, by her head. What I had been doing was putting my hand on her head through her hair and when the baby was born we both saw it." Even when fathers do not feel especially welcomed into the delivery, they share it in their own way. John, the father of a baby born in the seventies, remembers, "I was at the head of the bed at [both of my children's births]. I wasn't down by her feet. We were advised that if we were going to help with the breathing and all that we had to be next to them at the head of the bed. We had no role at the other end. Our role was pretty much to cheer for her. I didn't see much. I mean, they had everything covered by a waist-high curtain. So I didn't see anything until actually. . . . I mean, I never saw the cervix or anything like that. I had no role in either case with the umbilical cord. I didn't really see her until they brought her over and gave her to my wife."

The moment is almost always intense. Videos in birthing classes invariably show the father laughing and crying after the birth. Fathers' real-life experiences are usually similar. Few men make it through delivery without an emotional experience. Nicolas recalled, "I was beside myself. I just hit this wall of emotion. I started laughing and crying at the same time." Birth is also often magical. Mark, who lit candles for his wife at home in early labor, remembered, "There was something really unique there, really interesting. I almost felt like no one else was there. Like it was just [my wife] and me and this baby coming out."

But tears of joy and relief provide a window into the anxiety that fathers feel. Martin explained: "You're anxious about the baby. You hope everything goes well. You want her to be healthy. You don't want her to be in an incubator for a month and you come visit five hours a day. There are just so many things that can pass through your mind. It's all about this moment, and it's pretty exciting: but also nerve-racking. [I needed] a little bottle of courage. That would have helped. It was still a scary deal. I mean, all the toughest guys in the world, if you're going to be there and hold your wife's hand through the whole ordeal, it's scary to you, too.

Fathers' Moment in the Spotlight

If clipboards and stopwatches capture the public idea of fathers in labor, in delivery dads are supposed to cut the umbilical cord. In many cases, this is the most self-conscious ritual of the entire birth. Many physicians who have left fathers at the periphery bring them to cut the cord with symbolic flourish. Some dads want to do it; others simply do not. If the father is to cut the cord, the sterile scissors are handed to him and he is ushered into the bright glare of surgical lights. The physician usually clamps the umbilicus and holds the cord up with two hands to show the father where to put the scissors. In an act that carries tremendous weight in both human history and symbolic meaning, he cuts through the cord.

Talking to the men who perform this modern ritual, it is striking to realize how neutral many felt about the act. After the rush of emotions of birth and the relief of the anxiety of delivery, one might expect a third great wave of emotion as the father finally separates the new child and mother. For many men, this is the most directly that they become involved in the biology of parturition. But as dads described the cord and cutting it, most framed it in biological, not symbolic, terms. The memory of Mark, a father of three who is in his thirties, is illustrative: "I was surprised and kind of scared at how tough it was. I didn't want to hurt her or the baby, and this thing felt so solid and important. I had to just get my courage together and lean into the scissors and cut it."

The meaning of the act is explicitly defined in these conversations as incorporating fathers into the birth act. Martin, whose obstetrician liked to talk about football, remembered it this way. "He asked if I wanted to cut the cord and I said, 'No, no, I don't want to cut the cord.' And he said, 'I don't cut cords. Who wants to cut a cord?' So the nurse cut the cord. He was just messing with me, I guess, because he could see I was a nervous wreck."

The Director Makes Cuts

Father's involvement in cesarean section birth differs surprisingly little from that of vaginal birth. First, most men who experience cesarean births do so after accompanying their partners through conventional early labors. Most c-sections are unplanned and occur after physicians decide that labor is "dangerous." These "emergency" c-sections occur in a state of high tension. Doctors define what they consider a danger to the health of the baby or mother and respond with immediate, direct, and drastic intervention. Mothers' desires may be considered, but fathers' opinions usually carry little weight in the medical decision. If the physician advises a cesarean, most couples will acquiesce to the knowledge of the obstetrician and agree to the operation. Fathers cannot help but lose their emotional moorings as careful planning and preparation give way to emergency surgery. Kevin, whose first birthing ended in a cesarean, remembered this. "The doctor came in and said, 'We're going to do a c-section.' And they wheeled her out and threw some clothes at me and I put them on real fast. They just wheeled her out and I had to wait until they finished prepping her before they let me into the operating room. Then I sat right by her face and she could see me and I could see what they were doing, but they had the little shield and she couldn't see what they were doing. I could, and they just ripped her open. It seemed rough." Another dad, Jason, remembered, "His heart started fluttering, so we moved to an operating room. That part was really scary. I had a little camera and was taking pictures but by this time I couldn't really be near [her]. There were four or five other people all attending to her and I could choose to either be by her head or down at the other end to watch the baby come out. I was very torn. Because on one hand, it's like, here's the woman I love and she's in all this pain and scary things were happening, and on the other hand it was like, my child was about to come and I wanted to be there. On the other hand there wasn't really anything for me to do except try to help her."

Since fathers in cesarean deliveries have little to do to but hold their thumbs, surgery exaggerates the shift of power to physicians, reducing fathers (and perhaps mothers) to little more than observers. Most men are excluded from the preparations for the cesarean. As their partners are moved onto a gurney and into a surgical theater, dads are placed in ritual isolation, pacing the floor in a hall or waiting room. They are forced to wash themselves and wear scrubs, then are admitted into surgery. Physicians now control all aspects of the delivery. Once admitted, the father usually stands by the head of the mother, visually isolated from the operation as it proceeds, but in physical contact with his partner, with his hand in hers or on her shoulder or head. As the operation proceeds, it is common for men to move down below the barrier, with the permission of the doctor, in order to watch the removal of the child by the physician. Kevin described his son's delivery: "They just pulled [him] out. It's pretty amazing. They just . . . all sudden there's a little baby. He looked beautiful, I mean, he wasn't traumatized by having to go through the birth canal. Perfect little baby."

Cesarean fathers usually have time with their baby soon after birth, perhaps even more than in vaginal birth, for in this case mothers are often still occupied with surgery. As the cut is closed, the newborn is suctioned and weighed and swaddled, and perhaps given oxygen. Then when the nursing staff is content that all is well, the father has time to hold and cuddle his new son or daughter. In sum, the responses of the five men who talked about their c-section experiences were remarkably like those whose babies arrived vaginally.

Afterglow: Fathers and Babies

A father's first minutes with his new son or daughter brings a powerful rush of emotion. Cradling the infant in his arms, a father comes face to face with the changes that are occurring. He gets the opportunity to inspect his baby, her little nose, his scrunched-up little forehead, and the puffy little eyes. Touching this little being brings home the reality of the changes in the father himself. His connection to this new baby is powerful and permanent—and leaves most men forever transformed. Edward remembered, "I wasn't expecting to feel this way, but as soon as she handed me Becca, I like wanted to hold on tight and never let her go. I looked down at her and she was all red and still covered with that white stuff. She gave a little squeal and I just laughed and laughed and laughed. I'll never forget the smell of her in those minutes; it will stay with me forever. The nurses almost had to fight me to get her back again when it was time to take her to the nursery."

Fathers of newborns experience their new children with great intensity. The first minutes (or hours) with a newborn may be confused and conflicted, but most men are also profoundly involved and invested in this new being. Dads stare; they smile; they hold the little thing tight, and they marvel at its colors and shape and weight (or lack thereof). They laugh and lose themselves in the sights and sounds, the smells and feelings of this little being. Fathers feel a strong tactile awareness of their newborns. They want to touch and pick up the infant, and feel a strong sense of pleasure at holding the baby. Dads are aware of and express strong feelings about their babies' skin, struck by how soft and velvety it is.

Greenberg and Morris (1974) have called this experience "engrossment." Most fathers have a powerful feeling of attraction for their new baby, an emotion that seems to come out of nowhere and often surprises fathers with its intensity. Rather than a father's reaction to his child being based on personality or individual interests, it wells up from inside him. It is something that grips and hooks the father. The touch, sight, sound, and smell of the infant trigger an almost physical response. The imagery used by Greenberg and Morris is similar to that used to describe the release of hormones in the blood or the letdown of milk that mothers feel when they touch or gaze on their newborns.

Most fathers feel this engrossment in the first minutes or hours or days of having a baby. Greenberg and Morris noted that these dads inspect each part of the new child's body, tenderly touching each foot and hand, delicately extending the fingers and caressing the baby's pudgy little nose. Most men, like their partners, watch delightedly as the new baby purses its lips to their touch. The attraction to the infant seems to fill the father, its image and importance shutting out other thoughts and actions. The idea of "engrossment: to be made bigger," is literal in that the babies seem to be big enough to fill the father's thinking and feeling. Mark remembered, "I kissed him on the lips and he went like that and looked at me like this and I put him down on Mommy's tummy. There was something else too. At that point right when [my son] was born, it was incredible how I was kind of almost numb. Kind of almost taken in by the whole thing. I was in a daze. Not a daze, I was kind of out of it. Very overwhelming."

New fathers generally see their infants as perfect. Despite the surprises of a newborn, wrinkled and red and squeaky or squawking, fathers are overcome with the perfection that they perceive in the child that they have had. The sight of the newborn's face has an especially strong impact on new fathers. Greenberg and Morris quote a father of a newborn saying, "There was much more character in the child than I thought there was going to be at that stage in the face. I mean it didn't remind me of anybody, but it seemed to have a personality immediately. . . . It was absolutely incredible, the sight itself" (Greenberg and Morris 1974, 523).

The visual stimulation of seeing this new being up close is intensified for those fathers who hold their children in the first hour or so, when many babies are especially awake and aware. Dads experience the shock of the first eye contact with this new being, a glimpse that suggests that this little newborn is not just a body, but also has a mind of his or her own.

Men begin to understand that this new being is a unique individual. Until the baby rests in the father's arms, its identity has been thoroughly enmeshed in that of its mother. But holding him for the first time, a father has the opportunity to realize that the baby is an independent entity, physically capable of surviving without his mother, and able to develop a direct paternal relationship. Nicolas recounted "And holding him as soon as he was born, we made this connection. I mean, he was not even ten minutes old and I found that I was making a connection to this new person just by the sound of my voice. And that's when it hit me that I could do it and whatever would happen from that point on, that it was something I could handle."

Although nonparents are often struck by how all newborns seem to look the same, new fathers are aware of the unique features of their children, and the ways that their babies differ from other newborns. Dads talk about their babies as long or short, about the shape of their heads or the cut of their profiles. New fathers quickly distinguish their new babies in the nursery by looks, and within several hours most fathers can identify their children by touch. Many newborn fathers think that the infant resembles them or their wives. One father compared his three children as newborns. "My others both had my hair, but she came out looking like my wife. Three weeks later, she still does."

Not all fathers fall in love with their babies at first sight (or smell or sound). The feelings begin more slowly for some fathers, as they do for some mothers. After hours of intense focus on the birthing mother, many fathers find that they shift slowly to their new progeny. These men often want to usher their lover back to normalcy before turning attention to their child. Other men, who have had little experience with babies, are uncomfortable with such a small, young thing. Greenberg and Morris suggest that, among other things, the feeling of intimate connection can be promoted by physical contact between the two, and inhibited by the lack of it. Daren, a thirty-six-year-old state employee, remembered being less than engrossed with his first daughter. "I can't say it didn't feel natural. But it was like meeting a new person. And my personality isn't that I immediately bond with anyone that I meet for the first time. I wasn't totally comfortable. There was that sense of 'I'm going to have to get to know her.' My wife was taking a nap and I learned how to wrap her up and swaddle her, and learned how to hold her. Then I felt a little more at ease. Now, [two weeks later] we do so much together and we have so much fun together, it's just terrific."

Engrossment is more than a man's observations and feelings about his baby; it also brings a new self-identity. Most fathers respond to the sight of their newborns with a sense of being more mature and a growing self-esteem. As a father develops an awareness of his new baby, he begins a reflexive shift in his own identity. The father looks on his baby, and watches other people as they meet the infant, and feels different about himself, as if to say, "I have a child, therefore I am a father." With the new role come all the attendant rights and responsibilities. They are fathers!

With fathers at birth, the conventional imagery of mother and newborn expands to a threesome. Mother in the bed, baby in arms, and father moves between the two, supporting both. Although fathers sometimes get hazy about the long hours of labor, few fathers forget the dramatic first few minutes with the new child. The importance rarely fades from fathers' memories. Another dad, Rory, related, "It takes your breath away. You're the first one to hold her, because you've got to carry her from the weighing station and take her over to Mom. It's so special and also being there through the whole process."

Despite the powerful emotions engendered by the first moments of the child's life, a father is usually separated quickly from his offspring. Hospital policy dictates that infants be routinely removed to the hospital nursery, usually within a half-hour, to be weighed, measured, and evaluated. Blood is checked, temperatures stabilized, and antibiotics are administered. Fathers are sometimes allowed to accompany this process, especially at times of day when there are few births. The children are placed in rolling isolettes, and the father accompanies the nurse as she removes the child from the mother. The father holds tenuously onto his child with his eyes, restricted by hospital policy from carrying the new infant in his arms. The experience of Daren illustrates the problem.

> I had to make arrangements to pay for her room before they would let her go upstairs to her room. So I ran off to administration, got the room paid for and I get back, and we're finally ready to roll Debby away, and then they were going to take the baby to the nursery because they had to check her out, scrub her head, and do the things they do. So I followed Elizabeth's isolette instead. And we were glad I did. It's just incredible. The babies were stacked three on top of one another, it seemed like. And I'm watching her all the time. 'She's mine," I kept saying. I was afraid they were going to switch her on us.

Audience Applauds; Lights Dim

With the baby safely tucked into the nursery, or beside the mother in bed, it is time to inform the rest of the world of the great transformation. Grandparents, siblings, and friends need to be called and provided with the important data: the baby's sex, time of birth, weight, and length. These conversations usually take place from a pay phone in the hallway or lobby, or from the phone in the hospital room, unless the happy father is willing to trek outside the hospital, where cell phone use is permitted. In Nicolas's case, relatives were all outside in the hall. "The nurse came in and said, 'Everyone's waiting to hear. We haven't told them. We just said the baby's been born. We're going to let you make the announcement.' And so I went outside and told everyone that we had a boy and his name is going to be Adam. And everyone was just slapping my back and all that stuff and so I was just elated. It was an emotional high." Then after the grueling work and exuberant celebration of birth, fathers begin their reentry into the mundane world. Nicolas continued, "They finally said, 'You'd better go on home. Everything's fine here and your wife's going to go to sleep now.' And so I went to a bar and got a beer to celebrate. I told the bartender I was excited because I'd just had my first kid. He said, 'Well, congratulations, but you still have to pay for your beer.'"

Fathers, Conflict, and Biological Birthing

Men's birth performance has been lauded by a host of new birthing books, joked about on late night television, and evaluated by a generation of mothers with whom they birthed. But what do *men* think about their roles in birth? How do they feel about the roles that they were offered and the opportunities that they were given? Fathers' stories make clear that they are powerfully moved by their time in the birthing room. They talk about the benefits to themselves, their partners, and their babies. They speak of the intensity, the exhilaration, the joy, and the magic of being there. What they say is important for our understanding of fathers in birthing and how we may improve their experience.

"It takes your breath away"

The vast majority of men feel good about being part of birthing. One of the few surveys of fathers' own satisfaction shows that 88 percent of fathers have an overall positive experience. Men felt "in awe" and "honored," and that the experience was "miraculous" and "happily overwhelming" (Nichols 1993). Mark put words to the wonder that he felt:

> I held him for a few minutes while they did a few things and then put him on Mommy's tummy and he was there until the cord stopped pulsing and it was just so . . . Fathers who don't [attend] really deprive themselves. There's something that is stirred up on the inside that is really special. It

was as if a part of me hadn't woken up [until then]. Something innate. I
really started to feel a small voice talking to me and listened to it. And
from this perspective, you can almost say this voice I never heard before,
and so it was very, very deep. Very, very special, and very, very strong.

Other fathers were more objective, looking at what they did and liking what
they discovered about themselves. Nicolas had gone into birth with great expectations, but with real concerns about being able to do his part. Some years later
he looked back on the experience with a sense of accomplishment, saying "I
really surprised myself by taking a role I had wanted to take, but didn't know if
I could." Martin, who lost his previous baby to miscarriage, walked away from
his birth with a profound sense of accomplishment, saying, "Every baby I have
I'll be right there through the whole thing because, I mean, because the father's
the first one to see her because the mother can't see. It takes your breath away.
You're the first one to hold her because you've got to carry her from the weighing station, you got to do that first, and take her over to Mom. It's so special,
being there through the whole process."

In addition to the benefits to fathers themselves, attending birth had positive impacts on their relationships with their wives and partners. Many experienced a new power and intimacy. From the first years of the childbirth
revolution, Dick-Read was intensely aware of the importance of the bond
between lovers as procreative partners. He argued that the intimacy of sex fostered a relationship that gave men special skills in calming a woman in birth.
Fathers who have earned the trust and respect of their partners are in a unique
position to work with mothers who need a touchstone in the fear, pain, and confusion of labor and delivery.

Dick-Read's observation is reiterated by men seventy years later. A solid
relationship becomes a powerful tool in helping a mother cope with the travail
of labor and delivery. It becomes a well of resources from which a mother can
draw. Even established relationships can grow in the trials and tribulations of
birthing, as fathers may find that they have untapped skills and talents to share
and with which to support their partners in labor. An old friend of mine, a math
professor, illustrated this in saying, "We've always been a pretty good team, on
most everything, and it was like we were in there together. And it worked."

Couples find that, as they share this profound experience, it brings them
closer, developing their bonds in new and unexpected ways. Many fathers that I
talked with found that birthing provided a unique opportunity for developing

new empathy, care, and trust in their relationship. Mark, once again, remembered, "There was something very mental , something very ESP, something very deep between us that was happening. There was some communication, there was a link there."

Many fathers feel that being at the birth gives them a stronger bond with the new baby. Being an active part of birth becomes the first step in being a new kind of father. Mike said, "I held [my son] before [my wife] did. I got enough, I guess, of the attachment theory in me that you've got to be involved, you've got to do the cuddling and touching from the start. See, I was never touched by my father, never touched. I mean, not even a pat on the back. So it was a personal goal just to be the opposite." Nicolas put it this way.

> I think one of the proudest of things I like to think is that I am a good father. I think that I'm a better father than my own dad. And I think a lot of it has to do because I was involved in the whole birth. I think my sons have grown up knowing that their dad has always been there. They've heard the stories and they've seen the pictures. The second one, he's even seen videos. And so they know then they can see I was around my wife, that I took part. I think they understand that. They see that I was always there for them. I have been so far. And I think that that has been very important for all of us.

"I didn't really get it"

But there is more to the story. Many fathers also feel unsatisfied with the experience. They walk away from the birthing room with a sense of distance from the event and their partners. Men expressed misgivings about how little they could do to help, about failing in their role as coach, and about their frustrations with the nurses and the hospital. Although men would not have missed it for the world, they would do things differently if they could do it over again. No matter how positive the experience was, most fathers leave the birthing room with questions and concerns about what happened and their role in the process. The feelings are often diffuse and are difficult to define. Jason struggled to put the problem into words. "I didn't really get it, I guess. I didn't really understand what my role was. I got the impression that it was okay if dad didn't want to get too involved; that it was all right. So I really didn't understand what I was supposed to be doing, and I didn't understand what she was going to be going through, really."

Many men, both in my research and in other studies, reiterated Jason's reaction. Nichols' study documented men's satisfaction with their birth experience, but ambivalence was expressed as well. Although men were generally satisfied with the birth, they had less positive feelings about their involvement in the process. Forty-one percent of those interviewed had predominantly negative feelings about their involvement in the labor. For example, these men reported feeling "helpless" and "anxious"; others reported feeling "uncertain about what was going on" or "what to do." They suggested that they had been frustrated, scared, and tired, and were "happy it was over" (Nichols 1993, 102–103).

These feelings of conflict expressed by fathers in American hospitals were similar to those expressed by English fathers. Sociologists Lorna McKee and Margaret O'Brien pointed out that English men have feelings of helplessness in the face of the woman's experience of labor. One father reported, "I felt detached from the proceedings, you know, you feel . . . that there's not very much you can do." Worse yet, many fathers feel like impediments to the process. "[You] get that feeling you're just in the way, and the doctors keep talking to you and just . . . instead of getting on with the job they've got to tell you what's happening" (McKee and O'Brien 1982, 106).

Although birthing offers an opportunity to connect and grow with a partner, it also becomes a lightening rod for the problems within a couple's relationship. Just as it draws on a couple's strengths, birthing seems to seek out and exploit weaknesses. The emotional and physical demands of birthing expose the cracks in the foundation of even the best relationship. So the mother whose emotional needs are not met in daily life finds the emotional distance growing between them in labor; or the husband who spends his life compensating for a wife he finds inadequate will discover that the trials of birthing may only reinforce his perceptions.

The cauldron of birthing pushes relationships to extremes of strength and weakness. Fear and confusion force fathers to plumb the depths of both strengths and weaknesses. The result, inevitably, is a father's growing awareness of both the strengths and weaknesses of his relationship, seeing his partner in both the full glory of birthing and making what he considers shortcomings all the more apparent. Maybe most strikingly, a man sees himself in all the wonderful talents and skills that he brings to share in birth with his partner, yet is bitterly aware of his own shortcomings. As one dad put it, "You know, I really thought I could give her the help to do it the way I thought it should go.

And I learned I couldn't, and she couldn't, and I'm not sure what that means, but it wasn't good."

The Double Bind

In a society that is enamored with extreme sports, birthing is extreme living. It pulls for the strongest feelings and emotions, not to mention tremendous exertion. For the father, the birthing story is an intense drama that transforms his identity and relations with his partner, society, and his new child. After the long and often difficult travail of labor and delivery, the father is invariably transfixed and transformed by the final act in the performance: the birth of his child. As the baby makes its final slippery entry into the world, fathers go through what many describe as the most intense experience of their lives. It provides the suitable ritual climax, raising fathers and mothers to new heights of involvement and experience. Welcoming his new child is usually the most profound and positive aspect of a man's experience of birth. As the birth recedes into a man's past, the memories of pregnancy and labor fade. But the images, sounds, and even the smells of birth he carries with him throughout life.

Given that birthing is so intense, it is not surprising that many fathers walk away from the hospital with mixed feelings. They are elated and enamored, yet frustrated and confused. How do we understand the ambivalence that men feel in birthing? Although some of these conflicted emotions may be unavoidable, I suggest that much of the consternation felt by men is created by the roles that they are offered in hospital birthing. The biological and scientific perspectives that organize hospital birthing conflict with men's own spiritual, social, and psychological needs. To be a worthy coach, fathers are often forced to retreat into the perceptions offered by scientific rationality. They abandon the magic and mystery of birth for a false sense of control.

Not only are their needs ignored in hospital birthing, but many men feel that they fail as birth coaches. Men measure success in terms of mothers' experiences of birth. If mothers feel confusion, fear, or pain in birth, fathers feel like failures. As coaches, fathers do not see the difference between making *a* difference, and making *the* difference. Fathers fall victim to their own (and American society's) grandiosity. By suggesting that men are all powerful, any pain or fear by the mother is a sign of a dad's failure as father, defender, lover, and coach. On the other hand, the father who retreats into his own world feels even worse. He comes to see himself as either insensitive or incompetent.

Why do fathers assume roles in birthing that inevitably leave them feeling profoundly moved, yet peripheral and ineffective in the process? It is contemporary training for birth that leaves men in the double bind. Birthing classes become the prime means to impose the biological model on birth and train fathers in their conflicting and conflicted roles. Instruction and practice are intended to coordinate with hospital delivery, and emphasize the father's role as it conforms to the standard model of American men. The significance of the classes in creating conflict in men's experience of birth is clear: men with greater training for birth experienced more negative reactions than others did. While almost half the trained fathers reported negative experiences during labor, just over a third of the others reported negative experiences (Nichols 1993, 102). Why would the experience of labor be less fulfilling for a father who had trained for birth? The previous analyses of the medical birth and childbirth revolution suggest that fathers are taught inappropriate roles with unrealistic goals. The expectations created in childbirth training are frustrated by the reality of labor in a conventional hospital.

Is childbirth training counterproductive? A careful reading of the data suggests that it is not. Although childbirth training classes increased the level of dissatisfaction of fathers with labor, it also increased the level of their positive feelings at delivery. Although both prepared and unprepared fathers had positive experiences at birth, prepared fathers had significantly more intense positive feelings than did their unprepared counterparts. When asked to rank their experiences as "positive" or "very positive," over twice the portion of the prepared fathers ranked their delivery experiences as very positive: almost half of prepared fathers, compared to less than a quarter of the untrained fathers. Thus, although preparedness creates unrealistic role expectations for fathers in delivery, it provides them with the support that they need to truly experience it.

The double bind, then, becomes a double loss. Not only do men fail to successfully coach and defend their partner, but they also sacrifice much of their own experience of birthing in the process. Most walk away from the experience with a new sense of wonder and new appreciation for their partners and children. On the other hand, few fathers can travel through the valley of birth and come out unscathed by the messages and metaphors that it communicates about their relationships and roles. The final chapter explains why we ask a man to play this difficult role, and what the performance means for the new fathers.

7

Fathers, Birth, and Society

We have long forgotten the ritual by which the house of our life was erected.
–Walter Benjamin, "No. 113" (1979)

Kevin, who opened the first chapter, was initiated into fatherhood by the powerful rituals of hospital childbirth. As he cut the cord and handed out cigars, he filled a much larger role—he was the stage manager in the drama of birth. He performed a carefully scripted performance in birthing classes, the labor room, and during the final delivery. Kevin played the part of a good provider, a trained coach, and a supportive husband in the long and difficult birthing. He left the hospital exhilarated by the little bundle in his arms, yet he was confused and conflicted about what happened to the three of them during one of life's most important events.

The ambivalence felt by birthing fathers such as Kevin suggests that something is wrong, that there is a conflict between the messages that our society sends men and the fathers that they want to be. Although dads were brought into birthing to share the momentous event with mothers and babies, their stories suggest that hospital practice distances fathers from their feelings and their partners. Men are forced to choose between the rationality and power of being coach, and the experience of birthing in connection with mother and baby. They often walk away frustrated by their failure and unsatisfied with their success.

The solution is not to remove men from the birthing room, but rather to adapt our rituals to the kind of father we want them to be. We must integrate men into childbirth in a manner that fosters their identity as nurturing fathers, empathic partners, and responsible members of society.

The Problem

Clipboard and stopwatch in hand, a father is expected to be a mother's motivator, supporter, and guide. In pregnancy, he is to maintain her practice schedule, enforce dietary restrictions, and monitor her physical development. In labor and delivery, dad is to keep mom calm, cool, and collected. He counts her breaths, cheers her flagging energy, and is the rational voice in the intensity of biological birth.

Fathers' birth stories demonstrate that when men coach their partners, they focus much of their effort on power: controlling themselves, their partners, and the birth plan. Men know that the coach must make decisions and act on them. Nicolas put it this way, "I think I saw myself in the role of labor coach because . . . I was pretty much in charge of the whole situation." The well-prepared father goes into labor with a clear course of action; he has a blueprint to follow as the game gets going.

But this blueprint leaves little room for a man's capacity to be empathic and nurturing—two of the principle components of the new father. Our birthing ritual relies on three cultural beliefs about the idealized American man, beliefs that are as outdated as they are unattainable. American men in hospital birthing are caught between a rock and a hard place: if they fulfill the expectations created according to these outdated norms, fathers undermine their connection with both mother and child.

Stay Calm Cool and Collected: Do Not Get Too Involved

First, prepared childbirth practice demands that fathers deny their own emotional experience and stay reasonable in the face of their partners' irrationality. Training for birth teaches men that helping their partners and keeping the baby safe depends on their remaining rational. They learn that they can protect their partners from pain and fear by providing a rational presence to counter their emotionality. As Martin told his wife, "I am going to talk to you about what's going on because you may be a little bit whacked." Men are expected to be civilized and reasonable in the face of mothers' being, as Bradley put it, "nuttier than a fruitcake" (Bradley 1965, 108). The negative formulation of mothers as "nutty" both defines and aggrandizes their male opposites: fathers become logical and reasonable.

The idea of men as a tower of rationality is gratifying for many soon-to-be fathers. It conforms to the traditional model of masculinity in American culture in which men are ruled by their brains. The role of coach is based on a stereotypical idea that American men are rational and that their female partners are more easily swayed by emotion. As a man walks into the birthing room, he carries with him the baggage of this lifelong gender training. He finds it natural to try to ignore his own experience of childbirth as he ministers to his partner. One father reported proudly, "I was very prepared. I didn't have any fear. . . . I handled it very well and had a real good sense, really cool and confident."

Fathers' stories record their efforts to live up to the expectation of rationality during birth. Nicolas told me, "I think my wife would get sometimes a little scared about the changes that were happening to her body and so she just needed some reassurance from me and I would say 'No, remember reading this or remember we talked to your doctor and this is what happens.'" Many fathers' idea of rationality depends on their sense of personal accomplishment, and specifically their work. Dads tend to think that this gives them the tools to be good coaches. Martin explained, "I'm an engineer; I'm very practical. I have a philosophy minor and think things out in a logical way." This sense of responsibility to be a rational coach is mirrored by their expectation that their partners will be driven irrational by the labor itself. Martin continued, "When she decided she wanted an unmedicated birth, I said, 'Okay, but understand that I'm your coach. When we're there in the hospital if things aren't going right, I'm going to be talking to you and I promise not to try to talk you out of it, but I am going to talk to you about what's going on because you may be a little bit whacked.'"

Nicolas described how his wife's pain put him in the position of thinking for both of them.

> The nurse would make eye contact with both me and my wife, explain things to me, then to her, and then defer to me, asking, "What do you think?" And I would talk to [my wife], saying, "Well, this is the way we should go." And so I found myself taking charge. I think . . . [my wife] thought that the final decision would have to come from me because she was very distraught. As well she should be. And so I talked to the nurse and the doctor and I knew that if we had to make a decision it would be up to me and I'd tell her, "This is what we should do, hon. Do you want to do it?" And then go from there.

Nicolas felt an important part of his role in birthing was to *avoid* being someone "who was just babbling on and someone who was prone to histrionics or something like that. You know, I was someone who kind of knew what was going on and I also kept my demeanor and I wasn't overbearing or shouting." In birthing, he could be the civilizing force as his wife descended into physicality, the brain to her body, or as Lévi-Strauss might suggest, the culture to her nature. As another father told me, "I wanted to keep her from getting agitated because she's a very emotional individual. And so I tried to use some of the calming techniques that they had taught us in childbirth, which was looking at the picture and imagining something good and, you know, thinking good thoughts, and playing nice and calming music."

What happens to men as they struggle to stay cool and confident? Although the birthing revolution integrated fathers into birthing, this role of the rational male distances them from their own experience of birth. A father struggles to stay both rational and fully connected with his partner. He tries to empathize with a birthing mother from whom he is working to distance himself. Few fathers can do both, and most men are destined to fail at both; they suffer through birth as neither rational coaches nor empathic partners.

The Politics of Parturition: A Father's Power and a Nurse's Authority

There is another side to the father's role in helping a woman birth without pain and fear, and this aspect is organized around ideas about power, specifically power and the American man. Alternative childbirth models were developed in a time when fathers were idealized as the head of the household. This conventional American model of gender suggests that, even within the marriage of companionship, there is an imbalance of power. The ideal of masculinity embodies financial power, physical strength, public legitimacy, and private superiority. The feminine ideal is then defined in opposition to these characteristics. She is physically weaker and socially inferior. Therefore, as a mother is thought to descend into the uncontrolled animality of giving birth, a father is expected to assert himself over her. He is to exert his powerful presence to prevent her total disintegration. As Lamaze describes, the husband is to "command" his wife to relax.

Mark emphasized this role in working with his wife. "I was looking forward to being a coach. She always kind of needs a coach anyway. She needs to be reminded of stuff and it was really fun because she wanted to listen. A lot of times she won't like the coaching she gets from me; she gets a little bit defensive. But she ate it up and she listened." Despite gratifying the male ego, being given the role of power over a birthing mother has several drawbacks. First, the belief that a father could exert much power over a mother in birth derives from a highly idealized and largely outdated idea of gender. The same social changes that open the doors to the birthing room recognize and legitimize women's sources of power in their marriage. Even as the aphorism of the king of his castle is dying a timely death, we cling to a model of birth in which fathers are expected to exert power over mothers in birth. They rarely do. Nicolas's story illustrates the problem well: "She'd been in constant contractions for at least twenty-four hours and wasn't listening to me, to the help that I was trying to give her. I said, 'Look you've got to calm down' and she'd go, 'I don't have to calm down.' I'd say, 'Look, why don't you look at the picture.' She'd say 'I don't want to look at it!' I said, 'All right, all right. Just take it easy.' She said, 'You don't know how I feel right now.' I said, 'You're right, I don't.' I could just feel that she wasn't listening to me. . . . She just wouldn't listen to me because I'm her husband."

What fathers lack, nurses have. Nurses carry a good deal of authority with mothers and fathers. They have the aura of experience: they have assisted hundreds, perhaps thousands of mothers, and have probably given birth themselves. They also have the weight of technical knowledge. Nurses have been trained in medicine, both the indicators of normal birth and the symptoms of problems. Finally, they have the institutional backing of the hospital, with all its technological, legal, and social power. Nicolas was glad to turn responsibility over to someone else.

> I think she responded better when the nurse came in because the nurse was an authority figure. I think that's what helped. I really do. I was just her husband and I think she needed someone who was in authority, [someone about whom] she could say, "Okay, I'd better do this because this person's [telling me to.]" I think that it was definitely better that the nurse was a woman. I think if it had been a male coming in telling her to calm down she wouldn't have listened to him either. This was an older, matronly woman, who came on and said, "Now honey, you're going to have to relax," and told her straight out. My wife listened to her. She was like this mother figure coming in and telling my wife that this was the way it's going to be. "I'm not going to sugar coat it for you." she said, "You'd best listen to your husband and calm yourself down." And I think that definitely was it. It was a matronly woman who was a very imposing figure who calmed her down and got us through that afternoon.

More than their disappointment with failure, fathers are conflicted over their success as coaches. A man is caught between supporting his partner's power and being a coach with control over her. A father, as a partner, has the capacity to reinforce a woman's identity and perceptions, to empathize with her emotions and feelings. He can support her in her labor, recognizing and reinforcing her personal strengths and unique capabilities. This empathic connection, however, is fundamentally different from a relation that seeks to control a mother's actions, feelings, and behavior. A father's attempt to control birthing is in conflict with his ability to reinforce a mother's sense of agency. He can only increase his power by denying hers. Denying the power of a birthing woman demands that fathers create an alliance with physicians and hospitals.

Doctors, Hospitals, and Dads: "If You Can't Lick 'Em, Join 'Em"

As birthing proceeds, there are inevitable conflicts between the needs of the mother and the demands of the hospital. A father is caught in the middle. He has loyalties to his lover and partner, yet he is under the direction of a medical institution that seeks to assert standard operating procedures. According to the childbirth revolutionaries, dad's role includes protecting the mother from hospital and staff. Pelvic exams, fetal monitors, blood pressure cuffs, intravenous tubes, medications, blood work, catheters, and urine samples become offensive intrusions that distract a mother from the work at hand. Equipment is removed or replaced; nurses check progress at shift changes; and the mother is called out of the bathroom to submit to the technician's schedule.

Both Bradley and Lamaze envision fathers as the primary advocates of alternative childbirth practice in hospitals. Lamaze likens the father's roles to that of the French monitrice who lobbies against medication and intrusion. Bradley understands the inhospitable climate for alternative birthing in American hospitals and suggests that fathers are to educate staff and physicians about mother-centered birthing. Edward remembered, "We had fought off the nurse with the monitor, and tried to fend off the ones who kept wanting to check her, but when they showed up and wanted to remove her birthing bed and give her the old-fashioned regular one, I had enough. I said no they couldn't take it and raised a stink."

Changing standard procedure takes more than one man's voice. If a man bucks the system, he finds that the institution has considerable power over him, his partner, and his baby. Edward continued, "I put my hand on the bed frame and I argued with them. I forget what I said, but I took a real stand. They brought in the head nurse. Then my wife looked at me and asked me to please give them the bed, my fight was causing more disruption than the bed change would. For me that was a low point: I felt like I had really failed her."

In addition to having the responsibility to challenge staff in the practice of conventional birthing, fathers are expected to negotiate with these same staff for professional assistance. Nurses control routine materials, like bed sheets and bedpans. They have important information, such as test results and hospital policies. Staff even control access to a couple's physician. Once again, a double bind: fathers must fight to change hospital practice and at the same time maintain cordial relations with staff who have power over them. One husband, a serviceman giving birth in an army hospital, reported,

> Iris and I were by ourselves in the room and I was counting contractions and periodically the nurses would come in and say hello and check. The contractions were getting shorter and shorter, more frequent, and faster, so I went out to the nurse and said "I'm going to call the doctor right now. . . . I'm going to put you on the phone because this woman's going to have a baby." The reason they were not paying much attention was because my wife was not hollering, not screaming, not doing the . . . things that a woman in labor does. She was doing all the appropriate things that you do in Lamaze. So in any case, they weren't picking up on the clues and it wasn't until I put my foot down and said "We will call this doctor now!" that it happened. So [the obstetrician] said, "Oh, my God. I'll be right over." And we were literally running down the hall because this baby was coming.

Many men feel a need to defend partners from obstetricians themselves. Medical interventions by physicians are among the most difficult to confront. Not only do doctors have authority, but also a much broader range of knowledge. The desire to defend mothers from obstetricians spurs intense reactions. Joe recalled, "I almost wanted to punch the doctor out when my son was born because he wouldn't communicate to me. That was a feeling I had. But I felt like I wanted to punch him out because he didn't communicate, he was gruff and he probably had a big patient load and a lot of other things going on and he had problems with [delivering] my son. But, I had to ask for the information and I felt that was not the way to conduct a good doctor-patient relationship and make people feel comfortable with a very stressful situation."

Nicolas remembered, "I said, 'I'm not going to pretend to tell you how to do your job but I am going to tell you that we request a walking epidural.' And I wasn't trying to be aggressive or confrontational, I was just holding my ground. [I wasn't] going to let the nurse talk me out of it. Because my wife was just saying, 'I got to have relief.' And I knew that that's what she wanted and so we made sure that's what she got and it worked out great."

Although they expect fathers to promote alternative birthing, Bradley and Lamaze are no help in a father's struggle with physicians. As discussed in the fourth chapter, both revolutionaries assert that the obstetrician has ultimate authority. The father is expected to inform the physician of the advantages of prepared childbirth before the event, but the father's role is first and foremost to assure the birthing woman's compliance with the physician's demands. In hospital-run birthing classes, trainers are careful to stress that the physician makes the medical decisions. These classes are more reticent about defining the specific legal powers that patients have in the face of physicians' authority. As men become participants in birth, they do so by submitting to the authority of the physician in a role that the obstetrician defines. In fact, several court cases in the 1980s sustained the obstetrician's power to restrict men from observing the birth of their own children (American Bar Association 1996, 5:4–5).

The structure of power in hospital birthing forces a father to choose between the authority of the obstetrician and the agency of his partner. Those who accept the primacy of the medical institution have few immediate problems. In fact, fathers find great comfort in being able to relinquish their power. As one young dad told me, "I didn't feel a need to be in control, because as far as I was concerned, the doctors and the nurses were in control. I viewed it as their job and I am paying them to do that, so I had no intentions of even wanting to be in control."

If a father feels conflict when trying to defend his partner, his sense of calm is restored if he relinquishes his authority (and the mother) to the institution. The medical institution imposes meaning and practices on birth, uncontested by alternative ideologies. Nurses assert themselves through displays of technology and authority that allow dads to retreat into the objective world of medical charts. The doctor might ignore the father, or forge a masculine bond with him with casual conversation about football or deer hunting (or opera). In either case, the father is co-opted for the purposes of performing biological birthing.

Fathers are rarely aware of their integration into the power relations of hospital birthing, and they do not tend to be indignant about their low status on the team. On the contrary, most fathers are gratified by the alliance with the power of the institution. As masculinity in America is defined in relation to power, most men are aware of the indignities of being powerless, and seek legitimacy from those who have authority.

The process was evident with the nurse who turned to Nicolas and asked, "Would you mind stepping out?" The father who retains his sense of personal power by resisting the request is removed in handcuffs; those who remain must negotiate a means to be recognized and legitimized. Nicolas chose to acquiesce gracefully. In replying "No. I'll use that time to go talk to my in-laws," Nicolas found that his presence on the birthing team was legitimated. As Nicolas continued, "I was really surprised. They treated me as a participant, not as an interloper. I think they realized that I was taking a keen interest in what was going on." The short-term comfort from acquiescing to institutional power may well come back to haunt men with negative ramifications on familial relations. Like Kevin, who left the hospital feeling conflicted, we may wonder how this allegiance affected Nicolas's relationship with his wife and baby.

To Fight the Unbeatable Foe

The birthing revolution taught American men that they could protect their women from fear and pain of birth. Many fathers try to defend birthing mothers from the irrational emotions that increase fear and pain. But if pain-free and fear-free birth defines success, most men are destined for failure.

The strategies taught in birthing classes are powerful tools, but not silver bullets that dispel all birthing discomfort. The logic of the birthing models is impeccable: women fear birth, tense themselves, and increase the difficulty of birthing; if fathers help mothers relax, they permit a quicker and easier birth. Therefore, much of childbirth training involves fathers' efforts to stem mothers' discomfort through the confidence of reason, the control of breathing, and the relaxation of massage. Fathers are trained that this will help mothers stay focused and pain-free during what often is an extended labor. Despite the clarity of this biological approach, however, birthing cannot be reduced to a universal and predictable process. Focus and relaxation may help dramatically, but each birth follows its own unique path. Few women remain relaxed and confident through labor and delivery. Pain-free and fear-free birth is an ideal, not a standard by which to judge success.

Men often want to believe that they can not only make *a* difference, but can make *all* the difference. Most have a great desire to alleviate the pain of their partners and often take pride in protecting them from fear and danger. They become willing participants in a process that is doomed to fail. In short, fathers are expected to use a complex and flawed tool to accomplish an impossible task.

Some men quickly decide that they have neither the talents, skills, nor interest to coach labor. Others, however—those who take up the challenge—usually find that they cannot adequately fill the unrealistic role created by the childbirth movement. They feel incompetent in the face of biomedical birthing practice and ineffective in managing their partners. Kevin, whose particularly unhappy birth experience was recorded in the first chapter, remembered:

> You have this sort of important role to play, but not really any sort of authority. It's one of the few times I took a sort of back-seat kind of role. And so I think part of my feeling kind of bumbling is, on the one hand, I want to be decisive and take care of [my wife] and get her where she needs to be and get her comfortable as quickly as possible; but at the same time, [I'm supposed to] take a lead from her, and she's not sure what she wants or is feeling, either. It's the first time she's been through this whole process and she's in pain besides.

Even if a man realizes his limitations and lowers his expectations, who can watch his partner in exertion, exhaustion, or agony, and not wonder what more or different he could have done?

In sum, American fathers are expected to enact birth rituals that are based on both idealized and outdated ideas about American masculinity. Men are to remain powerful, rational, and in control during one of life's most moving experiences. In contrast, the rituals of Siriono or Bororo call on other women to attend to birthing mothers. Father, relieved of responsibility for managing labor and delivery, has the opportunity to focus on his own experience, rather than that of his wife. Rather than protect his partner, he focuses on this new person entering his world. Rather than attend birth as an objective outsider, those fathers retreat into their own spheres to experience ritual birth: the Bororo father dreaming his child into this world; the Siriono father hunting for the child's soul. American fathers, in contrast, are asked to embed themselves in actions that emphasize rationality and objectivity, which isolates them from both their emotions and their empathic connection with mother and child.

Fathers, Gender, and Science

In birth, fathers are expected to control themselves, the situation, and their partners. Men are to be rational under stress, manage their women, and respect authority. In these demands, our birthing ritual undermines a father's experience of birth, his capacity to nurture his child, and his ability to empathize with his partner.

Why are these roles foisted on fathers? Why must dads perform birth in a way that is insensitive to their needs and those of their partners? Fathers' roles make sense, and only make sense, in the context of the model of birth adopted by American hospitals. Biological birthing maintains the distinction between mind and body that has become a hallmark of science. By separating the subjective from the objective process, fathers' experience is by definition insignificant. The social and psychological transformations of men in birth are ignored because they are invisible to a perspective that focuses exclusively on the biological aspects of a woman's body. If Ernest Hemingway's physician failed to hear the screams of the birthing mother because they were insignificant to delivery, fathers' emotions have little hope of being recognized and legitimized in American hospitals.

American birthing depends on a scientific perspective that reinforces existing institutions of power in medical settings. Rather than a holistic perspective of birthing (which would integrate spiritual, psychological, and social aspects), our birthing practice derives from conventional attitudes about science, power, and gender. Fathers become the rational assistants in a biological process, under direction of technicians who manage birth along a prescribed path.

The link between science and gender has been well established in the history of science. In her groundbreaking theoretical work *Reflections on Gender and Science*, Evelyn Fox Keller argues that the development of scientific thought, from Plato and Aristotle through Bacon and Newton to modern science, has been laden with gendered concepts. Keller points out that men, rather than being neutral and gender blind, have adopted metaphors and analogies of gender to conceptualize the problems and processes of scientific thought and investigation. The homoerotic imagery of Plato's dialogues, informed by the mores of Athenian sexual culture, provides a crucial substrate to Plato's philosophical work. In the early seventeenth century, Bacon shifted the analogies used to describe the search for knowledge into the heterosexual arena. Marriage,

seduction, and conquest became the means to conceptualize the relation between the scientific observer and the natural subject. Nature needs to be dominated and domesticated as a woman is in marriage; science becomes the objective
entity, capable of rendering nature unthreatening and safe (Keller 1985).

Keller finds the basic roots of this dichotomous thinking in the psychological structure of gender. Based within the broad outlines of psychoanalytic theory, she draws on object-relations theory to explain the masculine enthusiasm
for objective and detached observation, as opposed to the emotional and connected experience of women. Boys seeking to establish sexual identity are forced
to define their distinctiveness from their mothers, and thus are forced to separate from the primary figure for their identification and affection. Girls, with no
pressure to isolate themselves from identification with mothers, are allowed to
retain the sense of relation and connectedness that characterizes early infantile
relations. Thus, women's experience of the world is one of greater subjective
involvement, where men's is characterized by objective detachment. Science
becomes gendered as it attempts to explore, describe, and explain worldly phenomena as detached and isolable entities. Women's ways of knowing are relegated to secondary and inferior status in contemporary society's understanding
of the world.

Fathers and Authoritative Knowledge

The medical profession brought this gendered perspective of science into the
power dynamics of birthing. The hospital birthing room became an arena for
competition and negotiation between a variety of systems of knowledge:
women's intuition, men's power, feminine spirituality, and masculine medicine. When a father enters a birthing class or maternity ward, he becomes
embroiled in a discussion about gender and power. The discourse is often subtle and symbolic, but is important in defining his perception of the process. To
understand the father's role in this debate, one must recognize the conflict
between the subjective knowledge of the birthing mother and the scientific
knowledge of the medical institution.

A woman's experience of labor and delivery provides her with a subjective
or intuitive understanding of the event. Intuition is the act of knowing without
recourse to rational thought: knowledge that does not rely on reason. Thus,
intuition is not inherently irrational, but rather is nonrational. The birthing
mother has recourse to this knowledge without undergoing the process of cate-

gorical evaluation, hypothesis testing, and generalization. (It is also important to note that intuitive understandings are not necessarily correct, either. Intuition demands that subjective states be converted into understandings. In the same way that data can support a scientific and logical hypothesis that is, in the final analysis, incorrect, intuitive understandings are a means of knowing, but not of infallible understanding.) Understanding provided by intuition is thus not right or wrong, but another way of knowing experience. Mothers experience and understand birth from their own subjective perspective.

The nonscientific understanding of birth extends beyond the birthing mother to all those with whom she shares her experience. Davis-Floyd and Davis (1996) have written a powerful account of the importance of this intuitive knowledge for midwives. Midwives apprehend this knowledge through their relation with the birthing mother, and therefore they promote and value their connection with laboring women. We can extend the concept of "knowledge through connection" to the father. Fathers have a multifaceted relation with mothers—as lovers, friends, and husbands. To the extent that husbands and partners maintain an emotional connection to laboring women, they have access to the intuitive understanding of birth. Connection, in this case, is exceedingly complex. Davis-Floyd and Davis write: "Connection . . . means not only physical, but also emotional, intellectual, and psychic links. It is not merely two-way, as with the connectedness of midwife to mother, or mother to child. If we were to diagram it, we might draw something like a web with strands connecting mother, child, father, and midwives" (1996, 243–244). Therefore, men-in-connection share an understanding of birth that is both immediate and intuitive. They create a sharing and mutually reinforcing community that validates the experience of the mother in the process of labor and birth.

The intuitive and subjective understanding of labor stands in direct contrast to the objective definitions of labor used in the medical community. Rather than experience, medicine depends on the scientific measures generated by fetal monitors, cervical checks, hospital clocks, and birthing diagrams.

Hospital birthing becomes an arena for conflict between medical and intuitive perceptions of birth. Most labor begins at home, where the couple has the opportunity to share the experience on their own terms. After the couple moves to the hospital, nurses, aides, doctors, and interns all bring their different and conflicting perceptions. As birth progresses from labor through transition to delivery, the scientific perspective gains in power and prominence. Given that the medical birth team feels it needs to coordinate decision-making and action, a competition is created that forces the various birthing perspectives into direct conflict. Symbolically speaking, the candles lit at home are snuffed out in the hospital room. In a hierarchy of knowledge, only one perspective can be dominant. This dominance has been termed the "authoritative knowledge." As such, it creates and recreates a perception of reality that is both self-contained and self-validating. In achieving dominance, the medical ideology asserts hegemony over ideas with less institutional power.

The conflict is played out and resolved in the theater of the birthing ritual. As the physician interacts with staff and parents, rights are defined and superiority given to the medical knowledge. The physician asks the nurse to get the fetal monitor report, both establishing a medical definition of the labor's progress and emphasizing the doctor's superiority on the birthing team. In reporting that the labor is not progressing fast enough, or that it is moving along at a good pace, the obstetrician asserts a scientific definition of what, to the mother, is the experience of birthing.

Authoritative knowledge is persuasive because it seems natural, reasonable, and consensually constructed. For the same reason, it also carries the possibility of powerful sanctions, ranging from exclusion from the social group to physical coerciveness (Jordan 1992). Thus, the couple that abandons the external fetal monitor when the nurse leaves the room is told that they are placing their baby in grave danger, or the mother who attempts to walk to the bathroom is told that she might fall and hurt the baby.

Pierre Bourdieu argues that social institutions and relations are critical for the ascendance of authoritative knowledge. Writing in 1977, he suggested:

[Formal schooling] succeeds in obtaining from the dominated classes a recognition of legitimate knowledge and know-how (e.g., in law, medicine, technology, entertainment, or art), entailing the devaluation of the knowledge and know-how they effectively command (customary law, home medicine, craft techniques, folk art, and language, and all the lore handed on in the hedge-school of the witch and the shepherd . . .) and so providing a market for material and especially symbolic products of which the means of production are virtually monopolized by the dominant classes (clinical diagnosis, legal advice, the culture industry, etc.). (Bourdieu 1977, 42)

As social science shifted from analyzing social institutions to the study of ideology, gender research focused on the hegemony of institutions that wield authoritative knowledge. In the same way that the American Medical Association disempowered midwives, the medical institution asserted power over the natural birthing movement, transforming it into classes and procedures for prepared birthing. Scientific and medical knowledge asserted dominance over mothers' and fathers' experience of birth. Birth becomes understood as a biological process and accepted as fact.

Fathers, Social Conflict, and Negotiation in Birthing

Recognizing these conflicting ideologies, it is easy to see why hospitals and physicians traditionally excluded fathers from birthing. If birth is defined as a biological act performed by (or on) women, then fathers had no place in the process. Observers take up space and time and energy that can be used more efficiently on patients. Moreover, without fathers, it was much easier to isolate the biological aspects of labor and delivery from the spiritual, psychological, and social context of birthing.

Americans' demands for a more family-centered birth opened a dialogue between the authoritative and the intuitive models of the process, and fathers' reintegration into birthing might strengthen the power of the latter perspective. A father's personal attentions to the mother, his efforts to calm her fears and manage her pain, and his own experience of the birth can legitimize and reinforce a woman's own understanding of birth. His presence calls up various aspects of a birthing woman: as a father, he elicits her identity as a mother; his being a husband emphasizes her being a wife; the fact that he was her lover makes clear that she loved. Birthing stories make it clear that fathers' involvement counters the medical message that birth is a simple biological process. The father's help, bringing ice chips or adjusting pillows, offers more than physical comfort. His touch, glance, and smile reinforce a mother's sense of herself. The simple presence of her partner across the room watching television is familiar, countering the unfamiliar sights, sounds, and smells of the hospital. As Edward remembered, "We were getting settled in the room and the nurse came in and gave my wife one of those silly hospital gowns that is open in the back. When my wife turned it down, saying she would wear her flannel nightgown, the nurse said with disdain 'Why do that, you'll just get blood all over it!' We just kind of looked at each other, laughed, and my wife put her own nightgown on."

Joining together, Edward and his wife could recognize the importance of familiar clothing and deflect the power of the nurse's statement.

In a more active sense, fathers often are successful in challenging the
impersonal policies and misguided practices of hospitals and physicians. Dads
who argue for a change of nurse, as Joe did, or for a better birthing bed can win
important battles in the struggle against the hospital's practice of birth. When
a husband supports his wife in convincing the physician to let her labor awhile
longer before intervention, he is promoting their idea of birth over that
imposed by medicine. As he reminds the nurse that they will keep the baby
with them and not release her to the nursery, he is asserting their rights against
those of hospital policy. Parents often score victories in the battle between
birthing models. The flannel nightgown may seem small, but for Edward it
became a symbol of what they wanted out of birth—and the possibility of
achieving it.

The Price Men Pay

Although men's involvement in birth has been profoundly positive for mothers,
the success that they enjoy comes at a high cost to fathers' experience. As couples share the joys of birth, men find themselves embroiled in a variety of unexpected and often unwelcome issues. Fathers' interventions encounter fierce
institutional resistance; and the fathers usually lose. Rather than the personal,
family-centered birth that couples envision, mothers are run through the standard process, having their birth defined and managed by medical models, scientific instruments, and hospital policies. Despite their efforts, men leave the
birthing room with the feeling that they have failed themselves, their partners,
and their children. Fathers' experience results from the larger social conflicts
concerning science, gender, and power. Fathers are caught between competing
ideologies of medicine; they also come into conflict with the existing structures
of power in hospital birthing.

First, as men become more involved in birth, they encounter a biological
model that does not recognize their significance. Men are most involved during
the intimate moments early in labor, often at home, while they and their partners manage and experience labor together. Not coincidentally, this is when
fathers feel the most connected with mothers, and when they feel that their contributions are important. This is the time that Mark lit candles and shared a
long romantic walk with Mary, for instance. But things usually change once a

couple reaches the hospital. Staff bustle in and out; tests are performed on the mother's body; and instruments spit out reports of the labor's progress. After experiencing early labor as full members of the team, fathers are replaced by technicians and specialists.

Even worse than unnecessary, fathers are often invisible in hospital birthing. Dads are transformed into aides or nursing assistants, as if their sole purpose were to make labor more efficient and delivery quicker. If fathers tire or fail to keep labor on schedule, as usually happens, they are shunted into an armchair or corner, handed a video camera or a TV remote, and expected to be content to observe. Only in the final moments of the birth are they permitted to come forth and occupy an important position in the birthing spotlight. Then, directed to the appropriate spot, fathers are told that by catching the baby or cutting the umbilicus, they are performing an important role in the birth of their child.

Just as the biological ideology is ignorant of mothers' understanding, it leaves no room for fathers' subjective and intuitive experience of birth. The distinction between mind and body ignores the psychological and spiritual dimensions of birth. If there is scant attention paid to a mother's experience of birth, there is even less to a father's. The essentialist aspect of the biological model ignores fathers because they are men. Birth is not just for bodies; it is for *women's* bodies. As fathers are believed to make their singular, cellular contribution at conception, their masculine responsibilities are fulfilled long before labor. Finally, by defining a single and specific individual as a patient, the medical system renders the father invisible to the process. His relationships as a husband, lover, father, and friend are only important in their capacity to facilitate the biology of birth. As the biology of birth moves forward, men find themselves pushed aside, or reduced to practical nurses, managing the most mundane and insignificant tasks in a highly choreographed drama.

Second, birthing fathers face social conflict in their relations with the structure of power in hospital birthing. When men enter the birthing room, they confront a system that is hostile to their participation and their power. To the extent that fathers lobby for any deviation from the standard procedure, they confront established systems and vested interests. As couples increasingly choose strategies of childbirth that differ from the medical norm, more men are asked to mediate between medical professionals and birthing women, not to mention the arriving child. Birthing rooms become an arena for conflict. The biological model does not include fathers as participants in birth or as advocates for the birthing mother. The medical community welcomes fathers into the medical setting to make labor and delivery more efficient, not to promote mother-centered or family-centered birthing. When fathers assert themselves to challenge the established process of birth or to question medical decisions, they experience hostility from hospital staff and physicians.

For couples who identify the inherent conflict between birthing couples and the medical establishment, this conflict can be an opportunity to join forces. Having a common enemy can create strong alliances, and couples might bond over their shared experience and resist medical understandings of birth. In practice, however, birthing makes it almost impossible to stand together against the pervasive, powerful system.

A birthing father has divided loyalties and little power. Despite his relation with the mother, a man must work with nurses and coordinate with physicians. It is critical that a father create a relation with the powerful managers of the birth process. Issues arise in most cases that pit the will and the good of the institution against those of the mother. Fathers can either challenge the medical system at great personal risk, or cooperate with the institution at great personal loss. If fathers are going to be present, nurses and physicians have a great deal to gain by integrating fathers into the existing structure of power in birth.

Fathers usually are assimilated into the existing medical system. The power assumed by the professionals, the rationality implied by the numbers and tests, and the security of seemingly infallible technology conspire to win men over to the dominant model of hospital birth. Despite the lip service paid to mothers' power and feelings, fathers become co-opted into a hierarchy of birthing that differs little from that despised era when dads were isolated in the maternity waiting room.

Thus, although fathers discover that birth is filled with wonder and beauty, there is often another side to their experience. Many men feel insignificant in the process or find themselves awash in a sea of loyalties. At a time when they are realizing what is often a long-anticipated dream, they are unsure of their role, rights, and responsibilities. Without a sense of their clear direction and control, they become willing members of a birthing team that respects neither their contribution nor experience.

Developing New Rituals for New Fathers

The American father is missing. The model of dad as the strong, silent family man and the head of the household is no longer salient, or even possible. The man of the house joins the paternal figure of Robert Young in the early television show *Father Knows Best* as a myth of American life. Professional careers, self-employment, and second jobs force fathers (and mothers) to devote themselves to work rather than to family. Some social scientists even suggest that fatherhood is dead, pointing to the demise of the traditional roles for men as breadwinners, authoritarian figures, and (with cloning) even sperm donors.

Despite the assertions of these prognosticators, fatherhood is not disappearing, just changing. From Robert Bly's search for fathers as role models to the 1996 Million Man March on Washington by fathers as role models, men are being called back to the family fold. (See Bly 1990 and Cottman 1995 for more on this subject.) The American search for fathers has been answered by a generation of young men who are reaching out to become the kind of fathers that they never had. After generations of being stern breadwinners, men are accepting the opportunity to be integrated into their children's lives.

The exciting changes in fatherhood are only the most recent transformation of the American paternal role. Fathers are as old as humanity itself and fatherhood has meant something different to each generation. Throughout time and space, fathers have asserted paternal presence in a bewildering variety of roles and relations. The Victorian patriarch would have been shocked by the doting fathers of the eighteenth century. Even today, no two societies or ethnic groups or religions agree on exactly what a father should do or how he should act. The Ibo father who asserts no interest in the biological paternity of his children would mystify the contemporary American father. The Kayapó father might criticize the suburban dad who shares his house with his children. Likewise, the 1950s father might be equally perplexed at his twenty-first-century grandson who changes diapers and cuddles his babies to sleep.

The New American Father

For many men, fatherhood is a grand opportunity to develop new skills and their nurturing selves. Those men for whom patience and compassion have been of little use at work, in school, or with friends, can at last discover their empathy and vulnerability as fathers. But today's dads have little help in developing this new, nurturing identity. They have neither the training nor the experience for the new job; nor are the historical models that they are offered much help.

First, American society provides no template for the new father. Historical models of fatherhood emphasize the father as the paterfamilias, the titular head of the family. The stereotypical American family was defined in the ideal of late nineteenth century Victorian society. Mothers developed affective bonds with children; fathers were distant and authoritarian, entering the nursery only to mete out punishment. Neither the factory nor the farm fostered fathers who shared the daily tasks of child care with mothers. As we look back, we see our own fathers and grandfathers as breadwinners and patriarchs, not wiping tears and tucking in babies. When fathers are asked to remember their interactions with their own dads, the most common memories are verbal and physical discipline, not nurturing activities such as long talks or reading or comforting (Hangsleben 1983, 267).

Popular culture offers few models for fathers to relate to the new child. In fact, most of the common perceptions are negative. The imagery of the rugged Marlboro man and the swashbuckling Wall Street entrepreneur are little help to the young father struggling to develop a relationship with his child. In fact, these images work against fathers' new identities. American society suggests that new fathers must overcome their natural and idealized masculinity to take on the nurturing role that is stereotypically feminine. (See Entwisle and Doering 1988 for more on this topic.)

Society is quick to tell men that the genetic cards are stacked against them as nurturing fathers. There is a common (mis)perception that women have an instinctive understanding of their nurturing role as mothers. Based on the everyday knowledge that female animals, such as cats and bats, care for their infants without lactation consultants, we assume that human females have a biological blueprint that lets them feed and hold and change babies without training. Moreover, we expect mothers to naturally feel a sense of attachment and affection for the new beings in their lives. In contrast, men in America have been thought to be following some biological and natural authority within the family. American society credits men no such natural nurturing role in the family. Fathers have been expected to stand over the mother and child, protecting the dyad and controlling the youngster as he or she grows. Although society expects that new mothers intuitively know what to do with new babies, people assume that new fathers do not. (Ask any new father how many times total strangers, usually older and well-meaning women, "correct" the way that he is holding his infant!) The father is expected to be instinctively able to provide for and protect the mother and new child, to keep the wolves away from the door, but he is thought to have no predisposition to nurture and care for his infant.

American society offers no training for this new fatherhood. We prepare individuals for a variety of highly specialized tasks, from driving cars to operating nuclear submarines. We have an educational system that prides itself on providing vocational training to be competent in jobs. But as men spend their early lives preparing to be successful in the work-a-day world or the boudoir, they are not trained in the art of fatherhood. Men are taught to be detached and rational actors in the world, capable of winning at tennis or office politics, but nurturing qualities are explicitly rejected as we train men to be this stereotyped and idealized male. For two decades we train men to be strong, objective, invulnerable, and independent, then we hand them a small, cuddly, vulnerable object to nurture and care for. If this is the mantle of fatherhood, men have good reason to feel bewildered.

A man becomes a father with an idea of what he wants to avoid, but less clarity about the role that he hopes to fill. Many want to avoid being like their own dads, wives, or contemporaries. They do not want to hit their children, and they do not believe in being too strict or too loose. But, once again, these ideas do not tell a man what a father is, but what he is not. A father of a seven-month-old put it this way: "I feel like . . . I'm just crawling through mud. . . . There is nothing clear. . . . I'm groping" (Jordan 1990, 15).

Since men have few models for their own role in fathering, they must create a role for themselves. Men are forced to learn their roles by trial and error (Yogman and Brazelton 1988). Rather than assuming a common and comfortable countenance, they are forced to discover and develop it on their own. Dads enter into fatherhood without a road map, trying on the new part of their personality as they might try on a new style shirt, seeing how it looks and what it feels like and how it changes their relationships with others. What could be more intense than to begin this process in the white-hot crucible of birthing?

Given that our present rituals place men in an untenable double bind, what new rituals should we create for tomorrow's new fathers? In the second chapter, I suggested that birthing ritual affects four primary areas of a father's world: a father's identity; his relation to his spouse; his connection with his child; and his position in the larger society. It is useful at this point to revisit these areas and look at a new kind of birthing ritual for fathers.

Fathers and Identity

A man spends his life developing identities. As a child, he learns to be a boy, a son, a nephew, a grandson, a playmate; as an adolescent, he struggles to find himself and be himself; as an adult, he works to become a man, a lover, a friend, and a husband. From the conception of his child, most especially his first child, a man begins to assume the identity of the father. He undergoes an internal transformation, accepting the rights and responsibilities of his new role. Through pregnancy, birth, and beyond, a man settles the mantle of fatherhood onto his shoulders.

In the same way that birth changes women into mothers, birth creates a new identity for men. But in the United States, contemporary fathers have far less socialization in the arts of parenthood. The nurturing talents of young men get little attention. As Margaret Mead (1928) pointed out some seventy-five years ago in her study of Samoan adolescents, American society provides a young woman with a schizophrenic gender identity. She is expected to be both Madonna and whore; both the nurturing and vulnerable mother, and the sexual and dangerous woman. Although Mead was clear about this psychological double bind for young women, the unnoticed benefit for women is that the duality offers a basis for the transition from womanhood to motherhood, allowing women to deny one aspect of their identities (the whore) and strengthen the other (the mother). Men have no such option. In developing their identities as males, American men have been forced to deny the nurturing and vulnerable aspects of their identities. The stereotypical American male develops a masculine identity around acts and attitudes of independence, aggression, and sexuality. Traditional concepts of American masculinity are not ambivalent. A man has no Madonna identity to draw upon, but only that of the unrepentant whore (or stud, to remain gender appropriate). When this stereotyped male picks up his infant child for the first time, he has had little experience as a vulnerable and empathic nurturer.

As today's men make the transition to being new fathers, they are forced to deny the attributes that were considered essentially masculine, and to embrace those that were viewed as feminine. One father wrote of the realization that he had about sitting in the gynecologist's waiting room in this way: "My work felt like an anchor to hold onto, mooring me to a more familiar world. There was an uncomfortable feeling within me as I sat there preoccupied. I wanted to be quiet, hushed, remembering schoolmarms who scold, not wanting to attract their attention. I wanted to impress with my composure. Hey man, I'm cool. Yet underneath it all lay a primitive fear or anxiety about women. . . . Pregnancy brings us back to that secret sea, the woman's world that men renounce in growing up" (Osherson 1986, 134).

American men in birthing need to do more than just deny personal characteristics that are traditionally considered masculine; they need the opportunity to assume gender characteristics that they previously considered feminine. Pregnancy and birthing can provide ritual to support this change. Recognizing the importance of birthing to fathers, be it in American birthing classes or Guaraní food taboos, men can borrow the nurturing and vulnerable characteristics of women. By ritualizing this process, we set men apart and make them and us aware of the change. Turner points out that rites of passage often include liminal periods when the neophyte has no social rank, office, degree, or (most significant here) gender. "Neophytes are sometimes treated or symbolically represented as neither male or female. Alternately, they may be assigned characteristics of both sexes, irrespective of their biological sex" (Turner 1977, 64). Men in pregnancy and birth can also distance themselves from their conventional roles as men; their sex becomes insignificant and their gender invisible. In terms of ritual meaning, they are either sexless or bisexual, what the psychologist Bruno Bettelheim (1954) terms human *prima materia*, undifferentiated raw material of human being-ness.

Neophytes in passage rites in other societies make themselves subject to the will and demands of elders. Childbirth training as ritual works in part because it does the same for birthing men in the United States. American men who have carefully cultivated their independence and sense of accomplishment (and perhaps authority) are expected to obey the requirements of a range of so-called experts. In office visits and on the floor of birthing classrooms, men find themselves quietly stripped of their identity as electrician, lawyer, or teacher; they are no longer Democrats or Libertarians, no longer of wealthy or modest means. In birthing, fathers find themselves in a position of inferiority, subject to the direction of physicians, medical staff, and birthing class leaders.

Pregnancy offers an important window of socialization during which fathers have a heightened awareness of the importance of the role that they are learning.

Although previous experiences do little to prepare fathers for their new roles, the influence of physcians, other parents, spouses, and (especially) childbirth classes have a great effect on the formation of fathers' roles after birth. The models that men are exposed to in childbirth classes and the information that they are given clarify their ideas about fatherhood and help them adopt their new identity (for more information, see Starn 1993; Jordan 1990).

The birth itself, performed after the long period of liminal preparation, acts as the culmination of this identity transformation. In the intensity of birth, fathers encounter and experience the fundamental shift in personal identity. Donning the appropriate medical garb, a father enters the secluded chamber and after the tense and often harrowing process of birth, is presented with a newborn baby. He leaves the birthing room with a new and fundamentally different identity: the role of father. He signs the birth certificate, sees to the circumcision, and attends the baptism. He returns to work and hands out cigars (or at least jokes about them). He goes home and receives family and friends. He begins the long process of discovering what he will do and what he will feel like in this new identity.

Fathers and Mothers in Birth

Pregnancy and childbirth are golden opportunities for men to create and recreate relationships with their partners. A new relationship is necessary, because couples invariably find that babies change everything. Who would have guessed how sentimental or nurturing he would become suddenly? Although some discoveries are new and wonderful, others are less so. She is so grumpy when she does not get enough sleep! She finds that her husband changed into a father that she has never met; she becomes a mother that he has never known. These two strangers need to forge a new relationship that also includes their baby!

In the midst of discovering themselves and each other, fathers and mothers discover that the baby brings a host of new responsibilities. The baby needs constant care, demanding more attention than any one person can adequately provide. As fathers rock babies to sleep and mothers rest, the dishes pile up in the sink and the groceries run out. In a society where time is already our most scarce resource, couples are forced to plan, schedule, and coordinate each minute of time and each ounce of energy to get all (or at least most) of the jobs done. Moreover, there are innumerable (and unexpected) decisions that need to be made: mother's milk or formula? What kind of formula? What about feeding schedules? Should the baby sleep on her back or belly? With or without a pillow and blanket? What about day care? Perhaps mothers made these choices in previous generations, but in the world of the new father, men are expected to be informed and have opinions about every aspect of a child's care. As couples strive to create a new kind of family, with both mothers and fathers as caretakers, there is no clear division of labor or unambiguous responsibility. Couples must negotiate and compromise, try and fail, until they discover the method of joint parenting that works for them.

The period of adjustment to parenthood is a time for new and exciting ideas and cooperative activities for couples, but it is also a time of greater conflict and confrontation. Neither fathers nor mothers sleep much: the baby needs a diaper, a bottle, a bath, or to nurse (and can not tell you which he or she needs); friends, neighbors, and family drop by to visit and watch. In short, the house descends into chaos. The increased stress and distress that a couple suffers in the first months of their baby's life only exacerbate the problem of establishing their new kind of relationship. It is no wonder that most couples' sense of marital satisfaction declines in the months after birth. Wives feel abandoned to the new baby, and fathers feel ignored and unappreciated (Tomlinson 1987).

Given the stress that a couple will experience after birth, it behooves them to go into the birthing room with a solid relationship. The quality of a couple's relationship during pregnancy is important for their adjustment to parenthood. Researchers from the Family Centre of the University of Victoria talked to husbands and wives during the pregnancy for their first child. They identified individuals who were securely attached to their partners, and others who felt more isolated and tenuous with their spouse. Then they returned when the baby was four to six months old to judge how the couples had adapted to their new babies. They found that the more secure the couple's relationship was before the birth, the easier the time that they had in managing the day-to-day problems of caring for their newborn.

Pregnancy can be a time to prepare not just for the arrival of the baby, but for the new intricacies and intimacies of a couple's relationship. When birthing educators are aware of the empathic connection created in birthing classes, they can shift their focus from mothers exclusively. Good classes already attend to all members of the family unit, discussing the prospects and pitfalls of their changing roles. Recent studies point out the effect of these interventions. The father's participation in childbirth classes and other aspects of his partner's pregnancy led to increased mutual dependence and an increase in supportive behaviors between the two (see, for example, Nichols 1993).

The identity that men develop in childbirth classes leads to "greater equality in marital relationships and is associated with lower rates of intrafamily conflict and violence, compared to traditional male-dominated marital relations" (Diemer 1997, 283). These benefits are a result of both the information that classes provide and the experiential learning that accompanies childbirth class exercises. When a man is asked to lie on the floor in a dark room and envision the child in his body, the awareness it provides allows him to step inside his wife's experience. This task is increasingly being accomplished explicitly, with new "daddy packs" that provide a strap-on pregnant belly and breasts to simulate the physicality of the pregnant mom. As a man focuses on his wife while she acts out the contractions that she expects to experience, he gains a new and visceral understanding of her experience. This empathy is critical for creating the bond and identities that both will rely on in the difficult transition ahead.

Childbirth classes can also teach strategies to cope with fear and stress; this can have the indirect effect of improving marital relations. In birthing classes, fathers and mothers are often asked to identify and recognize their own fears. Teachers can speak directly to those fears, giving couples the information both to minimize chances of problems and to deal with them if they come. What better way of bringing a couple together than to improve their awareness of and ability to cope with stress and tension?

Couples can come out of birthing classes not just knowing more about the baby and what to expect, but having shared concerns and experiences and a greater feeling of mutuality. When a mother and father work together to practice relaxation and positive feedback training, they increase their communication and ability to work as a team. In a study that interviewed pregnant parents during birthing classes and two months after birth, researchers discovered that the satisfaction that mothers and fathers feel with one another after the birth is directly related to the quality of their communication during pregnancy. Those couples who talked in birthing classes about how they intended to divide responsibilities and developed a realistic expectation of the other were more likely to feel good about their partner after the birth. In fact, in terms of marital satisfaction after birth, knowing what to expect of each other was more important than the actual contribution each partner made to manage the house (see, for examples, Coffman, Levitt, and Brown 1994; Gage and Christensen 1991).

In birth, fathers can avoid the conflicted roles of coaches by being companions. Although coaches perform an active role in directing and supporting birth, companions focus their attention on the mother: being with her and aware of her subjective state. As Paulo explained to me, "She just wanted to make sure that I was there; even if I wasn't doing anything, that I'd be there."

Contemporary American men are in a privileged position to share pregnancy and birth with their partners. Today's men and women share aspects of birthing biology that previous generations did not. Childbirth education classes provide men with the personal details of laboring physiology that only birth practitioners or experienced women would have had in previous generations. By the time that the baby is on the way, fathers are well versed in the complexities of menstrual cycles and bloody spotting. As gender barriers fall, men become increasingly available to share, even empathize, with a mother's birthing experience.

In addition, however, fathers often become important companions as women's other relations are disrupted in American society. As mobility has destroyed family support networks and isolated many women from their mothers, sisters, and friends, they turn to their husbands as their principle social contact. This is a return to companionate marriage, albeit in a post-industrial society. Women demand and men are allowed intimacy and connection in their relations. In childbearing, the companionship that begins in pregnancy becomes important to the relationship of the laboring couple. David remembered drifting into his role as a companion: "It just sort of felt natural once we got into the process. I felt like there was a certain point where I was doing what I was needed to do and that felt really good. I felt like we were really working in concert, we were giving birth together. I felt like a partner, the baby was inside her, but I was really playing a role and sort of helping her cope with the pain, helping her get ready to have this baby."

Controlled studies of men in birthing find that the majority of their activities are related to companionship, not coaching. In one study of forty couples observed in mid-labor, when the mother's cervix was dilated four to five centimeters, fathers rarely left the birthing room. Of their four primary means of helping mothers, the vast majority involved simple conversation and direct physical contact. The most common was verbal support—offering reassurance, humor, and sympathy—which men did almost two-thirds of the time. During almost half the time, partners were in direct physical contact with the mother, massaging her back or caressing her brow and arms. Other activities were less common. Men spent less than a tenth of their time doing standard nursing aide work—offering a cool washcloth, a bed pan, or ice chips. Men performed the most stereotypical coaching activity, choreographed breathing, only rarely (Nichols 1993).

When men were asked to rate which activities were most helpful, they most often mentioned the importance of personal contact. Psychological support accounted for one of the primary activities that men considered helpful: offering expressions of encouragement, prayer, or a simple statement that reassured the partner, such as "I love you," or providing a willing ear to listen to her experience. They also felt that the personal touch and physical assistance that they offered mothers was very helpful—massaging backs, helping them pace the halls and walk to the bathroom, or adjusting sheets and pillows. They could help mothers with water, ice chips, and bed or vomit pans. Men often mentioned their simple presence as a significant benefit for their wives. About a fifth of them thought that "just being there" was their major contribution (Nichols 1993).

Nurses, in contrast, were far less engaged with the mothers during the long hours of labor. Professional staff was present during less than a third of this intermediate labor period. When in the rooms, nurses spoke to mothers about half of that time and had far less physical contact with them than did fathers, touching them less than a tenth of the time. Nurses spent almost none of their time doing model breathing with the mother (Klein et al. 1981, 161–164).

In short, more than simply increasing their ability to work together mechanically, the couple, through their physical and emotional contact in birth, increases their opportunity for intimacy. As we invent new childbirth rituals, they need to forge this new kind of relation. The father's warm support can communicate his importance to the mother and his touch can create a physical bond to match their new relationship. The father can step into the mother's skin, at least symbolically, and discover new ways to empathize with his partner. In the classic couvade of the history books, men explicitly felt the pains of childbirth. In the contemporary hospital, the man gains a different kind of personal experience of his partner's condition, but one that can be as effective in building empathy. Isolated from the world and present next to her bed, the man has the ritual space, time, and energy to set aside his other roles and responsibilities and devote himself to feeling what his partner feels.

Fathers and Babies in Birth

Doctors, fathers, and mothers all agree that dads should attend childbirth. They are less clear, however, about *why* dads should be there. Do fathers really ease birthing for mothers? Do fathers have a moral obligation to accompany mothers on their dangerous passage? Do babies need fathers, who are theoretically rested and relaxed, to hold them while their mothers recuperate? These all may be true, but more important, science is documenting what fathers have already discovered: that being present at birth lays the groundwork for a man's relationship with his baby. As we create a new kind of fatherhood, our birthing rituals need to create the script for the father to start a new kind of relation with his child. The father reaches out to his new child; the baby catches his eye, grabs his finger, and melts into his arms; and a lifelong tie is created. Birthing can be the first step in a powerful and intimate bond between fathers and babies.

Although our culture does little to train males to be fathers, even scientists are finding that nurturing comes naturally to most men, possibly even driven by biology. The process has a variety of labels: bonding or attachment, if one is focused on the child; or engrossment, if one is thinking about the father. Early research suggested that babies imprinted on their parents, creating an indelible attraction for the adults who nurture them. These studies exaggerated the permanence and power of those first hours. We know that an infant learns a great deal in close association with a father during the early postpartum period. But there is little support for the proposition that an early and specific infant-father bonding period significantly affects the baby's future reaction to the father. On the other hand, there is growing interest in the possibility that the entire process of birthing ritual has long-term ramifications on the reaction of the father to the infant (Jones 1981).

The rituals that men perform throughout the entire birth process of getting pregnant, being pregnant, parturition, and those crazy days with a new baby can prepare the father to establish a complex and constructive relationship with the new infant. American marriage traditions provide the rituals for the creation of a new personal relationship. From the first crush to the final day of the honeymoon, a couple is expected to obey a complex set of (ever-changing) rituals. The rules of dating, courtship, engagement, wedding, and beyond almost literally choreograph the deepening intimate and affective tie between two people. Few sociologists would expect the time at the altar to be *the* fundamental force in forging the bond between the new couple. Likewise, we do not suggest that the time that a man spends in the birthing room determines his future tie to his child. But the entire process of birthing, from conception to snuggling with a newborn, does have a powerful effect on the father.

What birthing rituals would promote an intimate and emotional connection between father and child? We need to give the father support as he falls in love with and becomes attached to his new partner. First, fathers need information about this new little being. Pregnancy for men is an enculturation time; it is a time for socialization into the knowledge that is necessary to maintain a relation with a new child. Enculturation is carried out through three primary activities: observation, practice, and verbal exchanges. Pregnancy places men in a position to observe fathers and their relations with babies. Men who have never noticed the relationship between men and their children are now in situations where those activities are not simply present, but valued. In a study of 454 first-time fathers, men were asked to rank the most useful activities in socializing them into roles of fatherhood. Watching friends or relatives with babies ranked among the top categories for usefulness in learning about fatherhood, exceeded only by dads' conversations with spouses (Gage and Christensen 1991, 334).

Second, men can practice child care, changing a diaper on a plastic model or snuggling a doll in birthing classes. When his sister brings her own baby over to visit, the soon-to-be father may be offered the (often uncomfortable) opportunity of holding and changing his little nephew. Fathers need explicit training in the art and science of child care, in part to give them permission and a sense of responsibility. Classes in the care, feeding, and even the nursing of newborns are being increasingly taught to fathers. In fact, three-quarters of the men in the Gage study took parenting classes, and found them extremely helpful. Parenting training was on a par with watching friends as among the most useful things that a soon-to-be-father can do (Gage and Christensen 1991, 334).

Finally, and most dramatically, being a witness at birth is a golden opportunity to begin this new relationship. Sharing the experience with the mother, or just being in the room to witness the event, increases the father's confidence and his feeling of knowing his new child. We have invented a variety of rituals that formalize the event. The father catches the baby or cuts the cord or holds the naked little being against his chest. The specifics of the act are less important than that the act recognizes the growing bond between father and child. If engrossment is what he experiences, then the rituals that we create should promote and contain his feelings. Our treatment of fathers must both define and describe the bond that these men are creating with their children.

Fortunately, treating the father as a witness at birth conforms easily to the biological model of birth. Many dads come to the role of witness easily, even after an unsatisfying experience trying to coach the mother. Rather than controlling the event, the witness is allowed to step back and find the distance to observe. But few fathers retain that distance once their babies are born. Dad offers a ready pair of arms to hold his child and stare into the baby's eyes while the obstetrician and mother attend to the afterbirth. Sidelined during the delivery, dad now has energy to share with his baby as mother recovers from her most strenuous tasks. In doing so, the father may discover a new and powerful presence in their world.

Many men find the role of witness the most salient in the variety of things that they did in labor and delivery. Although he had been extremely active in assisting his wife in both labor and delivery, Martin promised, "I will never miss the birth of my baby. Just being there was the most important part." His strongest memories were of the first view of his newborn's blue-gray body sliding into the world. It started a relationship that he will carry through life.

Fathers and Society

Not only fathers, mothers, and children are calling for a new kind of fathers, but our religious leaders, politicians, social workers, and judges are also demanding that men shoulder responsibility for their children. If men are to rise to this social challenge, we need to assure that our birthing rituals create the kind of fatherhood that our society expects.

Just as birthing creates new relations for the father with his partner and child, so it also establishes his role in a broader culture and society. As the father attends to the mother and the baby, as he negotiates and collaborates with nurses and physicians, as he signs admission papers and birth certificates, he reinforces and reinvents his place in our more extensive social systems. He creates a new relationship with the church, the state, friends, and family.

What social relationships are created and reinforced in hospital birthing? Of primary interest here is the effect that birthing has on a man's relationship with larger institutions of power and his place in the social discourse concerning control and authority. How do men relate to medical institutions and the control that physicians and hospitals wield over mothers? Although fathers' presence in birthing would seem to challenge existing power structures, the data argue that their participation does not. On the contrary, birthing fathers are integrated into the existing hierarchy of power in hospital birthing.

Although birthing would ideally support the empathic and nurturing father, our rituals often emphasize his rationality and power. As men are recognized as powerful in American society, fathers are integrated into conventional systems of authority that exert themselves over female patients. In effect, birthing serves to reinforce fathers' power over mothers and to co-opt fathers' socially recognized authority into the system of control of birthing women. As medical birthing reinforces the father's power over the mother, it asserts its own power over him. Men find themselves disempowered and empowered in the same moment. They are empowered as men over women in society, yet disadvantaged in the face of scientific technology.

Understanding the complex process of both control and authority in birthing demands attention to the importance of gender and technology in the practice of biological birthing. Although biological birthing contradicts the image of the mother as a broken machine or birth as a pathological process, it attends closely to the idea that we can best understand and manage birth through a scientific perspective. Birth is not considered an emotional or a social process; it is seen as a physical act performed by women's bodies. As such, fathers are isolated from the process, defined as outsiders and individuals. But birth is directly influenced by American attitudes toward gender roles and relations. As their female partners slip progressively into what is seen as the irrational subjectivity of birthing, fathers are expected to assert their masculine power and authority over birthing mothers. Thus, as fathers engage in birthing ritual, they find themselves situated in the larger structure of gender relations, which in turn is embedded in the ideology of science and technology in contemporary America. The discourse concerning what is and what can be is carried out as each father forges forward into a new generation, creating his new identity and recreating his relations in the family and society.

NOTES

CHAPTER 1   AMERICAN FATHERS AND HOSPITAL CHILDBIRTH

1. Between 1996 and 2000, I interviewed fifty men about their experiences in childbirth. In the initial stage of my research, I performed unstructured interviews with thirty-two men drawn from my own personal network of friends and acquaintances. When I ran into a man who seemed to have a story to tell about childbirth, I would invite him to share a cup of coffee and talk about it. Often it resulted in an informal snowball sample, with men passing on the names of others who might have a story to tell. These early conversations detailed men's reports about their activities in and feelings about birth. (I generally avoided conversations with mothers who were anxious to report on their husbands' behavior.) Notes from these discussions were used then to formulate later research foci. In a sense, concepts of grounded theory legitimized this early information gathering, but my work has more in common with standard ethnographic methodologies that describe fathers' experiences in a holistic manner.

A second set of interviews focused on eighteen men and their experiences in hospital childbirth. Working with a set of open-ended questions, I invited men to discuss their expectations before birth, and then returned to detail their experience afterwards. Men were contacted through childbirth classes offered by several independent agencies that catered to a broad spectrum of couples. I, or a research assistant, attended several consecutive classes and then invited men to be interviewed. These interviews often took place in their homes or a coffee shop, without mothers attending. Interviews were limited to one hour each. They were taped and transcribed; the stories of six of the men are included here. The pool included Blacks, Hispanics, and Anglos; gays and straights; married and unmarried fathers; and men ranging from their teens to their sixties. Nevertheless, the work cannot adequately speak to the great diversity of men's experience (every man's birth experience is truly unique), but given the populations of the research areas, focuses on middle-class Anglos and Hispanics who give birth in American hospitals.

CHAPTER 2   COUVADE IN SOCIETY AND HISTORY

1. While seventeenth-century English literature inserts the voice of the commoner to critique the rationality of the developing civilized world, these early reports of couvade in other areas of the world served to fortify intellectuals' own sense of ration-

ality and civilization. They juxtaposed the supposed rational behavior of European men with that of the superstitious and uncivilized foreigner. The recent cultural critique in anthropology points out that the anthropologist must be aware of his or her own cultural context in documenting and analyzing another's culture (For a general discussion of this, see George Marcus and Michael Fischer's *Anthropology as Cultural Critique* [1986]). In fact, there is ample evidence that the anthropological understanding of couvade was manipulated to suit this attitude of superior rationality of the modern Western world. Even as anthropologists reanalyze the classic couvade, questions remain about the veracity of original reports. Metraux (1948) pointed out that the original reports of mimicry among South American Indians were themselves of suspicious accuracy. Yves d'Evreux, himself, admitted that his description of couvade was made with European models of birthing in mind. Even the report of Johann Bachofen is criticized for relying on Strabo's classical account and reporting ritual not practiced in the Basque country.

2. Bachofen's analysis gained wide notice, but the hypothesis about the evolutionary origins of couvade drew considerable skepticism. Rather than seeking to define the prehistoric past, most of the opposing arguments came from contemporary data that were flooding into academe from around the world. For example, Henry Ling Roth (1893), a British curator who made his name in documenting Tasmanian cultures, countered the argument about a transitional state between matriarchy and patriarchy with evidence from matrilineal societies, such as the Arawak and Melanesian, where couvade was both common and important.

3. Where Freud depended on case studies of single individuals, anthropologists collected ethnographic data to support their hypotheses. The Munroes found that along the Belizean coast, men commonly practiced extensive couvade. Psychological testing also showed that these men responded to questions of gender with, "feminine responses or exaggeratedly masculine responses." Thus, the team defined a negative correlation between the strength of masculine identity and the intensity of couvade reactions. In the time-honored process of anthropology, they moved from the ethnographic case study to cross-cultural analyses. The Munroes compared couvade ritual and masculine sex identity in American, Garifuna, and Bantu peoples. In this simple comparison, the research uncovered that couvade was practiced in those societies where men offered, "female-like responses on covert measures of sexual identity, and hyper-masculine reactions on overt measures." Moreover, in two of the societies, American and Garifuna, couvade was most evident in those groups where fathers were absent for extended periods during their sons' childhood (taken to suggest that these were men with weak sex role models). On a larger scale, the same authors undertook a cross-cultural statistical analysis of eighty-four societies. They compared residence and sleeping patterns, which were determined to be indicators of gender independence and the strength of masculine identity. They found that fathers' birthing ritual correlated with both, suggesting that couvade was institutionalized transexuality, a reaction to what was deemed cross-sex identification (Munroe and Munroe 1971).

4. It might be that these activities are a father's defenses against subjective involvement in pregnancy. Where women tend to read dozens of pregnancy books and pore over guides to childbirth and naming, men are instrumental. Fathers engage in projects that

have a clear product, which sociologists define as "goal driven behavior." Men's instrumental style may, in part, be understood in their rejection of active emotional participation in pregnancy: they pride themselves on the traditional functions of the husband and father role (Antle 1980, 445–453). On the other hand, it is important to remember that even though these activities are goal driven, men are processing their new identities as they exercise their masculine skills. It would be hard to rationalize the endless hours that many men expend on carving cribs and the care that they take in painting nursery baseboards solely in terms of the end result. These slow, tedious activities give men the opportunity to commune with their new child, even before it is born.

CHAPTER 4   BIRTHING REVOLUTION: MEN TO THE BARRICADES

1. Dick-Read wrote the book on natural childbirth, but he was not the first to take up the issue. In fact, nurses, physicians, and lay women had been advocating less medical intervention in birth in the United States even before Dick-Read published his manuscript in 1932. Female physicians were at the forefront of this nascent movement. As early as 1903, the basic techniques of prepared childbirth had been described by a female doctor named Mary Reis Melendy, in a complete medical guide for women. In the 1920s, Dr. Dorothy Reed Mandehall, a researcher for the Washington-based Children's Bureau, pointed out that the mortality rates for both mothers and infants were three times higher in hospitals than in home births. By 1937, another female physician, Gertrude Neilson, assailed the national meeting of the American Medical Association for its unnecessary and dangerous use of "twilight sleep." Pioneering agencies, such as the Chicago Maternity Center, Maternity Center in New York, and the Frontier Nursing Service worked to deliver healthy babies without unnecessary medical intervention (Davis-Floyd 1992, 168–170).

CHAPTER 5   BIRTHING CLASSES: TRAINING MEN TO BIRTH

1. A topic that deserves greater attention is the demise of the independent childbirth training program. With the advent of alternative birthing, individual women and independent agencies became important sources of birth training. As alternative birthing has been institutionalized within hospitals, the education process has increasingly been dominated by agencies that affiliate directly to physicians and hospitals. Childbirth education curriculum has been transformed from a radical message of maternal power to a process of socialization to medical culture.

CHAPTER 6   MEN'S EXPERIENCE OF BIRTH

1. In the past, the vast majority of obstetricians were male. Only 7 percent of the practicing obstetricians in 1972 were female. In this research, only two men delivered babies with women physicians attending. Today, women compose more than 25 percent of medical students, and an even larger portion of obstetricians-in-training are women (Ekeroma and Harillal 2003, 354). These female physicians will certainly change the practice of obstetrics. However, the experiences of the two fathers who birthed with female obstetricians were essentially the same as those working with men.

BIBLIOGRAPHY

American Bar Association. 1996. *The ABA Guide to Family Law: The Complete and Easy Guide to the Laws of Marriage, Parenthood, Separation.* New York: Three Rivers Press.

Antle, K. 1980. A Typology of Detachment/Involvement Styles Adopted during Pregnancy by First-Time Fathers. *Western Journal of Nursing Research* 2 (2): 445–453.

Apollonius Rhodius. 1912. *Argonautica.* Trans. R. Seaton. Cambridge: Harvard University Press.

Attia, A., M. el-Kakhly, F. Halawa, N. Ragab, and M. Mossa. 1989. Cigarette Smoking and Male Reproduction. *Archives of Andrology* 23 (1): 45–49.

Bachofen, J. 1861. *Das Mutterrecht.* Stuttgart: Krais & Hoffman.

Bakhtin, M. 1984. *Rabelais and His World.* Trans. H. Iswolsky. Bloomington: Indiana University Press.

Barnouw, V. 1950. *Acculturation and Personality among the Wisconsin Chippewa.* Menasha, WI: American Anthropological Association.

Beckerman, S., and P. Valentine, eds. 2002. *Cultures of Multiple Fathers: The Theory and Practice of Partible Paternity in Lowland South America.* Miami: University Press of Florida.

Bell, C. 1992. *Ritual Theory, Ritual Practice.* Oxford: Oxford University Press.

Benjamin, W. 1979. No. 113. In *One-Way Street, and Other Writings.* Trans. J. Edmund and S. Kinglsey, 45–107. London: New Library Binding.

Bettelheim, B. 1954. *Symbolic Wounds: Puberty Rights and the Envious Male.* New York: Free Press.

Bing, E. 1994. *Six Practical Lessons for an Easier Childbirth.* 3rd ed. New York: Bantam.

Bing, E., M. Karmel, and A. Tanzer. 1961. *Practical Training Course for the Psychoprophylactic Method of Childbirth.* New York: Center Printing Company.

Bly, Robert. 1990. *Iron John: A Book about Men.* Reading, MA: Addison-Wesley.

Boehm, F. 1930. The Femininity Complex in Man. *International Journal of Psychiatry* 2:444–469.

Bogren, L. 1983. Couvade. *Acta Psychiatrica Scandinavia* 68:55–65.

Bourdieu, P. 1977. *Outline of a Theory of Practice.* Trans. R. Nice. Cambridge: Cambridge University Press.

Bowers, F., ed. 1977. *The Dramatic Works in the Beaumont and Fletcher Canon*, vol. 4. Cambridge: Cambridge University Press.

Bradley, R. 1962. Fathers' Presence in Delivery Rooms. *Psychosomatics* 3 (6): 474–479.

———. 1965. *Husband-Coached Childbirth.* New York: Harper & Row.

Broverman, I., S. Vogel, D. Broverman, F. Clarkson, and P. Rosencrantz. 1972. Sex-Role Stereotypes: A Current Appraisal. *Journal of Social Issues* 28 (2): 59–78.

Brown, M. 1988. A Comparison of Health Responses in Expectant Mothers and Fathers. *Western Journal of Nursing Research* 10 (5): 527–549.

Buck, Pearl. 1931. *The Good Earth*. New York: John Day.

Butler, S. [1677] 1967. *Hudibras*. Ed. J. Wilders. Oxford: Clarendon Press.

Carlsen E., A. Giwercman, N. Keiding, and N. Skakkebaek. 1992. Evidence for Decreasing Quality of Semen during Past Fifty Years. *British Medical Journal* 305 (6854): 609–613.

Cavenar, J., and W. Weddington. 1979. Fatherhood and Psychosis: Case Report. *American Journal of Psychiatry* 136 (6): 490–491.

Cavenar, J., and N. Butts. 1977. Fatherhood and Emotional Illness. *American Journal of Psychiatry* 134 (4): 429–431.

Chabon, I. 1966. *Awake and Aware: Participation in Childbirth through Psychoprophylaxis*. New York: Delacorte Press.

Chagnon, N. 1997. *Yanomamo: The Fierce People*. 5th ed. Fort Worth: Harcourt Brace.

Charbouclais, C. 1856. *Dictionnaire des Superstitions, Erreurs, Préjugés et Traditions Populaires*. Paris: M. l'abbe Migne.

Chernela, J. 1993. Symbolic Interaction in Rituals of Gender and Procreation among the Garifuna (Black Caribs) of Honduras. *Ethos* 19 (1): 52–67.

Chidester, D., and E. Linenthal. 1995. *American Sacred Space*. Bloomington: Indiana University Press.

Clinton, J. 1985. Couvade: Patterns, Predictors and Nursing Management. *Western Journal of Nursing Research* 7 (2): 221–243.

———. 1987. Physical and Emotional Responses of Expectant Fathers throughout Pregnancy and the Early Postpartum Period. *International Journal of Nursing Studies* 24 (1): 59–68.

Coale, A., and M. Zelnick. 1963. *New Estimates of Fertility and Population in the United States*. Princeton, NJ: Princeton University Press.

Coffman, S., M. Levitt, and L. Brown. 1994. Effects of Clarification of Support Expectations in Perinatal Couples. *Nursing Research* 43 (2): 111–116.

Corea, G. 1985. *The Mother Machine: Reproductive Technologies from Artificial Insemination to Artificial Wombs*. New York: Harper and Row.

Cosby, B. 1986. *Fatherhood*. Doubleday: New York.

Cotgrave, R. 1611. *A Dictionarie of the French and English Tongues*. London: Adam Islip.

Cottman, M. 1995. *Million Man March*. New York: Three Rivers Press.

Cowan, C., and P. Cowan. 1992. *When Partners Become Parents: The Big Life Change for Couples*. New York: Basic Books.

Crocker, J. 1985. *Vital Souls: Bororo Cosmology, Natural Symbolism, and Shamanism*. Tucson: University of Arizona Press.

Crocker, W. 1990. *The Canela (Eastern Timira): An Ethnographic Introduction*. Smithsonian Contributions to Anthropology, no. 33. Washington, DC: Smithsonian Institution Press.

Cronenwett, L., and L. Newmark. 1974. Fathers' Responses to Childbirth. *Nursing Research* 23 (3): 210–217.

Curtis, J. 1955. A Psychiatric Study of Fifty-five Expectant Fathers. *United States Armed Forces Medical Journal* 6 (7): 937–950.

Davis-Floyd, R. 1992. *Birth as an American Rite of Passage*. Berkeley: University of California Press.

Davis-Floyd, R., and E. Davis. 1996. Intuition as Authoritative Knowledge in Midwifery and Home Birth. *Medical Anthropology* 10 (2): 237–269.

Davis-Floyd, R., and G. St. John. 1998. *From Doctor to Healer: The Transformative Journey*. New Brunswick, NJ: Rutgers University Press.

Dawson, W. 1929. *The Custom of the Couvade*. Manchester: Manchester University Press.

Dickens G., and W. Trethowan. 1971. Cravings and Aversions during Pregnancy. *Journal of Psychosomatic Research* 15:250–268.

Dick-Read, G. 1932. *Natural Childbirth*. London: William Heinemann.

———. 1944. *Revelation of Childbirth*. New York: Harper.

———. 1959. *Childbirth without Fear: The Principles and Practice of Natural Childbirth*. 2nd ed. New York: Harper.

Diemer, G. 1997. Expectant Fathers: Influence of Perinatal Education on Stress, Coping, and Spousal Relations. *Research in Nursing and Health* 20:281–293.

Draper, J. 2002. It's the First Scientific Evidence: Men's Experience of Pregnancy Confirmed. *Journal of Advanced Nursing* 39 (6): 563–571.

Du Tertre, J. 1667–1671. *Histoire Générale des Antiles*. 4 vols. Paris: T. Jolly.

Eakins, P. 1986. *The American Way of Birth*. Philadelphia: Temple University Press.

Ekeroma, A., and M. Harillal. 2003. Women's Choice in the Gender and Ethnicity of Her Obstetrician and Gynaecologist. *Australian & New Zealand Journal of Obstetrics & Gynaecology* 43 (5): 354–360.

Enoch, M., W. Trethowan, and J. Barker. 1967. *Some Uncommon Psychiatric Syndromes*. Bristol (England): John Wright.

Entwisle, D., and S. Doering. 1988. *The First Birth: A Family Turning Point*. Baltimore: Johns Hopkins University Press.

Fock, N. 1963. South American Birth Customs in Theory and Practice. In *Cross-Cultural Approaches: Readings in Comparative Research*, ed. C. Ford, 127–146. New Haven: HRAF Press.

Foster, G. 1960. *Culture and Conquest: America's Spanish Heritage*. Chicago: Quadrangle Books.

Foucault, M. 1973. *The Birth of the Clinic: An Archaeology of Medical Perception*. Trans. A. Smith. New York: Pantheon Books.

Frazer, J. 1890. *The Golden Bough: A Study in Comparative Religion*. Cambridge: Cambridge University Press.

———. 1910. *Totemism and Exogamy: A Treatise on Certain Early Forms of Superstition and Society*. London: Macmillan.

Freeman, T. 1951. Pregnancy as a Precipitant of Mental Illness. *Journal of Medical Psychology* 24:49–54.

Freud, S. [1913] 1950. *Totem and Taboo*. London: Standard.

Freund, P., and M. McGuire. 1991. *Health, Illness, and the Social Body*. Englewood Cliffs, NJ: Prentice Hall.

Gage, M., and D. Christensen. 1991. Parental Role Socialization and the Transition to Parenthood. *Family Relations* 40:332–337.

Gaskin, I. 1990. *Spiritual Midwifery*. 3rd ed. Summertown, TN: Book Publishing Co.

———. 2003. *Ina May's Guide to Childbirth*. New York: Bantam Books.

Gennep, A. [1908] 1960. *The Rites of Passage.* Trans. M. Vizedom and G. Caffee. Chicago: University of Chicago Press.

Gittleson, A. 1965. The Case against Natural Childbirth. *Harper's Bazaar,* June 16, 1965.

Goldman, I. 1963. *The Cubeo Indians of the Northwest Amazon.* Urbana: University of Illinois Press.

Goldsmith, J. 1990. *Childbirth Wisdom from the World's Oldest Societies.* New York: East-West Health Books.

Gray, J. 1993. *Men Are from Mars, Women Are from Venus: A Practical Guide for Improving Communication and Getting What You Want In Your Relationships.* New York: Harper Collins.

Greenberg, M., and N. Morris. 1974. Engrossment: The Newborn's Impact upon the Father. *American Journal of Orthopsychiatry* 44:520–531.

Greenblatt, S. 1988. *Shakespearean Negotiations: The Circulation of Special Energy in Renaissance England.* Berkeley: University of California Press.

Griswold, R. 1993. *Fatherhood in America.* New York: Basic Books, 1993.

Hangsleben, K. 1983. Transition to Fatherhood: An Exploratory Study. *Journal of Obstetric, Gynecologic, and Neonatal Nursing* 4:265–274.

Hannigan J., and Armant D. 2000. Alcohol in Pregnancy and Neonatal Outcome. *Seminars in Neonatology* Aug. 5 (3): 243–254.

Hazlett, W. 1967. The Male Factor in Obstetrics. *Child and Family* 6 (4): 3–12.

Heath, R. 1650. Clarastella. In *Clarastella: Together with Poems Occasionall, Elegies, Epigrams, and Satyrs,* 1 –27. London: Mosley.

Heinowitz, J. 1995. *Pregnant Fathers: Entering Parenthood Together.* San Diego: Parents as Partners Press.

Hemingway, E. 1972. The Indian Camp. In *The Nick Adams Stories,* 16–21. New York: Charles Scribner's Sons.

Holmberg, A. 1950. *Nomads of the Long Bow: The Siriono of Eastern Bolivia.* Washington, DC: American Museum of Natural History.

Holmberg, L., and V. Wahlberg. 2000. The Process of Decision-Making on Abortion: A Grounded Theory Study of Young Men in Sweden. *Journal of Adolescent Health* 26 (3): 230–234.

Hunter, R., and I. Macalpine. 1963. *Three Hundred Years of Psychiatry.* London: Oxford University Press.

Jackson, J. 1983. *The Fish People: Linguistic Exogamy and Tukanoan Identity in the Northwest Amazon.* Cambridge: Cambridge University Press.

Jacobus, M., E. Fox Keller, and S. Shuttleworth, eds. 1990. *Body/Politics: Women and the Discourses of Science.* New York: Routledge.

James, W. 1890. *Principles of Psychology.* New York: Henry Holt.

Jarvis, W. 1961. Some Effects of Pregnancy and Childbirth on Men. *Journal of the American Psychoanalytic Association* 10:689–700.

Jones, C. 1981. Father to Infant Attachment: Effects of Early Contact and Characteristics of the Infant. *Research in Nursing and Health* 4:193–200.

Jones, E. 1942. Psychology and Childbirth. *The Lancet* 6 June:695.

Jordan, J. 1992. *Women's Growth in Connection: Writings from the Stone Center.* New York: Guilford Press.

Jordan, P. 1990. Laboring for Relevance: Expectant and New Fatherhood. *Nursing Research* 39 (1): 1–16.

Karmel, M. 1965. *Thank You, Dr. Lamaze.* Garden City, NY: Dolphin Books.

Keller, E. 1985. *Reflections on Gender and Science.* New Haven: Yale University Press.

Kero, A., and A. Lalos. 2000. Ambivalence—A Logical Response to Legal Abortion: A Prospective Study among Women and Men. *Journal of Psychosomatic Obstetrics and Gynaecology* 21 (2): 81–91.

Kero, A., A. Lalos, U. Hogberg, and L. Jacobsson. 1995. The Male Partner Involved in Legal Abortion. *Human Reproduction* 14 (10): 2669–2675.

Kimmel, M. 1996. *Manhood in America: A Cultural History.* Boston: Free Press.

Kitzinger, S. 1996. *The Complete Book of Pregnancy and Childbirth.* New York: Knopf.

Klein, H. 1991. Couvade Syndrome: Male Counterpart to Pregnancy. *International Journal of Psychiatry in Medicine* 2 (1): 57–69.

Klein, R., N. Gist, J. Nicholson, and K. Standley. 1981. A Study of Father and Nurse Support for Labor. *Birth and Family Journal* 8 (3): 161–164.

Kolata, G. 1996. Sperm Counts: Some Experts See a Fall, Others Poor Data. *New York Times* 145 (50371): C10.

Lacoursiere, R. 1970. Fatherhood and Mental Illness: A Review and New Material. *Bulletin of the Menninger Clinic* 35:311–343.

Lamaze, F. [1956] 1970. *Painless Childbirth: The Psychoprophylactic Method.* Chicago: Contemporary Books.

Lamb, G., and M. Lipkin. 1982. Somatic Symptoms of Expectant Fathers. *American Journal of Maternal and Child Nursing* 7 (2): 110–115.

Lamb, M. 1977. Father-Infant and Mother-Infant Interaction in the First Year of Life. *Child Development* 48:167–181.

Leach, E. 1958. Magical Hair. *Journal of the Royal Anthropological Institute of Great Britain and Ireland* 11 (2): 147–164.

Leavitt, J. 1986. *Brought to Bed: Childbearing in America 1759 to 1950.* Oxford: Oxford University Press.

Lee, M., and V. Wong. 2002. POP! The First Male Pregnancy. http://www.malepregnancy .com.

Léry, J. [1578] 1990. *History of a Voyage to the Land of Brazil, Otherwise Called America.* Trans. J. Whatley. Berkeley: University of California Press.

Lévi-Strauss, C. 1962. *The Savage Mind.* Chicago: University of Chicago Press.

Licht, H. 1932. *Sexual Life in Ancient Greece.* London: Routledge and Kegan Paul.

Liebenberg, B. 1973. Expectant Fathers. In *Psychological Aspects of a First Pregnancy and Early Postnatal Adaptation*, eds. L. Shereshefsky and J. Yarrow, 103–114. New York: Raven Press.

Lowie, R. 1948. The Tropical Forests: An Introduction. In *The Handbook of South American Indians.* Bureau of American Ethnology Bulletin, vol. 4, no. 143, ed. J. Steward, 1–57. Washington, DC: United States Government Printing Office.

Mak V., K. Jarvi, M. Buckspan, M. Freeman, S. Hechter, and A. Zini. 2000. Smoking Is Associated with the Retention of Cytoplasm by Human Spermatozoa. *Urology* 3:463–466.

Malinowski, B. 1927a. *Sex and Repression in Savage Society.* New York: Meridian Books.

———. 1927b. *The Father in Primitive Psychology.* New York: W. W. Norton.

Maltbie, A., J. Cavenar, G. O'Shanick, and M. Volow. 1980. A Couvade Syndrome Variant: A Case Report. *North Carolina Medical Journal* 41 (2): 90–92.

Mann, T. 1955. *The Magic Mountain.* Trans. H. Lowe-Porter. New York: McGraw Hill.

Marcus, G., and M. Fischer. 1986. *Anthropology as Cultural Critique.* Chicago: University of Chicago Press.

Marsh, M., and W. Ronner. 1996. *The Empty Cradle: Infertility in America from Colonial Times to the Present.* Baltimore: Johns Hopkins University Press.

Marsiglio, W. 1998. *Procreative Man.* New York: New York University Press.

Masters, W., and V. Johnson. 1966. *Human Sexual Response.* Saint Louis, MO: Reproductive Biology Research Foundation.

Maybury-Lewis, David. 1960. *Akwe-Shavante Society.* Oxford: Oxford University Press.

McKee, L., and M. O'Brien. 1982. *The Father Figure.* London: Tavistock Publications.

Mead, M. 1928. *Coming of Age in Samoa: A Psychological Study of Primitive Youth for Western Civilization.* New York: William Morrow.

Meggars, B., and C. Evans. 1957. *Archaeological Investigations at the Mouth of the Amazon.* Bureau of American Ethnology Bulletin, no. 167. Washington, DC: United States Government Printing Office.

Melendy, M. 1903. *Perfect Womanhood for Maidens—Wives—Mothers; A Book Giving Full Information on All the Mysterious and Complex Matters Pertaining to Women.* Chicago: Monarch Book Co.

Metraux, A. 1946. The Ethnography of the Chaco. In *The Handbook of South American Indians.* Bureau of American Ethnology Bulletin, vol. 1, no. 143, ed. J. Steward, 197–371. Washington, DC: United States Government Printing Office.

———. 1948. The Tupinamba. In *The Handbook of South American Indians.* Bureau of American Ethnology Bulletin, vol. 4, no. 143, ed. J. Steward, 95–135. Washington, DC: United States Government Printing Office.

Michel, F. 1857. *Le Pays Basque: Sa Population, Sa Langue, Ses Moeurs, Sa Littérature et Sa Musique.* Paris: Firmin Didot Freres.

Miller, B., and D. Sollie. 1980. Normal Stresses during the Transition to Parenthood. *Family Relations* 29:459–465.

Mitchell, M. 1936. *Gone With the Wind.* New York: Macmillan.

Mooney, J. 1887. The Medical Mythology of Ireland. *Proceedings of the American Philosophical Society* 24:136–166.

Morton, J. 1966. Fathers in the Delivery Room—An Opposition "Standpoint." *Hospital Topics* 44:103–104.

Munroe, R., and R. Munroe. 1971. Male Pregnancy Symptoms and Cross-Sex Identity in Three Societies. *Journal of Social Psychology* 84:11–25.

Munroe, R., R. Munroe, and J. Whiting. 1973. The Couvade: A Psychological Analysis. *Ethos* 1 (1): 30–74.

Murphy, F. 1998. The Experience of Early Miscarriage from a Male Perspective. *Journal of Clinical Nursing* 7 (4): 325–332.

Nelson, F. 1999. *Passive Smoking and Health.* London: Health Education Authority.

Nichols, M. 1993. Fathers' Attendance during Labor. *Maternal Child Nursing Journal* 21 (3): 99–108.

Oakley, A. 1984. *The Captured Womb: A History of Medical Care of Pregnant Women*. New York and London: Basil Blackwell.

Ortner, S. 1996. *Making Gender: The Politics and Erotics of Gender*. Boston: Beacon Press.

Osherson, S. 1986. *Finding Our Fathers: How a Man's Life Is Shaped by His Relationship with His Father*. New York: Fawcett Columbine.

Paige, K., and J. Paige. 1981. *The Politics of Reproductive Ritual*. Berkeley: University of California Press.

Pasley, K., T. Futris, and M. Skinner. 2002. Effects of Commitment and Psychological Centrality on Fathering. *Journal of Marriage & Family* 64 (1): 130–139.

Plot, R. 1677. *The Natural History of Oxford-shire*. Oxford: Printed at the theatre.

Polo, M. [1298] 1984. *The Travels of Marco Polo*. Trans. T. Waugh. London: Sidgewick and Jackson.

Primrose, J. 1651. That the Husband Cannot Breed His Wives Childe. In *Popular Errours: Or Errours of the People in Physick*. Trans. R. Wittie. London: Bourne.

Puddifoot, J., and M. Johnson. 1997. The Legitimacy of Grieving: The Partner's Experience of Miscarriage. *Social Science and Medicine* 45 (6): 837–839.

Reed, R. 1996. Birthing Fathers. *Mothering* 78:50–55.

Reik, T. [1914] 1946. Couvade and the Psychogenesis of the Fear of Retaliation. In *The Psychological Problems of Religion*, 1:27–89.

Ribes, J., X. Lowe, D. Moore, S. Perreault, V. Slott, D. Evanson, S. Sevevan, and A. Wyrobek, 1998. Smoking Cigarettes Is Associated with Increased Sperm Disomy in Teenage Men. *Fertility and Sterility* 7 (4): 715–723.

Rochefort, C. 1665. *Histoire Naturelle et Morale des Iles Antilles de l'Amérique*. Rotterdam: L. de Poincy.

Romalis, C. 1981. Taking Care of the Little Woman. In *Childbirth: Alternatives to Medical Control*, ed. S. Romalis, 101–137. Austin: University of Texas Press.

Rosaldo, M. 1972. Women, Culture and Society: A Theoretical Overview. In *Women, Culture and Society*, eds. M. Rosaldo and L. Lamphere, 17–43. Stanford: Stanford University Press.

Rosenwasser, S., L. Wright, and R. Barber. 1987. The Rights and Responsibilities of Men in Abortion Situations. *Journal of Sex Research* 23 (1): 97.

Roth, H. 1893. On the Significance of Couvade. *Journal of the Royal Anthropological Institute of Great Britain and Ireland* 12:204–243.

Roth, W. 1915. An Inquiry into the Animism and Folklore of the Guiana Indians. In *Thirtieth Annual Report of the Bureau of American Ethnology*, 147–176. Washington, DC: United States Government Printing Office.

Rothman, B. 1982. *In Labor: Women and Power in the Birthplace*. New York: W. W. Norton.

Scully, D. 1994. *Men Who Control Women's Health: The Miseducation of Obstetrician-Gynecologists*. Boston: Houghton Mifflin.

Simkin, P. 2001. *The Birth Partner: Everything You Need to Know to Help a Woman through Childbirth*. 2nd ed. Boston: Harvard Common Press.

Simmel, G. 1955. *Conflict*. Trans. K. Wolff. New York: Free Press.

Skjeldestad, F. 1986. Induced Abortion: Decision and Need for Medical Information. *Scandinavian Journal of Primary Health Care* 4 (4): 225–230.

Spiro, M. 1961. An Overview and a Suggested Reorientation. In *Psychological Anthropology: Approaches to Culture and Personality*, ed. F. Hsu, 459–498. Homewood, IL: Dorsey Press.

Starn, J. 1993. Strengthening Family Systems. *Association of Women's Health, Obstetric and Neonatal Nurses: Clinical Issues* 4 (1): 35–43.

Stearman, A. 1989. *Yuquí: Forest Nomads in a Changing World*. New York: Holt, Rinehart, and Winston.

Stein, L. 1987. Male and Female: The Doctor-Nurse Game. In *Conformity and Conflict: Readings in Cultural Anthropology*, eds. J. Spradley and D. McCurdy, 67–77. 6th ed. Boston: Little, Brown.

Steinbeck, J. 1939. *The Grapes of Wrath*. New York: Viking Press.

Stender, F. 1965. *Husbands in the Delivery Room*. Bellevue, WA.: International Childbirth Education Association.

Stewart, R. 1968. Natural Childbirth, Fathers Rooming In or Whatever. *Medical Times* 91:1065–1068.

Strabo. [AD 18–23] 1903. *The Geography of Strabo*. Trans. H. Hamilton. London: George Bell and Sons.

Strickland, O. 1987. The Occurrence of Symptoms in Expectant Fathers. *Nursing Research* 36 (3): 184–189.

Suitor, J. 1981. Husbands' Participation in Childbirth: A Nineteenth-Century Phenomenon. *Journal of Family History* 6 (3): 278–293.

Taylor, D. 1951. *The Black Carib of British Honduras*. Viking Fund Publications in Anthropology, no. 17. New York: Wenner-Gren Foundation for Anthropological Research.

Tenyi, T., M. Trixler, and F. Jadi. 1996. Psychotic Couvade: Two Case Reports. *Psychopathology* 29 (4): 252–254.

Tolor, A., and P. di Graza. 1976. Sexual Attitudes and Behavior Patterns during and Following Pregnancy. *Archives of Sexual Behavior* 5 (6): 539–553.

Tomlinson, P. 1987. Spousal Differences in Marital Satisfaction during Transition to Parenthood. *Nursing Research* 36:239–243.

Trethowan, W. 1972. The Couvade Syndrome. In *Modern Perspectives in Psycho-obstetrics*, ed. J. Howells, 68–93. New York: Brunner/Mazer.

Trethowan, W. H., and M. Conlon. 1965. The Couvade Syndrome. *British Journal of Psychiatry* 3:57–66.

Turner, V. 1977. *The Ritual Process: Structure and Anti-Structure*. Ithaca, NY: Cornell University Press.

Tylor, E. [1865] 1975. *Primitive Culture: Researches into the Development of Mythology, Philosophy, Religion, Art, and Custom*. New York: Gordon Press.

———. 1873. *Primitive Culture*. London: John Murray.

———. [1888] 1977. On a Method of Investigating the Development of Institutions; Applied to Laws of Marriage and Descent. *Journal of the Royal Anthropology Institute of Great Britain and Ireland* 18:256–269.

Ulrich, L. 1990. *A Midwife's Tale: The Life of Martha Ballard*. New York: Knopf.

Vellay, P. 1966. *Childbirth Without Pain*. Trans. D. Lloyd. New York: Dutton.

Veyne, P. 1987. The Roman Empire. In *A History of Private Life: From Pagan Rome to Byzantium*, ed. P. Veyne, trans. A. Goldhammer, 214–233. Cambridge: Harvard University Press.

Wainwright, W. 1966. Fatherhood as a Precipitant of Mental Illness. *American Journal of Psychiatry* 1:40–44.

Walzer, S. 1998. *Thinking about the Baby: Gender and the Transition to Parenthood.* Philadelphia: Temple University Press.

Weales, G., ed. 1967. *The Complete Plays of William Wycherley.* New York: New York University Press.

Wilson, S. 1964. The American Way of Birth. *Harper's Magazine,* Sept. 29, 1964, 54.

Wood-Martin, W. 1902. *Traces of the Elder Faiths of Ireland: A Folklore Sketch.* London: Longman, Green and Company.

Yogman, M., and T. Brazelton. 1988. *In Support of Families.* Cambridge, MA: Harvard University Press.

Yves, E. [1614] 1864. *Voyage dans le Nord du Brésil Fait durant les Années 1613 et 1614.* Leipzig: A. Franck.

Zilboorg, G. 1931. Depressive Reactions Related to Parenthood. *American Journal of Psychiatry* 87:927–962.

INDEX

ABOUT THE AUTHOR

RICHARD K. REED is an associate professor in the Department of Sociology and Anthropology at Trinity University in Texas. His work explores birthing in American hospitals as ritual, specifically the process by which men make the passage to fatherhood. This is part of his larger interest in masculinity as an ever-changing cultural construction. Reed's interest in the topic grows not just out of life experience as the father of two children, but from his work among the Guaraní of Paraguay and the sympathetic birth ritual performed by all Guaraní men who become fathers.